MODERN IRISH LITERATURE AND CULTURE

A Chronology

HISTORICAL NOTE: The historically defined, centuries-old four provinces of Ireland are Leinster, Munster, Connacht, and Ulster. Ulster traditionally included the six counties of present-day Northern Ireland as well as three other counties located in today's Republic of Ireland: Donegal, Monaghan, and Cavan. During the earlier periods treated in this book, Ireland remained under English domination (formalized in the Act of Union of 1800). The controversial treaty of 1921 divided the island into Northern Ireland—which kept the six most Protestant counties within the United Kingdom—and the Free State, made up of the twenty-six predominantly Catholic southern counties, which became the Republic of Ireland or Eiré (with the approval of its constitution in 1937, and full, formal independence in 1949).

MODERN IRISH LITERATURE AND CULTURE
A Chronology

James M. Cahalan

G.K. Hall & Co.
An Imprint of Macmillan Publishing Company
New York

Maxwell Macmillan Canada
Toronto

Maxwell Macmillan International
New York Oxford Singapore Sydney

G.K. Hall & Co.
An Imprint of
Macmillan Publishing Company
866 Third Avenue
New York, NY 10022

Maxwell Macmillan Canada, Inc.
1200 Eglinton Avenue East, Suite 200
Don Mills, Ontario M3C 3N1

Macmillan Publishing Company is part of the Maxwell Communication Group of Companies

Library of Congress Catalog Card Number: 92-15105

Printed in the United States of America

printing number
1 2 3 4 5 6 7 8 9 10

Library of Congress Cataloging-in-Publication Data

Cahalan, James M.
    Modern Irish literature and culture : a chronology / James M. Cahalan.
      p. cm.
    Includes bibliographical references and index.
    ISBN 0-8161-7264-1
      1. English literature—Irish authors—Chronology.   2. Ireland—
  History—18th century—Chronology.   3. Ireland—History—19th
  century—Chronology.   4. Ireland—History—20th century—Chronology.
  5. Northern Ireland—History—Chronology.   6. Ireland in literataure
  —Chronology.   7. Irish literature—Chronology.   I. Title
  PR8718.C35   1992   92-15105
  820.9'9415—cd20   CIP

To the memory of my grandmother,
Mabel Virginia Tway (1887–1987)

CONTENTS

....

MODERN IRISH LITERATURE AND CULTURE

A Chronology

....

INTRODUCTION

....

While several surveys of modern Irish literature (some of which are listed in my bibliography) are available, no comprehensive chronology of the subject has ever before been published. *A Chronology of Irish History since 1500* (1989), by J. E. Doherty and D. J. Hickey, has recently appeared, and the same authors (listed under Hickey and Doherty) also brought out an extremely useful *Dictionary of Irish History, 1800–1980* (1987); both books are available from Gill and Macmillan in Dublin. As in the case of Jim O'Donnell's *Ireland, the Past Twenty Years: An Illustrated Chronology* (1986)—a helpful though less readily obtained source concerning the not always easily documented events of recent years—I discovered these reference works quite late in my research and cite only relatively small-scale events listed in them. They complement the present book nicely, since I focus primarily on literature (along with several of the subjects with which literature has been thoroughly intertwined in Ireland, including history, politics, social issues, and the other arts), and also because their style and organization are significantly different from mine. These chronologies of Irish history are composed of very minute, precise entries (typically, a phrase or a sentence or two), while Hickey and Doherty's dictionary contains alphabetically organized entries on authors and subjects. The entries in my literary chronology are generally longer and more cohesive, aimed at relating literature to history and other aspects of Irish culture and also including many more explanatory details, illustrative quotations, and the like.

One would do well to consult my chronology together with Hickey and Doherty's *Dictionary of Irish History,* as well as Robert Hogan's *Dictionary of Irish Literature* (1980). One can

1

move profitably from the present reference work to Doherty and Hickey's *Chronology,* for example, looking up "O'Connell, Daniel" in the index to their historical work in order to follow up on the more specific, precisely dated activities of this great nineteenth-century leader, or to their *Dictionary* for a summary in a single entry of his career. (Similar to this *Dictionary* is Peter Newman's *Companion to Irish History* [1991], so recently published that I could not consult it prior to the completion of my book.) One can also consult Brian de Breffny's *Ireland: A Cultural Encyclopedia,* which is particularly helpful for concise information about extraliterary but crucially relevant subjects such as art, music, and architecture. My debt to these previous reference works—and to such landmark historical surveys as Terence Brown's *Ireland: A Social and Cultural History, 1922–1985* (1985) and Roy Foster's *Modern Ireland, 1600–1972* (1988), as well as to such useful literary surveys as Roger McHugh and Maurice Harmon's *Short History of Anglo-Irish Literature* (1982)—will be obvious from my citations of these works. Along with my book, students will also want to consult a recent history such as Roy Foster's and perhaps follow up with some of the sources identified in his bibliographical essay. My chronology is designed for students and scholars intending to go further in the study of Irish literature. It is a beginning rather than an end; no one could ever "cover" every date and every event, and I hope that this book whets the appetites of others to pursue their own studies and present their own findings.

I have sought to make this book a readable, interesting narrative, not merely a list of dates and events. This means that while following the structure of a year-by-year chronology, within each year I have sought to organize entries in a readable sequence, following clearly labeled categories, often seeking to make thematic connections. To make this work as "user-friendly" as possible, under each year I have grouped together and labeled all entries that fall into the same category. Such headings as "Architecture," "Art," "Drama," "Education," "Fiction," and "Poetry" are listed alphabetically within each year. Entries focused on politics as traditionally defined—legislative acts, rebellions, the activities of labor unions, and so on—are listed (without a special heading) before the other categories, at the beginning of each year where they occur, in order to help set a historical context for literary and other kinds of information. These unlabeled entries predominate early in the chronology, while its later parts consist of many more entries on literature and the arts. The organization and headings should make it easier for the reader to read selectively by category—to scan for the unlabeled entries immediately following dates in order to trace political events, for example, or to look for "Drama" headings in order to piece together the story of the development of the Irish theater. I also include at the beginning of the chronology a set of three dozen brief biographical sketches of some particularly recurrent literary and historical figures in this work, in order to provide the student with basic facts about William Butler Yeats, for example, before one encounters the numerous entries on Yeats's diverse activities and accomplishments spread across parts of two centuries. Please see my explanatory note at the beginning of those sketches for references to the several biographical dictionaries that are available. Additionally, within the chronology itself, birth and death dates are incorporated at the first mention within the lifetime of each Irish writer (and many politicians and other figures).

This chronology has a particular historical emphasis. Much as J. C. Beckett's classic study *The Making of Modern Ireland, 1603–1923* (1966) and Foster's more recent book both examine the deep roots of "modern" Irish history, similarly, "modern" Irish literature has often been dated from 1800 or earlier rather than from the late nineteenth or early twentieth century as in the case of modern American or British literature. Originally I was invited to write a chronology confined to the turn-of-the-century Irish Literary Revival, the period of Yeats, Lady Gregory, Synge, Joyce, O'Casey, and the other writers who made Irish literature truly and fully "modern." However, following Beckett and Foster, I was determined to begin earlier, and therefore have included the era beginning in the early seventeenth century when the Irish first started to aspire to the kind of nationality that transcended thinking in terms of the different, conflicting, small kingdoms that had traditionally occupied the island. I also wanted to bring the story up to the present. The writers of the Literary Revival were profoundly interested in and influenced by the events and writers of the earlier periods, and in an important sense the Literary Revival—understood as the impressive growth of Irish writing aimed primarily at Irish readers but also speaking to many other readers around the world—has never ceased, even though Irish writers and events have developed and changed a great deal since the turn of the century.

For these reasons, my chronology begins with the seventeenth century and ends in February 1992, when I am finishing this introduction. But I must point out that I emphasize the period since about 1800 to the present much more than earlier times. There are entries on every year since 1858, while entries on earlier periods are deliberately confined to only the most significant events. Reading this book from the beginning, one moves swiftly from 1601 into the early nineteenth century and then encounters considerably more detailed information about the nineteenth and twentieth centuries. In effect, briefer information about the seventeenth and eighteenth centuries serves as an introduction to a more focused treatment of the nineteenth and twentieth centuries. My aim is not to suggest that less happened during the earlier centuries or that they were not as important. Rather, I wish to attend chiefly to the most immediate contexts for modern Irish literature, while recognizing its particular roots in "the making of modern Ireland, 1603–1923," from the time when the Irish first aspired to nationality until the time when they finally achieved it in partial form. I felt that I could best be faithful to my subject in this way. It is also true that my page limitation has mandated less detail about the earlier periods in the face of more detail about the modern era. Again, one can consult Doherty and Hickey for many more specific items about Irish history, including the epoch of 1500–1800.

In order to facilitate a context for novice readers coming to Irish history in medias res in 1601 (the first date in my chronology), let me briefly set the earlier historical scene. England had established its imperial hegemony in Ireland in the Middle Ages. Yet up until 1600 Ireland still existed in a state that had persisted from medieval times: the authority of the royal English government extended nominally over all of the country but was systematically exercised only within "the Pale," a relatively small area surrounding the seat of government in Dublin. Most of the rest of Ireland was fragmented into fifty or sixty virtually independent regions, each ruled by a native chief or *rí* (king) or by an Anglo-Irish noble. During the 1590s Donegal chieftains Red Hugh O'Donnell and Hugh O'Neill joined forces in order to try to stop the anglicization of their Gaelic areas of Ulster; O'Neill won the Battle of the Yellow Ford in 1598 and found himself at the head of a national movement that the English feared might subvert their dominance in Ireland. The seventeenth century was a time when the traditional Gaelic way of life was overwhelmed by the far more powerful forces of Protestant settlement (or "plantation") of the best farmlands of Ireland, accelerated by Cromwell's reign of terror in 1649 and culminating in the victory of Protestant King William at the Battle of the Boyne in 1690. The triumph of Protestantism over Catholicism in Scotland and England gave the English added motivation—particularly their fears of a Catholic enemy at their back to the west while Catholic France lay waiting to the east, and the possible use of Ireland as a staging area for invasion by Catholic forces from the Continent—to conquer its neighbor, which was a relatively easy foe given its own divided, factional heritage. This grim period is the point at which I take up the story in outline form.

At the same time that I structure this reference work with helpful headings for the reader, I deliberately interlink literature, history, and other relevant subjects in terms of how I treat people and events within each entry and throughout this book. History does not function merely as "background" to literature, in the old historicist way. Instead, I write with the conviction that history is an arena in which writers participate and make their mark. Within literary studies, recent new historicists such as Jerome McGann advocate and practice literary research methods according to which the contents of a contemporaneous newspaper editorial may be as germane to the understanding and interpretation of a poem by Keats as the poem's structure and rhyme scheme. New historicists also openly admit their own subjectivity and self-interest in reading history, literature, and culture. Such an approach could not be further from the once prevalent New Critical obsession with the literary text alone.

Of course, in the case of Ireland, long before the arrival of new historicism, one was likely to recognize that Shelley's thesis that poets are the unacknowledged legislators of the world was not quite accurate. In the case of someone such as Yeats—who became an Irish senator and, thinking back about *Cathleen ni Hoolihan* (1902) in "The Man and the Echo" (1932), worried, "Did that play of mine send out / Certain men the English shot?"—a poet could in fact be a widely acknowledged legislator in Ireland. Pádraic Pearse and other future rebels were in Yeats's audience in 1902, mesmerized by his seductive Poor Old Woman who convinces a young man to lay down his life for Ireland, and in response they staged the Easter Rising of 1916, a dramatic more than a pragmatic event. Yeats not only reacted to the Easter Rising, as in his poem "Easter 1916"; he and other writers of the Literary Revival crucially helped to create the cultural world that made the Rising possible. Like Yeats and like two other leaders of the Easter Rising executed in 1916, Thomas MacDonagh and Joseph Plunkett, Pearse was also a published poet, and he wrote short stories and edited newspapers and magazines in both Irish and English. In 1916 MacDonagh not only helped lead the Rising but also published a scholarly study of Irish literature (*Literature in Ireland*) and was a professor at University College, Dublin.

Indeed, in Ireland poets have been politicians, politicians have written short stories, short story writers have published critical studies, and university professors have led revolutions. This reality leaves one with the feeling that one cannot merely write about Yeats and Pearse and fix them immovably onto the page. In some sense Yeats, Pearse, and many other such figures seem to be still writing their own history, literature, and culture. Especially when a MacDonagh publishes poetry and his own survey of Irish literature at the same time that he helps stage a revolution, it can also be said that not only are we scholars writing, recording, and analyzing the deeds of Irish writers and activists; they may also be writing *us*. (J. Hillis Miller has made a similar remark about James Joyce, but his sense was linguistic and less historical.) On the other hand, when narrating throughout this book all the events that occurred and publications that appeared in the past, I use the past rather than the present tense (employed by many other chronologists). I somehow feel more secure— however elusive my security may be—with figures and events defined in the past tense; as a matter of taste I happen to find the "historical present tense" a bit tedious and precious; and most importantly, the past tense allows me to distinguish the typical contents of my entries from remarks that do require the present tense. An example of this last distinction would be a comment about the residual nature (indeed, the frightening increase) of unemployment in Ireland since the early 1970s: I might need to

note something to the effect that at a particular time "unemployment became a severe problem, and this is still the case today."
My admission that we can never be done "fixing" Yeats and
others in historical immobility, and my remark that such figures
may sometimes, somehow seem to "read" us—both of which may
appear unusual in a reference book such as this—are not meant to
suggest that we cannot determine facts or effectively interconnect
Irish literature, history, and culture. Even older scholars of Irish
literature often wrote almost necessarily as new historicists of
sorts, long before that term was known: for example, Richard
Kain in *Dublin in the Age of William Butler Yeats and James Joyce*
(1962), William Irwin Thompson in *The Imagination of an
Insurrection: Dublin, Easter 1916. A Study of an Ideological
Movement* (1967), and Malcolm Brown in *The Politics of Irish
Literature: From Thomas Davis to W. B. Yeats* (1972), to name
only three. Perhaps the necessarily interdisciplinary character of
Irish literature and Irish studies has much to do with the small,
intense makeup of the place—after all, the island is about the size
of Massachusetts or West Virginia. It has been remarked that in
Dublin, a literary movement consists of two or more writers who
cordially despise each other.

While this chronology is avowedly interdisciplinary, to be fair
I should note that not every field of human endeavor has found its
way into my text, for the same kinds of reasons that mandated my
historical emphasis on more modern times as explained above.
For example, Irish films are cited here, but sports—except for the
1884 founding, significant in broad cultural terms, of the Gaelic
Athletic Association—are not. Nor have I been able to include the
natural sciences (except for the 1940 founding of the Dublin
Institute for Advanced Studies), largely due to the paucity of
readily available information about this subject—as recently
pointed out by John Wilson Foster, who argues that the history of
the natural sciences in Ireland is related to Irish cultural history in
general. Legislative acts and unemployment rates figure in my
book, but insurance and exchange rates do not. Again, this is not
because I find these and other omitted aspects of Ireland unimpor-
tant or uninteresting; I love sports and pay close attention indeed
to the exchange rate, especially when traveling there. Rather,
while casting my gaze in interdisciplinary directions but faced by
the limitations of space, I have had to confine myself to the

subjects that seem to me most directly, repeatedly, and meaning-
fully related to Irish writers and the culture in which they have
operated. Still, the reader will find this book to be more than a
dated list of literary works.

My sources, as cited parenthetically throughout my text and
listed at the end, range from the original first issue of the *Irish
Times* in 1823 to Doherty and Hickey's chronology and other
surveys of Irish history and literature. That is to say, I have sought
to combine citations from primary, rare, specific sources together
with secondary, easily obtained, and general ones. I should note
that my bibliography is a list of all the secondary works (from
nineteenth-century periodical articles to recent critical books) that
I have cited specifically by page number in my chronology as well
as a few others mentioned separately in this introduction. As such
it does not include the myriad primary works of literature
discussed or mentioned throughout my text—from Mícheál Ó
Cléirigh's *Leabhar Gabhála* (The book of invasions, 1631) to
Thomas Murphy's *Conversations on a Homecoming* (1992), with
James Joyce's *Ulysses* (1922) and a great many other primary
literary works published in between. Publication information on
these numerous primary works is often complicated by the
multiple editions that many of them have gone through, and
would have been overly cumbersome for reference purposes here
because of the overwhelming number of primary works that I
mention. Also, this kind of information, at least concerning
traditionally canonical works, is already available in such sources
as Roger McHugh and Maurice Harmon's *Short History of Anglo-
Irish Literature* (1982), Harmon's *Modern Irish Literature, 1800–
1967: A Reader's Guide* (1968) and his *Select Bibliography for the
Study of Anglo-Irish Literature* (1977), E. H. Mikhail's *Annotated
Bibliography of Modern Anglo-Irish Drama* (1981), both volumes
of Stephen Brown's *Ireland in Fiction* (published decades apart, in
1919 and in 1985), and the bibliographies of other surveys of Irish
literature (several of which are enumerated in my list of works
cited); more definitive lists can be compiled by examining the
National Union Catalogue and the catalogues of the Library of
Congress in Washington and the National Library in Dublin.

Nor do I attempt anything like a comprehensive bibliography
of scholarship and criticism on Irish literature; such information
can be found in other sources such as the two Modern Language

Association books edited by Richard Finneran and the handbooks by Thomas Bartlett and Maurice Harmon. Therefore, I do not include a number of other scholarly works that have influenced my own thinking. In short, my bibliography is a concise list of secondary works cited.

I should add that, as in my three previous books on Irish fiction, I define "Irish literature" as writing in the Irish language as well as in English, rejecting the term "Anglo-Irish literature," and therefore I include Irish Gaelic works; unless italicized in cases where translated versions have been published, all translations of book titles are my own. Proinsias MacCana's *Literature in Irish* (1980) is an excellent brief overview of this important part of my subject, and the novice should also consult at least one of the several works that introduce some of the many ways in which the Irish language has extensively influenced the English language as spoken and written in Ireland (see the entries listed under Ó Muirithe and McCrum in my bibliography).

My chronology pays particular attention to Irish periodicals; indeed, I believe I can claim to have included here the most comprehensive chronology of Irish periodicals available. Ever since the seventeenth century, Irish newspapers and journals have consistently constituted a major interdisciplinary cultural arena. Poets and politicians intermixed in their pages; fiction writers got their start there; popular leaders as well as creative writers contributed to them; novelists edited them; their reviews registered the reception history of Irish plays, fiction, poetry, speeches, and events. In the case of someone such as Thomas Davis, the nineteenth-century Young Ireland leader, it becomes difficult to separate the poems from the speeches and the texts from the events. I should recognize here two particularly useful books that have helped me compile my chronology of Irish newspapers, magazines, and journals: Barbara Hayley and Enda McKay's *Three Hundred Years of Irish Periodicals* (1987), which contains essays by seven contributors focusing on different kinds of journals, and Hugh Oram's *The Newspaper Book: A History of Newspapers in Ireland, 1649–1983* (1983).

I would like to thank several other individuals and institutions who have helped make this book possible. Without research grants from Indiana University of Pennsylvania (IUP) and the Faculty Professional Development Council of the Pennsylvania

State System of Higher Education, it would have been much more difficult to complete this work than it has been. I am grateful as always to the staff of the IUP Library, particularly Carol Connell, Janet Clawson, and Larry Kroah, the library's director. My graduate assistants Mark Crilly and Margery Vagt provided key assistance. Mark retrieved many sources for me at the beginning of this project. During the last stages of my work, Margery checked and inserted a great many authors' dates, raised questions that allowed me to make some useful additions and changes, and compiled much of the index. The staff of the National Library of Ireland provided considerable help during the summer of 1991; in particular I want to thank Linda McNamara. Three fellow members of the Irish-language, electronic-mail newsgroup GAELIC-L@ IRLEARN—Paddy Matthews, Dónall Ó Baoill, and particularly Marion Gunn (GAELIC-L host)—helped me arrive at better English translations of five book titles, among my many translations of original Irish Gaelic titles listed in this work. I appreciate the sage assistance of my editors, Philip Holthaus and Catherine Carter, and also Elizabeth Holthaus, formerly of G. K. Hall, who helped get me started on this project. Last but not least, thanks to Lea Masiello, Clare Masiello Cahalan, and Rose Masiello Cahalan, who journeyed to Dublin with me in pursuit of dates, names, and events.

Indiana, Pennsylvania
February 1992

BIOGRAPHICAL
SKETCHES OF
RECURRENT FIGURES

••

The following set of three dozen brief biographical entries is intended to help the reader in following some of the particularly recurrent figures whose myriad activities are reported throughout the chronology that follows. This section is intended as merely a brief "reader's aid," not as a substitute for a full biographical dictionary, a few of which I want to recommend here. The most extensive source for Irish writers is Anne Brady and Brian Cleeve's *Dictionary of Irish Writers* (1985), and for fuller entries (but fewer writers) one can consult Robert Hogan's *Dictionary of Irish Literature* (1980). Hickey and Doherty's *Dictionary of Irish History, 1800–1980* (1987) provides entries on hundreds of Irish notables, while Roy Foster's *Modern Ireland, 1600–1972* incorporates brief biographical footnotes on numerous leaders (including those before 1800 not contained in Hickey and Doherty). Brian de Breffny's *Ireland: A Cultural Encyclopedia* (1983) has entries on many architects, artists, and other figures outside of literature. Perhaps the best source for biographical information on figures beyond literature is Henry Boylan's *Dictionary of Irish Biography* (1988). The student looking for basic information and overviews of entire careers can find them in these books.

The brief entries that follow do not simply duplicate facts contained in my chronology: some items listed here did not work their way into the chronology, and as one might more readily expect, many items of information in the chronology concerning these people are not listed in these very short sketches. The entries below are intended to identify these people, place them in context, and list a few of their most significant accomplishments. The

11

thirty-seven figures listed here are truly the most *recurrent,* a categorization that does not correspond simply to those who might be evaluated as most *major.* For example, Oliver Cromwell's career is not sketched here, even though his impact on Ireland was indisputably very major indeed; I have written elsewhere about the popular as well as historical reverberations of Cromwell's Irish career (see my *Great Hatred, Little Room,* 24–26).

Given the emphasis of this chronology as explained in my introduction, however, Cromwell's deeds are summarized on a single page at the beginning, so the reader will have no trouble finding and following him in the chronology; also, I include here sketches only of *Irish* writers and leaders. Nor will the reader have any difficulty following Thomas Davis, the very influential Young Ireland leader and writer, because of the brevity of his career. On the other hand, to give a different kind of example, the activities of Peadar O'Donnell, an important but neglected twentieth-century writer and leader, are scattered throughout quite a number of entries ranging across many years (from 1921 to 1985), so the brief sketch below of his career is much more necessary, to help the reader in situating O'Donnell.

I should also note that I do not attempt to sketch here the career of any living Irish writer or leader. The facts concerning the living will develop further even before this book appears in print; also, with the recent deaths of both Samuel Beckett and Seán O'Faoláin, the list of indisputably major writers with careers beginning early in the century (and thus particularly calling for clarifying inclusion in this "reader's aid") seems significantly shorter if not at closure.

Having recorded these caveats and recommendations of biographical reference books, I hope these few sketches assist readers in tracking the following figures through my chronology.

Beckett, Samuel (1906–89), the greatest absurdist dramatist and fiction writer of the mid- to late twentieth century: born near Dublin; educated at Trinity College, Dublin; lecturer at École Normale Superieure, Paris, 1928–30, and at Trinity College, Dublin, 1930–32; friend of James Joyce in Paris during the 1930s; published *Proust* (critical study), 1931; *More Pricks than Kicks* (short stories), 1934; *Murphy* (novel), 1938; active in French resistance movement during World War II; published last novel in

English, *Watt,* 1953 (but written considerably earlier); henceforth wrote mostly in French, including his trilogy of novels *Molloy,* 1951, *Malone meurt (Malone Dies),* 1952, and *L'innomable (The Unnamable),* 1953; his great plays *En attendant Godot (Waiting for Godot),* 1953; *Fin de partie (Endgame)* and *All That Fall,* 1957; *Krapp's Last Tape,* 1958; and *Comment c'est (How It Is)* (novel), 1961; awarded Nobel Prize for Literature, 1969; *Breath* (play), 1970; mostly very short works of fiction and drama in his last years.

Carleton, William (1794–1869), one of the best fiction writers of the nineteenth century, the first from Gaelic Ireland to write in English: born in county Tyrone, in an Irish-speaking area, the youngest of fourteen children of a poor tenant farmer; a gifted student of the Gaelic "hedgeschools" of the era; joined the Ribbonmen (agrarian revolutionaries), 1813, but later renounced their violence (the subject of his great story "Wildgoose Lodge"); did not succeed in gaining admission to Maynooth Seminary; lost a schoolmastership in Carlow; went to Dublin, converted to Protestantism, and met Caesar Otway, editor of the *Christian Examiner,* in 1826; serialized his first stories in the *Examiner,* subsequently collected as *Traits and Stories of the Irish Peasantry,* 1830, 1833; published first novel, *Fardorougha, the Miser,* serially, 1837–38; *Rody the Rover* and *Valentine McClutchy* (novels), 1845; wrote for the *Nation,* 1845; *The Black Prophet* (novel), 1847; *The Emigrants of Ahadarra* and *The Tithe Proctor* (novels), 1848; later fiction, such as *The Black Baronet,* was inferior.

Clarke, Austin (1896–1974), one of the best poets since Yeats: born in Dublin; educated at Belvedere College and University College, Dublin (UCD), where he studied Old Irish literature; succeeded Thomas MacDonagh as lecturer at UCD in 1916; published early poetry, inspired by Irish epic models, in such books as *The Fires of Baal,* 1921, and *The Cattle-Drive in Connacht,* 1925; shifted to shorter lyrics in *Pilgrimage,* 1929; wrote such prose romances as *The Bright Temptation,* 1932, and *The Singing Men of Cashel,* 1936; *Night and Morning,* 1938, a pivotal volume of poems with further shift to short, often satiric verses; *The Viscount of Blarney and Other Plays,* 1944; *Poetry in Modern Ireland* (criticism), 1951; *Ancient Lights* (poems), 1955;

Later Poems, 1961; *Mnemosyne Lay in Dust* (poems), 1966; *Collected Poems,* 1974.

Connolly, James (1868–1916), Irish socialist labor leader and Easter 1916 martyr: born in Edinburgh, Scotland, of Irish immigrant parents; joined the British army for economic reasons at age fourteen, 1882; deserted and returned to Edinburgh, 1889; came to Dublin as an organizer for the Dublin Socialist Society, 1896; founded the Irish Socialist Republican Party, 1896; founded and edited the *Workers' Republic* newspaper, 1898; went to America where he was active as a socialist organizer, 1903–10; returned to Ireland to serve as organizer in Belfast for James Larkin's Irish Transport and General Workers' Union (ITGWU), 1910; author of *Labour in Irish History* and *Labour, Nationality, and Religion,* 1910; led the ITGWU during the lockout of the workers by the Dublin Employers' Federation, while Larkin was imprisoned, 1913; founded the Irish Citizen Army to defend workers, 1914; published *The Reconquest of Ireland,* 1915; led the Citizen Army and joined forces with Pádraic Pearse's Irish Volunteers in the Easter Rising, 1916; executed by the British, 12 May 1916.

Davitt, Michael (1846–1906), founder of the Land League: born in Straide, county Mayo; emigrated with his family in 1851 to Lancashire, England, where he lost his right arm while working in a mill at age eleven; joined the Irish Republican Brotherhood (IRB), 1865; IRB organizing secretary, 1868; sentenced for IRB activities to fifteen years in prison, 1870; released, 1877; went to America where he worked with Fenian leader John Devoy on a "new departure" combining nationalist and land concerns; formed the Land League of Mayo, 1878; founded the National Land League, 1879; helped establish the Ladies' Land League and the American Land League, 1880; met the American socialist Henry George and was impressed by his writings about land nationalization; elected member of Parliament for county Meath while in prison, 1882; convinced Parnell to form the National League after the Land League was proscribed, but grew apart from Parnell (who was not nearly so radical as Davitt on land issues); published *Leaves from a Prison Diary,* 1885; gave evidence on Parnell's behalf during the investigation of his reputed role in the Phoenix Park murders, 1889; edited the *Labour World* in London,

1890–91; anti-Parnellite member of Parliament for North Meath, 1892 and South Mayo, 1895–99; published *Life and Progress in Australasia,* 1898, as a result of his trip to Australia and New Zealand three years earlier; published *The Boer Fight for Freedom,* based on his earlier observation of the Boer War as a correspondent, 1902; published *Within the Pale* about his trip to Russia, 1903; published *The Fall of Feudalism* (memoir), 1904.

de Valera, Eamon (1882–1975), nationalist rebel and longest serving (and most recurrent) head of state of the Irish republic, "Dev," "the Chief": born in New York but raised in county Limerick; educated at Blackrock College and University College, Dublin; joined the Gaelic League, 1908; enlisted in the Irish Volunteers, 1913; last commander to surrender in the Easter Rising, yet spared execution by the British due to his U.S. citizenship, 1916; elected Sinn Féin member of Parliament for East Clare, 1917; chief of the Irish Volunteers, 1917–22; president of Sinn Féin, 1917–26; elected president of the first Dáil Éireann (Irish parliament), April 1919; visited America in search of U.S. and League of Nations support, 1920; elected president of the Irish Republic, August 1921; resigned upon the ratification of the Anglo-Irish Treaty by the Dáil, 15 December 1921; founded the antitreaty Cumann na Poblachta (Society of the republic); led antitreaty IRA during the Civil War, 1922–23; arrested and imprisoned, 1923–24; established the Fianna Fáil (Soldiers of destiny) party, November 1926; led the first Fianna Fáil government after agreeing to join the Free State Dáil, 1932–37; elected president of the council of the League of Nations, 1932; had major influence on the Irish Constitution, 1937; served as taoiseach (prime minister) and minister of external affairs, 1937–48; minister of education, 1939–40; defeated for the first time in a national election, 1948; returned again as taoiseach, 1951–54 and 1957–59; president of the Irish republic (a more ceremonial position), 1959–73.

Edgeworth, Maria (1767–1849), the first great Irish novelist: born in Reading, England; moved to Edgeworthstown, county Longford, with her father, Richard Lovell Edgeworth, an influential Anglo-Irish educator and politician, 1782; collaborated with her father on *Essays on Practical Education,* 1797, and *Essays on*

Irish Bulls, 1803; helped make Edgeworthstown a model progressive estate; published her most celebrated novel, *Castle Rackrent,* 1800; other Irish novels include *Ennui,* 1809, *The Absentee,* 1812, and *Ormond,* 1817; subsequently declared that she was too saddened by conditions in Ireland to write about it further.

Gregory, Lady Augusta (1859–1932), cofounder with Yeats of the Irish dramatic movement and popularizer along with Hyde of a newly authentic Irish-English style of writing: born in county Galway; married Sir William Gregory in 1880; widowed in 1892; theater movement planned at her home, Coole Park, in a meeting including Yeats and others, 1897; collaborated with Yeats on *Cathleen ni Hoolihan* (play), 1902; *The Pot of Broth* (play), 1902; redaction of Ulster cycle, *Cúchulain of Muirthemne* (prose mythology), 1902; *Twenty-Five* (play), 1903; *Spreading the News* (play), 1904; sequel to *Cúchulain, Gods and Fighting Men* (prose mythology), 1904; *The Gaol Gate* (play), 1906; *The Rising of the Moon* (play), 1907; *Our Irish Theatre* (memoir), 1913; son Robert killed in World War I; as Abbey director participated in rejecting O'Casey's *The Silver Tassie* and Denis Johnston's *The Old Lady Says "No!,"* 1928.

Hyde, Douglas (1860–1947), Gaelic League founder, first (titular) president of the Irish Republic, playwright, translator, scholar, and professor: born in Sligo and raised in county Roscommon; educated at Trinity College, Dublin; cofounded the Irish Literary Society in London, 1891; president of the National Literary Society, Dublin, 1892; gave a celebrated speech, "The Necessity for De-anglicising Ireland," 1892; founded the Gaelic League, 1893; published his bilingual collection of *Love Songs of Connacht,* very influential in its use of Irish English, 1893; wrote the first play in Irish for the Dublin stage, *Casadh an tSúgáin* (The twisting of the rope), 1901; professor of modern Irish at the National University of Ireland, 1908–32; resigned as president of the Gaelic League because he felt it had become too involved in politics, 1915; Irish Free State senator, 1925–26; president of the Irish Republic, 1938.

Joyce, James (1882–1941), chief innovator of the modern novel and one of the two most celebrated figures (with Yeats) in modern Irish literature: born in Dublin, oldest son of a large family that suffered the economic decline of his father, John Joyce; educated at Jesuit schools and University College, Dublin; published review of Ibsen in the *Fortnightly Review,* 1900; *The Day of the Rabblement,* a pamphlet critiquing the theater movement, 1901; left Dublin with Nora Barnacle for Paris, Zurich, and Trieste, 1904; "The Holy Office," a satiric broadsheet poem, 1905; *Chamber Music* (poems), 1907; "Gas from a Burner" (satiric poem), 1912; *Dubliners* (short stories), published after much delay, 1914; *A Portrait of the Artist as a Young Man* (novel), 1916; *Ulysses* (novel), 1922; helped organize *Our Exagmination* [*sic*] *Round His Factification for Incamination of Work in Progress,* a book of essays on what would be *Finnegans Wake,* 1929; *Finnegans Wake* (novel), 1939.

Kavanagh, Patrick (1904–67), the most important poet in the generation after Yeats: born in county Monaghan, whose countryside he immortalized in his poems; self-educated; *Ploughman and Other Poems,* 1936; *The Green Fool,* autobiography of his life in Monaghan, 1938; moved to Dublin, where he became a leading "character" and subsequently friend of Flann O'Brien and Brendan Behan, 1939; *The Great Hunger* (long poem), 1942; *A Soul for Sale* (poems), 1947; *Tarry Flynn* (novel), 1948; *Come Dance with Kitty Stobling* (poems), 1960; *Collected Poems,* 1964.

Larkin, James (1876–1947), "Big Jim," the central leader along with James Connolly of the Irish labor movement; born in Liverpool of Irish parents; raised in county Down in the north of Ireland; returned to Liverpool in 1885, became a dock foreman, and was fired for joining a strike; sent to Belfast as an organizer of the National Union of Dock Labourers and also formed a Dublin branch of the union, 1907; founded the Irish Transport and General Workers' Union (ITGWU), 1909; president of the Irish Trades Union Congress, 1911; major leader of the workers during the 1913 lockout; imprisoned as a result, 1913–14; went to America where he was active in the International Workers of the World (IWW or "Wobblies"), 1914–23; imprisoned, 1920–23; returned to Dublin in 1923 to a big reception, but was then expelled from the ITGWU by antisocialists and founded the Workers' Union of Ireland, 1924; labor spokesman in the Irish

Senate, 1926–32, 1937–38, and 1943–44; memorialized today by a statue in the middle of O'Connell Street in Dublin.

Lever, Charles (1806–72), the most commercially successful Irish novelist of the nineteenth century and one of the most entertaining and interesting: born in Dublin; educated at Trinity College, Dublin, in medicine; traveled in the United States and Canada, 1829; worked as a doctor during the cholera epidemic in county Clare, 1832; *The Confessions of Harry Lorrequer* (novel) serialized in the *Dublin University Magazine,* 1839; *Charles O'Malley, the Irish Dragoon* (novel), a rollicking smash success, 1841; edited the *Dublin University Magazine,* 1842; *The O'Donoghue* and *St. Patrick's Eve* more somber novels published at the beginning of the Great Hunger, 1845; moved to Florence, Italy, 1847; *The Martins of Cro Martin* (novel), 1856; named British consul to Trieste, 1867; *Lord Kilgobbin* (novel), 1872.

Moore, George (1852–1933), Joyce's rival as leading novelist of the Literary Revival period, older and better known than Joyce during Moore's lifetime but later eclipsed by him: born in Dublin, the son of Catholic gentry; educated at Trinity College, Dublin; lived in Paris, 1873–80, and then in London, 1880–1901; first novel, *A Modern Lover,* in the style of Zola, 1883; *A Mummer's Wife* (novel), 1885; *A Drama in Muslin,* first novel set in Ireland, 1886; *Parnell and His Island* (prose nonfiction), 1887; *Esther Waters* (novel), 1894; moved to Dublin and was active in the Literary Revival, 1901–11; *The Untilled Field* (short stories), 1903; *The Lake,* his best Irish novel, 1905; returned permanently to London, 1911; *Hail and Farewell,* a three-volume memoir, 1911–14; *A Storyteller's Holiday* (stories), 1918.

O'Brien, Flann (1911–66), the leading Irish satirist of the twentieth century: born Brian O'Nolan in Strabane, county Tyrone; educated at University College, Dublin, where he earned an M.A. in Irish; first novel, *At Swim-Two-Birds,* published under his characteristic fictional pseudonym, "Flann O'Brien," 1939; as "Myles na gCopaleen," began writing "Cruiskeen Lawn" (the little full jug), the most popular and longest running satiric column of the century, for the *Irish Times,* 1939; *An Béal Bocht (The Poor Mouth),* satiric novel in Irish, 1941; *Faustus Kelly* (satiric Dublin play), 1943; *The Hard Life* (novel), 1961; *The Dalkey Archive* (novel), 1964; *The Third Policeman* (novel), 1967, actually an earlier, previously unpublished version of *The Dalkey Archive.*

O'Brien, Kate (1897–1974), one of the most accomplished Irish novelists of this century: born in Limerick (memorialized in her novels as "Mellick"), the daughter of middle-class Catholics; educated at University College, Dublin; first novel, *Without My Cloak,* 1931; *The Ante-Room* (novel), 1933; worked as a governess in Spain, the setting of her novels *Mary Lavelle* (1936) and *That Lady* (1946); her best novel, *The Land of Spices,* 1941, ludicrously banned because of a single veiled reference to homosexuality; *The Last of Summer* (novel), 1943; *My Ireland* (memoir), 1962.

Ó Cadhain, Máirtín (1907–70), the greatest Irish Gaelic fiction writer: born in county Galway; lost his job as a schoolteacher because of his IRA activities in the 1930s; *Idir Shúgradh agus Dáiríre* (Half in jest, half in earnest) (short stories), 1939; spent five years during World War II in an internment camp; *An Braon Broghach* (The dirty drop) (stories), 1948; *Cré na Cille* (Churchyard clay) (novel), 1949; became Irish government translator, 1949; *Cois Caoláire* (Beside the inlet) (stories), 1953; appointed lecturer at Trinity College, Dublin, 1956; *An tSraith ar Lár* (The swath laid low) (stories), 1967; elected professor, 1969; *An tSraith Dhá Tógáil* (The swath raised up) (stories), 1970.

O'Casey, Seán (1880–1964), one of the two or three best Irish dramatists: born in Dublin as John Casey, self-educated and the son of working-class (or lower-middle-class) Protestant parents; worked as a laborer and became deeply committed to the labor movement; appointed secretary to the Irish Transport and General Workers' Union (ITGWU) under James Larkin, 1913; published *The Story of the Irish Citizen Army,* 1919; first successful play, *The Shadow of a Gunman,* 1923; *Juno and the Paycock* (play), 1924; *The Plough and the Stars* (play), greeted by protests because of its unsentimental portrait of the Easter Rising, 1926; moved permanently to England; *The Silver Tassie* rejected by the Abbey Theatre, 1928, but subsequently staged in London; *The Star Turns Red* (play), 1939; *I Knock at the Door,* 1939, the first of a six-volume autobiography appearing through 1954; *Purple Dust* (play), 1940; *Red Roses for Me* (play), 1942; *Cock-a-Doodle Dandy* (play), 1949; *The Bishop's Bonfire* (play), 1955.

Ó Conaire, Pádraic (1883–1928), the writer who modernized Irish Gaelic prose, though he suffered financially for doing so and therefore often wasted his talents while trying to support himself: born in Galway; went to sea and then worked in the British civil service in London; won a prize for his short story "Páidín Mháire," 1904; *Bairbre Ruadh* (Red Barbara) (play), 1908; *Deoraíocht* (Exile) (novel), 1910; *An Chéad Chloch* (The first stone) (stories), 1914; *Seacht mBuaidh an Eirghe-Amach* (Seven battles of rebellion) (prose nonfiction), 1918; *An Crann Géagach* (The branching tree) (stories), 1919; *Brian Óg* (Young Brian) (novel), 1926; *M'Asal Beag Dubh* (My little black donkey) (stories), 1944; *Scothscéalta* (Selected stories), 1956.

O'Connor, Frank (1903–66), the Irish writer most devoted to the art of the short story: born in Cork as Michael O'Donovan, the son of working-class Catholics; like Seán O'Faoláin, an earlier follower of Daniel Corkery who subsequently turned away from Corkery's comparatively conservative nationalism; served with the republican antitreaty forces during the Civil War, 1922–23; librarian of Cork County Library, 1925–28, and then of the Ballsbridge library in Dublin, 1928–38; first volume of stories, *Guests of the Nation,* 1931; *The Saint and Mary Kate,* 1932, and *Dutch Interior,* 1940, his only two novels; *Bones of Contention* (stories), 1936; *Crab Apple Jelly* (stories), 1944; *The Common Chord,* (stories), 1947; *Irish Miles* (travel book), 1947; *Traveller's Samples* (stories), 1951; visiting lecturer at Harvard, 1952 and 1954; *Stories,* 1952; *More Stories,* 1954; *Domestic Relations* (stories), 1957; *An Only Child* (autobiography), 1961; *The Lonely Voice: A Study of the Short Story,* 1962; *Collection Two,* 1964.

O'Connell, Daniel (1775–1847), the first great Irish nationalist popular leader, the "Emancipator," the "Liberator," the "Counsellor": born in Carhen, county Kerry; educated at St. Omer school; called to the bar, 1798; opposed the Act of Union in his first speech, 1800; founded the Catholic Association, 1823;

elected Catholic member of Parliament for county Clare, provoking the granting of Catholic Emancipation, 1828; reelected, 1829; founded the Repeal Association in opposition to the Union, 1840; first lord mayor of Dublin, 1841; called off a massive Repeal rally at Clontarf, north of Dublin, when the authorities proscribed it, 1843; as a result scorned by Young Ireland leaders and nonetheless sentenced to a year in prison, May 1844; sentence removed by House of Lords, September 1844; witnessed the beginning of the Great Hunger, 1845; died at Genoa while en route to Rome, where his heart was buried according to his own Catholic request.

O'Donnell, Peadar (1893–1986), socialist leader, editor, and novelist: born and raised in county Donegal; schoolteacher; organizer for the Irish Transport and General Workers' Union (ITGWU), 1916; joined the IRA, 1918; took the antitreaty side in the Civil War and was imprisoned, 1922–24; published first novel, *Storm,* 1925; jailed during struggle over land annuities, 1927; *Islanders* (novel), 1928; *Adrigoole* (novel), 1929; *The Knife* (novel), 1930; founder member of Saor Éire (Free Ireland), 1931; edited IRA newspaper, *An Phoblacht* (The republic), 1925–34; *The Gates Flew Open* (political memoir), 1932; founded Republican Congress, 1934; *On the Edge of the Stream* (novel), 1934; edited the *Bell,* 1946–54; *The Big Windows* (novel), 1955; *Proud Island* (novel), 1975.

O'Faoláin, Seán (1900–91), a writer whose influence as editor and nonfictional prose writer as well as fiction author made him the dean of Irish letters in the period after Yeats: born John Whelan in Cork, and grew up with the century; educated at University College, Cork, and Harvard, where he earned an M.A. in literature; fought with the republican antitreaty forces during the Civil War, 1922–23; lecturer at Boston College after completing his M.A., 1929; returned to Ireland and published his first volume of stories, *Midsummer Night's Madness,* 1932; other collections include *A Purse of Coppers,* 1937, *Teresa and Other Stories,* 1947, *The Man Who Invented Sin,* 1948, *The Stories of Seán O'Faoláin,* 1958, *I Remember! I Remember!,* 1961, *The Heat of the Sun,* 1966, and *Foreign Affairs,* 1976; also wrote the novels *A*

Nest of Simple Folk, 1933, *Bird Alone,* 1936, *Come Back to Erin,* 1940, and *And Again?,* 1979; also published influential biographies including *King of the Beggars,* 1938, on Daniel O'Connell, and *The Great O'Neill,* 1942; other influential prose nonfiction includes *The Irish,* 1947, and *The Short Story,* 1948; founded and edited the *Bell,* the most influential journal at midcentury, 1940–46; *Vive Moi!* (autobiography), 1964.

O'Flaherty, Liam (1896–1984), realistic-naturalistic fiction writer and socialist: born on Inis Mór in the Aran Islands; studied at Rockwell College, Blackrock College; and University College, Dublin; enlisted in the British army, 1915; wounded in France, 1917; traveled to and worked in London and then in South and North America, 1918–20; occupied the Rotunda building in Dublin for four days as leader of a group of unemployed men, January 1922; published first stories and first novel, *Thy Neighbour's Wife,* 1923; befriended London editor and reader Edward Garnett, 1923; first volume of stories, *Spring Sowing,* 1924; novel about the IRA, *The Informer,* 1925; married Margaret Barrington, 1926; *The Tent* (stories), 1926; *The Life of Tim Healy* (biography), 1927; *The Mountain Tavern and Other Stories,* 1929; *Two Years* (memoir), 1930; *The Puritan* (novel), 1931; *I Went to Russia* (memoir), 1931; separated from Margaret Barrington and published *Skerrett* (novel), 1932; *Shame the Devil* (autobiography), 1934; *The Short Stories of Liam O'Flaherty* and *Famine* (novel), 1937; lived in Connecticut, South America, and the Carribean, 1940–46; returned to Dublin, 1946; *Two Lovely Beasts and Other Stories,* 1948; *Dúil* (Desire), collection of stories in Irish, 1953; *The Stories of Liam O'Flaherty,* 1956; *The Pedlar's Revenge and Other Stories,* 1976.

O'Grady, Standish James (1846–1928), the writer whom Yeats described as "the father of the Irish Renaissance": born in county Cork, to a comfortable Protestant family; educated at Trinity College, Dublin; called to the bar but turned to journalism, history, and fiction, publishing his two-volume *History of Ireland,* 1878, 1880; *Early Bardic Literature of Ireland* (criticism), 1879; *The Crisis in Ireland* (prose nonfiction), 1881; *Toryism and the Tory Democracy* (prose nonfiction), 1886; *Red Hugh's Captivity* (novel), 1889; *The Coming of Cuculain [sic]* (novel), 1894; *Ulrick* *the Ready* (novel), 1896; *The Flight of the Eagle* (novel), 1897; edited the *All-Ireland Review,* 1900–1907.

Parnell, Charles Stewart (1846–91), Irish nationalist parliamentary leader and "uncrowned king of Ireland": born in Avondale, county Wicklow; educated in England; member of Parliament for county Meath, 1875; a leader of Irish "obstructionists" in Parliament, 1877–78; president of the Land League, 1879; head of the Irish Parliamentary party, 1880; imprisoned in Dublin by the British, October 1881; released under terms of the "Kilmainham Treaty," May 1882; helped convert British prime minister William Gladstone to the cause of Irish Home Rule, December 1885; accused of involvement in the Phoenix Park murders of the British chief secretary and undersecretary, 1887; vindicated as the victim of a forger, February 1889; cited as lover of Captain O'Shea's wife in O'Shea's divorce petition, December 1889; as a result of scandal, abandoned by many supporters, 1890; defeated in election, December 1890; married Kitty O'Shea, June 1891; died, 6 October 1891.

Pearse, Pádraic H. (1879–1916), educator, bilingual writer, and chief leader of the 1916 Easter Rising: born in Dublin; learned Irish at a Christian Brothers school; earned a degree at Dublin's Royal University; called to the bar but did not practice as an attorney; very active in the Gaelic League, beginning in 1896; editor of the newspaper *An Claidheamh Soluis* (The sword of light), 1903–9; founding schoolmaster of St. Enda's, his model nationalist boys' school outside of Dublin, 1908–13; founding member of the Irish Volunteers, November 1913; toured America to raise money for his school and the Volunteers, 1914; delivered a celebrated nationalist oration at the funeral of the Fenian O'Donovan Rossa, August 1915; planned the Easter Rising, led the Irish Volunteers, and read the "Proclamation of Independence" from the steps of Dublin's General Post Office, Easter Monday 1916; surrendered five days later; executed by British, 3 May 1916.

Russell, George ("Æ") (1867–1935), poet, social activist, and influential editor and mentor of younger writers: born in county Armagh; studied at the Dublin Metropolitan School of Art; first volume of verse, *Homeward: Songs by the Way,* 1894; his pen name "Æ," short for "aeon," encapsulating his visionary views; joined the Irish Agricultural Organisation Society, becoming secretary; edited the society's journal, the *Irish Homestead,* beginning in 1895; *Deirdre* staged by the Abbey Theatre, 1902; *New Poems,* 1904; *Collected Poems,* 1913; *The National Being* (essays), 1916; *The Candle of Vision* (poems), 1919; edited the very influential *Irish Statesman,* 1923–30.

Shaw, George Bernard (1856–1950), the playwright whose career was the longest and most successful of any modern dramatist: born in Dublin, the son of an unsuccessful Protestant merchant; left school at age fifteen and worked in a land agent's office; moved to London with his mother and sister, 1876; wrote several unsuccessful novels; joined the socialist Fabian society, 1884; began reviewing for the *Star,* 1888; first play, *Widowers' Houses,* 1892; wrote *Mrs. Warren's Profession* (play) but was refused a license for it, 1893; became drama critic for the *Saturday Review,* 1895; *Man and Superman* (play), 1903; *Candida* (play), 1904; in an unusual reversal, *John Bull's Other Island* turned down by the Abbey Theatre but staged in London, 1905; *The Shewing Up of Blanco Posnet* banned in London but produced at the Abbey, 1909; *Pygmalion* (play), 1912; protested executions of leaders of the Easter Rising, and unsuccessfully defended Roger Casement, 1916; *St. Joan* (play), 1924; awarded Nobel Prize for Literature, 1925; *The Intelligent Woman's Guide to Socialism and Capitalism,* 1928.

Somerville, Edith (1858–1949) and **Violet Martin** ("Martin Ross," 1862–1915), the cousins who formed the closest highly successful coauthorship in modern literature: Somerville born in county Cork and Martin in county Galway, both to Ascendancy families whose Big Houses were on the decline; met in 1886 and formed the friendship that would be the most important in their lives; first novel, *An Irish Cousin,* 1889; best novel, *The Real Charlotte,* 1894; Martin suffered a riding accident that left her in poor health for the rest of her life, 1898; most successful sequence of stories *The Experiences of an Irish R.M.* (1899), *Further Experiences of an Irish R.M.* (1908), and *In Mr. Knox's Country* (1915); Martin's death left Somerville in deep mourning but determined to write in her spirit, 1915; *Irish Memories* (memoir), 1917; *An Enthusiast* (novel), 1921; best solo novel, *The Big House of Inver,* inspired by an earlier letter from Martin and published under both of their names, 1925.

Stephens, James (1882–1950), the "leprachaun of Irish literature" not only because of his very small stature but also because of his popular, myth-based book *The Crock of Gold:* born in Dublin; worked as a clerk; *Insurrections* (poems), 1909; made an auspicious debut as a fiction writer with *The Crock of Gold* and *The Charwoman's Daughter,* both 1912; *The Hill of Vision* (poems), 1912; *Here Are Ladies* (stories), 1913; appointed registrar of the National Gallery, 1915; *Reincarnations* (poems), 1918; *Deirdre* (prose mythology), 1923; *In the Land of Youth* (prose mythology), 1924; moved to London, 1925, where he became a popular BBC announcer; *Collected Poems,* 1926; *Etched in Moonlight* (stories), 1928; asked by James Joyce in the 1930s to finish *Finnegans Wake* if Joyce himself could not do so.

Swift, Jonathan (1667–1745), the first great Irish writer in English and the leading pioneer of satire: born in Dublin; educated at Kilkenny Grammar School and Trinity College, Dublin; became secretary to Sir William Temple, 1689; ordained in the Anglican Church of Ireland, 1694; first important prose work, *The Battle of the Books,* 1697; met Esther Johnson ("Stella" in his writings), who would die in 1728; returned to Dublin, following Temple's death, to serve at St. Patrick's, 1699; published satire on Christian sects, *A Tale of a Tub,* 1704; appointed dean of St. Patrick's, 1713; met Esther Vanhomrigh ("Vanessa" in his writings), apparently to be his lover and his child's mother, who would die in 1723; *Gulliver's Travels,* 1726; *A Modest Proposal,* his great satire on Irish poverty and hunger, 1729; sunk into madness in his later years.

Synge, John Millington (1871–1909), the outstanding playwright of the early Literary Revival period: born in Rathfarnham, near Dublin; educated at Trinity College, Dublin; lived and wrote for several years in Paris, where he met Yeats in 1896; visited Aran Islands during summers of 1898–1902; first play, *In the Shadow of the Glen,* 1903; *Riders to the Sea* (play), 1904; *The Well of the*

Saints (play), 1905; *The Playboy of the Western World* (play), greeted by riots in reaction to its portrait of the harboring of a self-proclaimed murderer, who refers to women's "shifts," and *The Aran Islands* (prose nonfiction), 1907; died of Hodgkin's disease; *Deirdre of the Sorrows* staged after his death with his lover, Molly Allgood, in the lead, 1910.

Tone, Theobald Wolfe (1763–98), chief leader and republican idealist of the 1798 rebellions, often viewed as the founder of modern Irish nationalism: born in Dublin; educated at Trinity College, Dublin, where he imbibed Irish Protestant idealism; founded the United Irishmen and instigated an abortive voyage of a French fleet toward Ireland, 1791; published his *Argument on Behalf of the Catholics of Ireland*, 1791; lived in exile in Paris, in close contact with French republicans, 1795–98; led a more dramatic French expedition to Ireland to take part in the 1798 risings; committed suicide after capture.

Wilde, Oscar (1854–1900), the leading character of the "art for art's sake" movement in London and the playwright who (along with his fellow Dubliner Shaw) revolutionized modern British drama: born in Dublin; educated at Trinity College, Dublin, and Oxford University, where he was awarded the chief poetry prize for "Ravenna"; satirized as a flower-wearing esthete in Gilbert and Sullivan's operetta *Patience*, 1881; toured America where he created a sensation entertaining his audiences, 1882; first play, *Vera, or the Nihilists*, 1883; *The Picture of Dorian Gray* (novel), 1891; *Salome* (play) and *Lady Windermere's Fan* (play), 1892; *A Woman of No Importance* (play), 1893; his masterpiece, *The Importance of Being Earnest*, staged to rave reviews just as events unfolded that would destroy him, 1895; sued the Marquis of Queensbury, father of Wilde's lover Lord Alfred Douglas, for libel after Queensbury accused him of homosexuality, but instead convicted and sentenced for homosexuality, 1895; *The Ballad of Reading Gaol* (poem), 1898; died in France; *De Profundis* his bleak, posthumously published prose "testament," 1905.

Yeats, William Butler (1865–1939), the greatest modern poet, the chief architect of the Irish Literary Revival, and one of the two (with Joyce) most celebrated figures in modern Irish literature:

born in Sandymount in Dublin, son of a notable painter, John Butler Yeats, and older brother of modern Ireland's best-known painter, Jack Yeats; studied art in Dublin and London; *The Wanderings of Oisin* (long poem) and *Crossways* (first volume of poems), 1889; helped found the Irish Literary Society in London, 1891; *The Countess Cathleen* (play), 1892; *The Celtic Twilight* (stories), 1893; *The Rose* (poems), 1893; planned Irish dramatic movement with Lady Gregory and others at her home, 1897; *The Secret Rose* (stories), 1897; *The Wind among the Reeds* (poems), 1899; *The Countess Cathleen,* one of the initial productions of the new Irish theater, Dublin, 1899; *Cathleen ni Hoolihan* (play), 1902; *In the Seven Woods* (poems), 1903; *On Baile's Strand* (play), 1904; *Deirdre* (play), 1906; *The Green Helmet* (poems), 1910; *Responsibilities* (poems), 1914; married Georgie Hyde-Lees, 1917; *The Wild Swans at Coole* (poems) and *The Only Jealousy of Emer* (play), 1919; *Michael Robartes and the Dancer* (poems), 1921; moved into a restored tower, Thoor Ballylee, near Lady Gregory's home, 1922; first Irishman to be awarded the Nobel Prize for Literature, 1923; became a member of the Irish Senate, 1923; *The Tower* (poems), 1928; *The Winding Stair* (poems), 1929; *The Words upon the Window-Pane* performed, 1930, and published, 1934; *Purgatory* (play), 1938; *The Death of Cuchulain* (play), 1939; *Last Poems,* 1939.

MODERN IRISH LITERATURE AND CULTURE
A CHRONOLOGY

••

1601

In December at the Battle of Kinsale in county Cork, the English, led by Montjoy, defeated the northern chieftains Hugh O'Neill (1540–1616) and Red Hugh O'Donnell (1571–1602) and other Gaelic leaders, having already repulsed their Spanish allies. Nearly 5,000 Spanish allies of the Irish had managed to land, but O'Neill and O'Donnell were hampered by having to join them from the north after a long march and with little consolidated Irish support.

1607

By this date Hugh O'Neill and Red Hugh O'Donnell, following their attempts to stop the anglicization of their Gaelic areas of Ulster, had been permanently vanquished by the English and, along with several other Irish leaders, O'Neill had fled to the European Continent in September. He preferred life in exile to surrender. This action was forever remembered as "the flight of the earls" or "wild geese."

Poetry

"Now stolen is the soul from Éire's breast," lamented one poet, reacting to these events. Another, Aindrias Mac Marcais (whose dates are unknown), wrote in "The Deserted Land," a poem originally in Irish translated here in prose, "Tonight Ireland is lonely. The banishment of her true race causes the cheeks of her

29

men and her fair women to be wet. . . . Away from us the choicest
of the sons of Ireland are journeying without anyone stopping
them" (Deane et al., 1991, 1: 279–80).

1608

A short-lived rebellion led by Cahir O'Doherty (1587–1608), a
Gaelic aristocrat, in Derry was followed by the expansion and
acceleration of the Protestant plantation scheme in Ulster.

1612

Prose Nonfiction

Sir John Davies's (1569–1626) *A Discovery of the True Causes
Why Ireland Was Never Entirely Subdued* was an imperialistic
British account of the conquest in Ireland, full of arrogant pride in
what was described as "a *Perfect Conquest.*"

1613

As part of the anglicization and plantation of Ulster, in March the
city of Derry was incorporated as "Londonderry" (Doherty and
Hickey 1989, 36). To this day, in a linguistic and geographic
version of sectarianism, Protestants call the city "Londonderry"
while Catholics continue to refer to it as "Derry." At the same
time, massive amounts of choice acreage in Ulster were reas-
signed, by governmental fiat, from Catholic farmers to Protestant
Church of Ireland bishops, Trinity College, in Dublin, the city of
London, and various Protestant aristocrats.

1614

In May it was proclaimed that "all titular archbishops, bishops,
deans, vicars-general, Jesuits, friars, seminary priests, and other
priests, depart the realm of Ireland before the 30th of September,"
and in June British lord deputy in Ireland Arthur Chichester
(1563–1625) was instructed to force the Irish to practice Protestantism rather than Catholicism (Doherty and Hickey 1989, 36).

Despite these fiats, evidence of the mounting political domination of Protestantism, most of the native Irish population would remain Catholic. This was a century in which, increasingly, the small Catholic middle and upper classes were devastated, while the general Catholic population (mostly poor tenant farmers and even poorer laborers) were reduced to a slavelike status.

1618

A system of fines was enacted in an attempt to enforce the removal of Catholics from their lands and the segregation of Catholics from Protestants.

1620

Prose Nonfiction

Of the Commonwealth of Ireland by Fynes Moryson (1566–1630) was another imperialist essay from the British point of view.

1622

By this date nearly 8,000 English settlers had settled in counties Down and Antrim in Ulster.

1626

Archbishop Ussher (1581–1656) and twelve other Protestant bishops declared in November that "to grant the papists a toleration or to consent that they freely exercise their religion and profess their faith and doctrines, was a grievous sin" (quoted in Doherty and Hickey 1989, 38).

1628

The system of fines enacted ten years earlier was now amended, permitting Catholics to live on some of the lands earlier bequeathed to Protestants, but with steep rents and severe restrictions.

1629

In Dublin Protestant archbishop Bulkeley, the mayor, and English troops tried to stop a Mass service at a Franciscan chapel, but Catholic rioting foiled the attempt and forced the archbishop to seek refuge (Doherty and Hickey 1989, 39).

1631

Irish Language and Literature

Micheál Ó Cléirigh (1575–1643) completed a revised version of *Leabhar Gabhála* (The book of invasions), a historical account written in early modern Irish Gaelic (Doherty and Hickey 1989, 39).

1634

Irish Language and Literature

Seathrún Céitinn (Geoffrey Keating) (1570–1644) completed his *Foras Feasa ar Éireann* (Basic information about Ireland), which he had begun fourteen years earlier (Doherty and Hickey 1989, 37). This was the first history of Ireland written in Irish Gaelic and also an influence on and source for the formation of the modern Irish Gaelic language and its literature.

1637

Drama

The first theater in Dublin, the Werburgh Street Theatre, opened, but closed a few years later during the political and military upheavals of the 1640s (McHugh and Harmon 1982, 143).

1641

The southern Leinsterman Rory O'More (1620–52) led bitter Ulster Catholics in an uprising against the Protestant settlers, beginning a larger war that eventually exposed Ireland to a more total English conquest. O'More's attack on Dublin Castle failed partly because the government had been warned by a relative of one of the rebels.

The Ancient Order of Hibernians (AOH) was founded (Hickey and Doherty 1987, 11). It would develop into a nationalist opponent of the Protestant Orange Order, and in the nineteenth century spread to the United States, where it became a formidable Irish-American organization.

1642

In July Owen Roe O'Neill (1590–1649), who had been fighting with the Spanish army in Flanders, returned to Ireland from the Continent, and subsequently led last-ditch native Irish attempts (continuing through the 1640s) to stave off English domination of Ireland.

1645

The papal nuncio, Cardinal Rinuccini (1592–1653), came to Ireland to try to help solidify Catholicism in Ireland, but instead divisions among Irish Catholics deepened, particularly between those who combined their Catholicism with nascent Irish nationalism and those Catholics who remained loyal to English rule.

1649

Oliver Cromwell (1599–1658) arrived in Ireland in August, landing at Ringsend in Dublin. In September his 8,000 infantry and 4,000 cavalry slaughtered more than 3,000 men, women, and children in Drogheda, north of Dublin, and within eight months the English forces broke native Irish Catholic resistance and opened the way for nearly total Protestant domination. Over the next couple of years, Cromwell's army wreaked devastation similar to that at Drogheda at Carrickfergus, Wexford, Kilkenny, Clonmel, Carlow, Waterford, Limerick, and Galway. Thousands were killed, and survivors were sent to the West Indies in large numbers, more than 8,000 to Barbadoes alone. Cromwell's forces claimed more than a million acres of the best Irish farmland in the wake of their campaign of terror. In contrast to his reputation in English history as a reformer, in the Irish mythos Cromwell lives on in the image of a devil. More stories about him have been preserved in collections of Irish folklore than any other historical personage except for Daniel O'Connell.

Periodicals

Ironically, yet appropriately, given the nature of the influx of the English language into Ireland, Cromwell's invading army published the *Irish Monthly Mercury* in Cork on two occasions, in 1649 and 1650: "Ireland's first faltering newspaper, it depicted simply the Cromwellian victories, the chronicle of his gory progress across Ireland" (Oram 1983, 21).

1650

Irish Language and Literature

Páirlimint Cloinne Thomáis (Parliament of the descendants of Thomas), an Irish Gaelic prose parody composed around this date by an anonymous Munster writer, satirized those now on the rise as a result of changes in landholding in southern Ireland (Doherty and Hickey 1989, 52).

1654

May 1 was the deadline for all "transplantable persons" (primarily Catholic farmers in the midlands) to remove themselves to the west; they "should be liable to death if found east of the Shannon after that date" (Beckett 1966, 107). "To Hell or to Connacht" was the popular slogan.

1662

Drama

In October the Smock Alley Theatre in Dublin opened under the direction of John Ogilby (Doherty and Hickey 1989, 57). Until the late nineteenth century, such Dublin theaters were essentially provincial sites for staging British dramas.

1663

Periodicals

A Dublin bookseller, Samuel Dancer, brought out fifteen issues of the *Mercurius Hibernicus* or *Irish Intelligencer* newspaper (Oram 1983, 23).

1665

Fiction

Richard Head's (1637–86) *The English Rogue* was the first novel to feature an Irish protagonist. It played up "stage-Irish" stereotypes for obviously commercial reasons ("stage-Irish" refers to the long-standing stereotype of the Irishman as a clever, violent, drunken vagabond). The night that Head's hero spends in Ireland —sleeping among cows, pigs, and geese—not only reflects such stereotypes but also looks far ahead to their inflation by modern writers such as Myles na gCopaleen (Brian O'Nolan, better known as Flann O'Brien).

1667

Jonathan Swift (d. 1745) was born in Dublin.

1669

George Fox (1624–91), founder of the Religious Society of Friends, visited Ireland and organized the first Quaker meetings there.

1673

The Test Act in effect excluded all but Anglicans from public life by requiring officeholders to receive the Church of England's sacraments (Doherty and Hickey 1989, 59).

1677

Irish Language and Literature

Francis Molloy published a grammar of the Irish language in Latin, *Grammatica Latino-Hibernica* (Doherty and Hickey 1989, 59).

1681

The outlaw and rebel Redmond O'Hanlon, later celebrated by the novelist William Carleton and many Irish balladeers, was caught and shot dead in April, but lived on in the popular imagination as an Irish Robin Hood, an outlaw "rapparee" who sought to subvert English colonial settlement in Ireland.

Oliver Plunkett (b. 1629), Catholic archbishop of Armagh, was executed in July because of a supposed "Popish plot"; his remains were subsequently preserved in the cathedral at Dundalk, county Louth, and he was eventually canonized (in 1975).

1685

Periodicals

At the Leather Bottle tavern in Skinner's Row directly opposite Christ Church cathedral and near Dublin Castle, Robert Thornton published the *Dublin News-Letter* on the front and back of a single sheet (Oram 1983, 23–24).

1687

English Catholic King James II appointed the Catholic partisan Tyrconnel as chief minister in Ireland, thereby enraging Protestants, particularly those in the North.

1688

In the face of large-scale Protestant opposition in England, Catholic King James II fled to France. In November his throne was claimed by his Protestant daughter, Mary, and her husband, William of Orange. James then called Irish troops to his support. In December the town of Londonderry shut its gates against a new garrison from the Catholic Tyrconnel, the Protestants there declaring "No surrender!"

1689

In March King James II arrived in Ireland, landing (like the Spanish in 1601) at Kinsale in Cork, and advanced on Londonderry, thus beginning the most celebrated siege in Irish history with James's Catholic forces surrounding the Protestants inside the walled city of Derry. Thousands starved in Derry, but this did not sway the Protestant commanders, Major Henry Baker and the clergyman George Walker (1618–90). After nearly four months, King William's ships finally brought relief forces, and the Jacobite army broke camp, beginning a disheartened retreat south. Protestant victory followed at the battles of Boyne and Aughrim in the following year.

Jonathan Swift became secretary to Sir William Temple in London.

Periodicals

Andrew Cook printed the *Dublin Intelligencer* newspaper from 1690 to 1694 (Oram 1983, 24).

1691

The Treaty of Limerick instituted an anti-Catholic "Penal Age" that persisted throughout the eighteenth century. No Catholic was permitted to purchase land on a lease exceeding thirty-one years, to own a horse worth more than five pounds, or to bequeath his land by will to his oldest son—it had to be divided equally among all his sons, thus ensuring the extreme subdivision of holdings that was to afflict an overpopulated Ireland. Catholic priests were forced to celebrate Mass—now an illegal act—in caves and other remote places. Conversion to Protestantism freed an Irishman from the "Penal Code," and so some "conformed." A "hidden Ireland" (in Daniel Corkery's phrase) of Catholic, usually Gaelic-speaking peasants, whose religion was illegal and whose culture was devastated, suffered under the thumb of England and an elite Anglo-Irish upper class.

Prose Nonfiction

The Political Anatomy of Ireland by William Petty (1623–87) was a more tolerant account from the English point of view, looking ahead to the writings of Arthur Young in the next century.

1692

In November many Catholic landholders were outlawed for having supported King James II; they were forced to forfeit 3,921 estates amounting to 1,060,792 acres (Doherty and Hickey 1989, 65).

1698

Drama

Young playwright George Farquhar's (1677–1707) *Love and a Bottle* was staged in London. Born in Derry and educated at Trinity College, Dublin, Farquhar was one of the earliest in the long tradition of Irish playwrights—subsequently including Richard Brinsley Sheridan, Oscar Wilde, and George Bernard Shaw—who would make their names in London after being brought up in Ireland, and who specialized in English satire and comedy enhanced by their outsider status as Irishmen living in English society. More generally, Farquhar reflected the long-standing necessity of the Irish people provoked by far greater opportunities outside of Ireland, to seek their fortunes elsewhere. A contemporary commentator noted of his characters, "Farquhar's gentlemen are Irish gentlemen, frank, generous, eloquent, witty, and with a cordial word of gallantry always at command" (quoted in Martin 1980, 14).

Prose Nonfiction

William Molyneux (1656–98) published his pamphlet *The Case of Ireland's Being Bound by Acts of Parliament in England Stated.* On 27 June it was condemned by the English Parliament as "of dangerous tendency to the Crown and people of England" (quoted in Doherty and Hickey 1989, 66).

1700

Drama

The Way of the World consolidated William Congreve's (1670–1729) position on the London stage as master of the comedy of manners. This Protestant Anglo–Irishman was Jonathan Swift's contemporary at Kilkenny College and Trinity College, Dublin, and was one of the leading Irish comedians in London, along with Farquhar and, later, Sheridan.

1703

Periodicals

Thomas Hume began publishing the *Dublin Gazette* or *Weekly Courant* in Essex Street in Dublin, and it survived for twenty-five years.

A more frequent and long-lasting Irish newspaper, *Pue's Impartial Occurrences,* appeared three times a week, continuing until 1773.

1704

Fiction

Jonathan Swift (1667–1745) published his *A Tale of a Tub* and *The Battle of the Books.*

Periodicals

The *Dublin Mercury* newspaper was launched and "stayed on course until 1760" (Oram 1983, 26).

1707

When the Act of Union between Scotland and England was enacted in May, the Irish House of Lords expressed a hope for such a union between Ireland and England (Doherty and Hickey 1989, 68).

Fiction

Swift wrote his two allegories of English oppression of Ireland, *The Story of the Injured Lady* and *An Answer to the Injured Lady,* though they were not published until much later (see 1746 entry).

1713

Jonathan Swift reluctantly returned to Dublin to take up the deanship of St. Patrick's Cathedral—in his words, to die "like a rat in a hole," but actually to emerge, almost against his own will, as the most important voice in eighteenth-century Irish literature and history.

1715

Periodicals

The *Cork Idler* was the first newspaper published in an Irish town outside of Dublin; the *Limerick Newsletter* followed in the next year (Oram 1983, 31).

1719

In a recommendation that did not succeed, it was proposed in the English House of Commons that every practicing Catholic priest or friar found in Ireland after 1 May 1720 be branded on the cheek (Doherty and Hickey 1989, 71).

1720

In April the Declaratory Act mandated the supremacy of the British Parliament over the Irish one, with the English House of Lords identified as the final court of appeal for all Irish litigation (Doherty and Hickey 1989, 71).

Prose Nonfiction

Swift published *A Proposal for the Universal Use of Irish Manufacture,* in which he recommended boycotting English goods in favor of Irish ones. He urged "utterly rejecting and renouncing everything wearable that comes from England," and attacked landlords in Ireland "who by unmeasurable screwing and racking their tenants all over the kingdom, have already reduced the miserable people to a worse condition than the peasants in France, or the vassals in Germany and Poland."

1724

Music

John and William Neale's *Collection of the Most Celebrated Irish Tunes* contained twenty tunes by the famous Irish harper Turlough O'Carolan (1670–1738) (Doherty and Hickey 1989, 73).

Prose Nonfiction

Swift's *Drapier's Letters* included "A Letter to the Whole People of Ireland," which further advocated Irish economic self-reliance. Swift wrote: "'Tis true indeed that within the memory of man the Parliaments of England have sometimes assumed the power of binding this kingdom by laws enacted there, wherein they were at first openly opposed by Mr. Molyneux" (see 1698 entry). He insisted, "All government without the consent of the governed is the very definition of slavery." Soon thereafter, Primate Boulder

reported in alarm that in Dublin the *Drapier Letters* were having
"a most unhappy influence in bringing on intimacies between
Papists and Jacobites and the Whigs." Swift's *Maxims Controlled
in Ireland,* published in this same year, pointed out that in Ireland
"five children in six who are born, lie a dead weight upon us, for
want of employment," and described areas "where the wretches
are forced to pay for a filthy cabin, and two ridges of potatoes . . .
to whom death would be the best thing to be wished for" (quoted
in McHugh and Harmon 1982, 74–75).

1725

Periodicals

The *Dublin Journal* began and continued until 1825. George
Faulkner (1699–1775), its publisher, was Jonathan Swift's printer.
This Anglo-Irish newspaper was an early antecedent of today's
Irish Times. One of the *Dublin Journal*'s early issues included
what was said to have been the first illustration ever used in an
Irish newspaper, "a crude but effective woodcut showing a dentist
pulling a patient's tooth" (Oram 1983, 28).

1726

Fiction

Swift's masterly fantasy-satire *Gulliver's Travels* appeared. Swift
blended elements from travel narratives, the emerging novel,
periodical essays, and a variety of other genres to create a
one-of-a-kind, while he and his masterpiece prefigure such later
Irish satirists as Joyce, Eimar O'Duffy, and Beckett.

1728

Prose Nonfiction

Swift's *A Short View of the State of Ireland* was released. Here he
advanced compelling suggestions for the reform of the economic
and political system in Ireland—which reappeared (in satiric
derision) at the end of his *Modest Proposal* in the following year,

by which time he had despaired of the likelihood of the acceptance of his suggestions.

1729

Poetry

Aoghan Ó Rathaille (b. 1675) died. Along with Eoghan Rua Ó Súilleabháin (1748–84), Ó Rathaille was one of the great county Kerry poets in Irish rediscovered and celebrated much later by Daniel Corkery in his book *The Hidden Ireland* (1924). In poems such as "Gile na Gile" (Brightness of brightness), Ó Rathaille perfected the *aisling,* or vision poem, a political allegory in the form of an interview between the poet and a *spéir-bhean* ("sky woman") who personifies Ireland and prophesies that her lover will return and bring relief to the country. Such poems often contain an amalgam of Irish, classical, and Christian allusions (Murphy and MacKillop 1987, 43).

Prose Nonfiction

Swift published his famous *Modest Proposal for Preventing the Children of Poor People in Ireland from Being a Burden to Their Parents or Country, and for Making Them Beneficial to the Public,* in which his satiric persona slyly suggests that both hunger and overpopulation in Ireland could be solved if poor babies were "offered in sale to the persons of quality and fortune through the kingdom" to cook and eat. This practice would be effective since "a child will make two dishes at an entertainment for friends," and, though fairly expensive, is "therefore very proper for land-lords, who, as they have already devoured most of the parents, seem to have the best title to the children."

1731

Cultural Institutions

The Royal Dublin Society (RDS) was founded. Later, the RDS was responsible for such important institutions as the National

Library, the National Gallery, the National Museum, and the Botanic Gardens (Hickey and Doherty 1987, 509). The RDS's annual Dublin Horse Show each August remains one of the city's most popular events.

1732

Periodicals

The *Dublin Evening Post* began as a rival to the *Dublin Journal,* but survived only a few years (Oram 1983, 30–31).

1736

Periodicals

Hamilton's Advertiser or *Dublin Daily Advertiser* was Ireland's first attempt at a *daily* newspaper (Oram 1983, 31).

1737

Periodicals

The Belfast *News-Letter* was begun by Francis Joy and "survives to this day, making it the oldest newspaper in continuous publication in Ireland" (Oram 1983, 32).

Prose Nonfiction

The Querist was a collection of pithy questions about the state of Ireland, by George Berkeley (1685–1753), the Anglican bishop of Cloyne and celebrated philosopher. Born in Kilkenny and educated at Trinity College, Dublin (Ireland's oldest university, founded in 1592), Berkeley was an important philosopher whose work influenced subsequent Irish writers, most notably Yeats. He was an idealist "who opposed the prevailing mechanistic and materialistic view of the universe; 'we Irish do not hold this view,' he wrote" (McHugh and Harmon 1982, 78).

1739

An unprecedented frost this winter (lasting into 1740) caused a famine for two years that killed about 400,000 people or about one-eighth of Ireland's population (Doherty and Hickey 1989, 76).

Architecture

The Parliament House in Dublin, designed by Sir Edward Lovett Pearce in 1728, was completed; additions to the building were made in 1785 and 1792. In the late eighteenth century it served as the site of the home-rule "Patriot Parliament," but was sold to the Bank of Ireland after the Act of Union of 1800 (de Breffny 1983, 190). Located across from the main gate into Trinity College, today the building serves as a bank but has preserved some of the parts of the old parliament building, which are often open for public view.

1745

Jonathan Swift (b. 1667) died in October. He left a large sum of money to aid in the foundation of a mental hospital in Dublin, having written in his anticipatory *Verses on the Death of Dr. Swift* (1739):

He gave the little Wealth he had,
To build a House for Fools and Mad:
And shew'd by one satyric Touch,
No nation wanted it so much.

Swift was quite right: Ireland's rate of mental illness remains the highest in Europe today.

1746

Prose Nonfiction

Written much earlier, in 1707, and echoing William Molyneux's *Case of Ireland's Being Bound by Acts of Parliament in England* (1698), Swift's first Irish pamphlet, *The Story of the Injured Lady,* was published.

1747

Drama

In January rioters at the Smock Alley Theatre in Dublin, angered because the proprietor Thomas Sheridan (Richard Brinsley Sheridan's father) had assaulted a Galwayman who had frightened the actresses during a performance, destroyed most of the theater (Doherty and Hickey 1989, 77).

1752

Peter Wilson compiled the *Dublin Directory,* which became better known later as *Thom's Directory* after it was taken over by Alexander Thom in 1844 (Hickey and Doherty 1987, 560). *Thom's Directory,* the eighteenth-century Dublin equivalent of the telephone directory and yellow pages, is perhaps best known today as an important source for Joyce scholars, since James Joyce made extensive use of it to add realistic detail to his portrait of Dublin in *Ulysses.*

Fiction

William Chaigneau's (1709–81) *The History of Jack Connor,* the first novel set predominantly in Ireland, was a bildungsroman focused on a young man who grows up during the early eighteenth century in Ireland, runs off to London and Paris, abandons his Irishness (becoming "John Conyers"), but subsequently returns to Ireland. There he is guided and educated by Lord Truegood. Chaigneau in *Jack Connor* established the conventional role of the authorial persona who serves as an intermediary between Irish characters and English readers.

1754

Drama

Further riots (see 1747 entry) at Dublin's Smock Alley Theatre were provoked by proprietor Thomas Sheridan's attempt to censor Voltaire's *Mahomet the Imposter*. This episode ended Sheridan's career in Ireland (Doherty and Hickey 1989, 79).

1756

Fiction

Thomas Amory's (1691–1788) *The Life of John Buncle,* the second part of which appeared ten years later, concerned an Irish Unitarian who leaves Ireland, goes to England, is repeatedly married and widowed, meets diverse Irish friends, and ends up immersed in utopian fantasies. Buncle's eccentricies are linked to his Irishness, and the formless nature of his tale was to persist as a significant feature in the Irish novel.

Prose Nonfiction

Edmund Burke's (1729–97) ironic treatise, *Vindication of Natural Society,* appeared. Born in Dublin and educated at Trinity College, Burke was Ireland's most important political philosopher. Outside Ireland he became best known for his conservative *Reflections on the Revolution in France* (1790), but inside Ireland he argued on moral and pragmatic grounds against the anti-

Catholic Penal Laws; Burke was an Anglican, but his mother and wife were both Catholics. Burke would be an important figure for Yeats, and his writings have pragmatic political implications that remain influential and much debated today.

1760

Drama

Henry Mossop (1729–74) reopened the Smock Alley Theatre in Dublin as a rival to Spranger Barry's Crow Street Theatre (Doherty and Hickey 1989, 80).

Poetry

During the years 1760–63 James Macpherson (1736–96) published his pseudo-Celtic *Ossian,* in a volume whose full title was *Fragments of Ancient Poetry Collected in the Highlands.* Ostensibly a translation of a Gaelic bardic manuscript, the work was in fact Macpherson's own composition, inspired by what he knew of Scots-Gaelic mythology and folklore. This very popular book helped to inspire interest in the traditions of Ireland and Scotland.

1761

The Catholic, scholarly gentleman Charles O'Conor (1710–90) wrote to a friend concerning the Penal Laws, "Former governors punished us more as Irishmen than latter governors have punished us as Papists, and the present governors do not punish us at all. Our afflictions proceed entirely from the laws, not from them" (quoted in Foster 1988, 206).

1763

In the north the underground "Oakboy" movement (paralleling the more widespread Catholic antitithe "Whiteboy" movement in the south, as well as the Presbyterian "Steelboys" of south Antrim a few years later) was organized in protest against taxes on road building, and involved working-class Protestants as well as Catholics. This was one of the earliest resistance efforts against the tithes—required payments by Catholics in support of the Protestant Church of Ireland and its Anglican clergy.

Art

James Barry's (1741–1806) early painting *The Conversion by St. Patrick of the King of Cashel* broke new ground by illustrating a subject from Irish history (de Breffny 1983, 40).

Periodicals

The *Freeman's Journal* was founded by Charles Lucas (1713–71) and Henry Brooke (1703–83); it became a forum for Irish nationalism by reprinting, for example, Thomas Paine's *Common Sense*. It was to become "one of the most powerful newspapers in Ireland towards the end of the following century, yet collapsed in 1924" (Oram 1983, 34).

1765

Drama

The "stage Irishman"—such a great success later, in the nineteenth-century plays of Dion Boucicault—appeared, for perhaps the first time since *Henry V*'s MacMorris (who had stumbled onto Shakespeare's stage muttering, "Ireland ish my nashun"), in the character of Teague, a resourceful and witty Irish servant, in the Englishman Sir Robert Howard's London play *The Committee*. The characteristic stage Irishman drinks, fights, and makes a fool of himself, but gains the audience's indulgence because of his ready wit.

1766

Periodicals

Limerick poet and historian John Ferrar (1740–1800) founded the *Limerick Chronicle,* "still published today by the *Limerick*

Leader. The *Chronicle* is the oldest newspaper in the Republic"
(Oram 1983, 35).

1767

Drama

Henry Mossop played Richard III at the Crow Street Theatre in
Dublin, which he now owned along with the Smock Alley Theatre
(Doherty and Hickey 1989, 81).

Fiction

Laurence Sterne (1713–68), who was born in county Tipperary
but left Ireland for good at age ten, completed his fictional
masterpiece, *Tristram Shandy.* Not strictly speaking an Irish novel
because its characters are ostensibly upper-class English people, it
is typically treated as one of the most unusual specimens of the
eighteenth-century English novel. However, like his fellow trans-
planted Irishmen and predecessors Farquhar, Congreve, and
Sheridan (and later, Wilde and Shaw) who wrote for the stage,
Sterne's presentation of English life was widely comic, indeed
absurdist. Along with Swift's *Gulliver's Travels* (1726), *Tristram
Shandy* emerges as an early precursor to such twentieth-century
experimental novels as James Joyce's *Finnegans Wake* and Flann
O'Brien's *At Swim-Two-Birds* (both 1939). Sterne stops at nothing
in *Tristram Shandy:* one of its pages consists simply of a blank,
darkened rectangle.

The first highly successful Irish novelist who took Irish life as
her subject matter, Maria Edgeworth (d. 1849), was born.

1768

Irish Language and Literature

Bishop John O'Brien of Cloyne published an Irish dictionary in
Paris in order to assist priests working in Irish-speaking areas
(Wall 1969, 84).

1770

Poetry

Oliver Goldsmith's (1728–74) *The Deserted Village* was published. This enormously successful poem, though set nominally in England, was based on Goldsmith's knowledge of conditions in Ireland, and especially of depopulated and abandoned villages victimized by exploitive landowners. Born in county Westmeath, the author of such major contributions to English literature as *The Vicar of Wakefield* (1766) and *She Stoops to Conquer* (1774) was educated at Trinity College, Dublin.

1771

Fiction

Henry Brooke's bildungsroman *The Fool of Quality* focused on a young Protestant, Harry Moreland, who is trained to be a good landlord by a moral guide, his Uncle Henry. His moral earnestness calls to mind the works of Arthur Young and Maria Edgeworth.

Periodicals

The *Hibernian Magazine* began and ran until 1812 (Doherty and Hickey 1989, 82).

1772

Periodicals

The *Derry Journal* began and remains today the third oldest newspaper in Ireland, after the Belfast *News Letter* and the *Limerick Chronicle* (Oram 1983, 35).

1773

Irish Language and Literature

Archbishop John Carpenter of Dublin, an Irish scholar himself, informed the pope that the bishops of Ireland believed it essential that the students of the Irish College in Rome be "trained in both native languages" (quoted in Wall 1969, 83–84).

1774

Fiction

Like Swift in his "Modest Proposal," Charles Johnstone (1719–1800) clearly allegorized English oppression of Ireland, by means of an Oriental fantasy, *History of Arsaces*.

1775

Drama

Richard Brinsley Sheridan's (1751–1816) *The Rivals* was one of the greatest successes of the Augustan stage in London. In the Irish context it was perhaps most remarkable for the character of Sir Lucius O'Trigger, a highly amusing Anglo-Irish "stage Irishman." Sheridan, the son of Smock Alley Theatre founder Thomas Sheridan (see 1747, 1754 entries) was born in Dublin.

1776

Prose Nonfiction

Arthur Young (1741–1820)—agriculturalist, traveler, and the best-known eighteenth-century English chronicler of Ireland—journeyed to Ireland. He noted that Catholics made up 75 percent of the population but held only 5 percent of the land.

1777

Prose Nonfiction

Arthur Young became agent to Lord Kingsborough in county Cork, serving until 1779 and writing his well-known book, *A Tour of Ireland* (see 1780 entry).

1778

Full property rights were granted to Catholic landholders contingent on their subscription to an oath of allegiance to the British crown.

1779

The first St. Patrick's Day march was held in New York (Doherty and Hickey 1989, 84).

1780

Irish Language and Literature

The Gaelic poet Brian Merriman (1740–1805) wrote "Cúirt an Mheadhon Oidhche" ("The Midnight Court"), a long satiric poem in modern Irish about sexual conventions in eighteenth-century Ireland. Merriman attacked men who would not marry unless they received a good dowry, women eager to marry, and celibate priests. This thousand-line tour de force is divided into a prologue, three monologues, and an epilogue, and describes an assembly of women ruled over by Aoibheall, queen of the fairies.

Prose Nonfiction

From the other side of the cultural divide between English and Irish, upper class and lower class, Arthur Young published *A Tour of Ireland,* the best-known eighteenth-century English chronicle of Ireland, a liberal and sympathetic portrait described by Maria Edgeworth at the end of her novel *Castle Rackrent* (1800) as "the first faithful portrait" of Ireland.

1781

Architecture

Architect James Gandon (1743–1820) came to Dublin to build the Customs House. The first stone was laid on 8 August, and this dominant building opened ten years later (Doherty and Hickey 1989, 86).

Fiction

Charles Johnstone's *The History of John Juniper* was yet another episodic bildungsroman about a young Irishman who gets into trouble.

The Triumph of Prudence over Passion was an anonymous novel presenting the advantages of being an unmarried woman and advocating the rights of women to political freedom. It adopts a pro-Irish stance, at one point describing Irish-Nationalist Volunteers as "staunch patriots."

1782

The Declaratory Act was repealed and the very old Poynings' Law amended, meaning that Irish legislation could no longer be changed in England and bringing into effect "Grattan's Parliament" (so called after the Dublin politician Henry Grattan) or the "Patriot Parliament," the Irish home-rule Parliament in Dublin that continued until the Act of Union in 1800. The way was also opened for the establishment of Roman Catholic schools, but the Protestant Church of Ireland continued to dominate the school system. Later the period of the "Patriot Parliament" symbolized a kind of golden age for nationalists, especially for leaders of Ascendancy (upper-class Protestant) background, such as Charles Stewart Parnell and W. B. Yeats. In "The Tower" Yeats was to champion the Anglo-Irish Ascendancy of this period, "The people of Burke and of Grattan / That gave, though free to refuse."

Periodicals

The *Volunteer Journal* was founded, associated with the Nationalist Irish Volunteers and subsequently calling for Ireland's complete independence—provoking legislation against it in 1784 (Foster 1988, 240).

1783

Cultural Institutions

George and William Penrose established the celebrated crystal factory in Waterford (de Breffny 1983, 98). Waterford crystal is still famous today for its clarity and precisely cut decorations.

1784

Art

The sculptor Christopher Hewetson's memorial to Provost Baldwin was ensconced at Trinity College, Dublin.

Poetry

The great Kerry poet in the Irish language, Eoghan Rua Ó Suilleabháin (b. 1748), died. A schoolmaster and migrant farm laborer, Ó Suilleabháin is best remembered for his *aislingí* or vision poems.

1785

Cultural Institutions

The Royal Irish Academy was founded. It celebrated Irish antiquities, appealing to members of the gentry as part of the more general movement of romanticism.

1786

Architecture

Building began on the Four Courts, the chief group of courtrooms in Dublin, by architect James Gandon; it opened ten years later (Doherty and Hickey 1989, 89).

1788

Cultural Institutions

The Linenhall Library was founded under its original name, the Belfast Society for Promoting Knowledge or Belfast Reading Society, and housed in the old White Linen Hall—before moving a century later, in 1896, to its present site, where it is a rich depository of Irish materials (de Breffny 1983, 133).

Periodicals

Thomas McDonnell purchased the *Hibernian Journal.* Under his ownership this newspaper supported the United Irishmen, but after his death in 1809 its new owners turned it around into a progovernment organ. It ceased publication in 1822 (Hickey and Doherty 1987, 224).

1789

Poetry

Charlotte Brooke (1740–93) published *Reliques of Irish Poetry,* with translations of five "Ossianic" poems—more authentic varieties of the kind of very popular poetry forged by James Macpherson in the 1760s—which increased English readers' interest in Celtic mythology and literature.

1791

Inspired by the American and French revolutions, Theobald Wolfe Tone (1763–98), Napper Tandy (1740–1803), and others founded the United Irishmen. The French fleet recruited by Tone on Ireland's behalf, though intending a campaign against English forces, was broken up by storms and forced to return home.

Prose Nonfiction

Tone published his *Argument on Behalf of the Catholics of Ireland,* strongly arguing against Protestant domination and Catholic oppression.

1792

Periodicals

The *Northern Star,* reflecting the Irish-nationalist views of Belfast United Irishmen, was founded by Samuel Neilson (1761–1803) and circulated its radical views as far as Dublin, Edinburgh, and London (Oram 1983, 41).

1793

The Relief Act granted Catholics (those who could produce forty shillings) a parliamentary vote and limited civil and military rights. However, Catholics were still not permitted to serve as members of Parliament.

1794

In May the United Irishmen were banned by the government, causing their reconstruction as an oath-bound, increasingly radical (though middle-class) secret society.

Fiction

William Carleton (d. 1869), the great nineteenth-century fiction writer, was born.

1795

Wolfe Tone traveled to Paris to pursue the task of international conspiracy with the French.

In opposition to Tone's United Irishman, the Orange Order

was founded in county Armagh. This Protestant, Unionist organization continues to hold parades today every July 12 in Northern Ireland, in commemoration of King William's victory at the Battle of the Boyne in 1690.

Architecture

Carlisle Bridge (later O'Connell Bridge), designed by James Gandon, was opened in Dublin (Doherty and Hickey 1989, 91).

Education

Maynooth College near Dublin was founded and quickly established itself as the most prestigious Catholic seminary in Ireland.

Music

John Bunting's *General Collection of Ancient Irish Music* appeared. It was later adapted in the *Irish Melodies* of the celebrated poet Thomas Moore (1779–1852) (McHugh and Martin 1982, 113).

Periodicals

The presses of the radical Belfast *Northern Star* newspaper printed some issues of *Bolg an Tsolair* (the *Gaelic Magazine*) (Oram 1983, 41).

Poetry

The phrase "the Emerald Isle" as descriptive of Ireland came from a poem or song by William Drennan (1754–1820) called "Erin": "When Erin first rose from the dark-swelling flood, / God bless'd the green island, He saw it was good; / The Emerald of Europe, it sparkled, it shone; / In the ring of this world the most precious stone!" Drennan was a Belfast Presbyterian and founding member of the United Irishmen (Deane et al. 1991, 3:318, 327).

1796

Instigated by Wolfe Tone, who believed in "open war" against England (and is viewed by many today as the founder of modern Irish republicanism), a French expedition of forty-three ships carrying 15,000 men very nearly landed at Bantry Bay in west Cork, foreshadowing the 1798 rising.

1797

Periodicals

In September the first issue of the *Press,* an organ of the United Irishmen, was published by Arthur O'Connor. It was suppressed in March 1798 (Doherty and Hickey 1989, 96).

Prose Nonfiction

Richard Lovell Edgeworth (1744–1817) and Maria Edgeworth's two-volume *Essays in Practical Education* advocated their utilitarian, pragmatic educational ideals.

1798

An unorganized nationalist uprising broke out around Dublin in May and was suppressed within a week.

A bloody, sectarian rebellion in county Wexford, led by United Irish men from the Catholic gentry class, lasted from 26 May to 21 June and ended with a devastating defeat at Vinegar Hill.

Short-lived risings in the North were led by Henry Joy McCracken (1767–98) and Henry Munro—Protestant ancestors of some of the same "loyalists" or "Unionists" who insist today that commitment to the United Kingdom is their chief priority.

In August the French landed at Killala in county Mayo, but not in nearly the numbers that Wolfe Tone had brought to Bantry Bay two years earlier. Led by General Humbert and accompanied by ragtag Irish peasant pikemen, the French chased the garrison forces from Castlebar (in the celebrated "races of Castlebar") and set up a short-lived "Republic of Connacht" that ended when they were surrounded at Ballinamuck on 8 September. The French were sent home; Irish rebel forces were killed in large numbers; and Tone committed suicide while awaiting execution.

1800

After a bitter debate generating dozens of pamphlets pro and con, and on the second attempt (with a narrow defeat in January 1799), the Act of Union was passed in August (and took effect on 1 January 1801), abolishing the Dublin Parliament in College Green and enacting direct rule from Westminster.

Ireland's population reached between 4,500,000 and 5,000,000, thereby having doubled since 1700. The traditional explanation is increased fertility—facilitated by the proliferation of small farm holdings, early marriage, and better nutrition due to cultivation of the potato—though causes now seem more complex. Ireland, as Roy Foster notes, "failed to participate in the kind of nineteenth-century industrialization that could sustain . . . population growth within an economy structurally unable to cope with it" (1988, 219).

Fiction

Written mostly between 1793 and 1796, Maria Edgeworth's first Irish tale, *Castle Rackrent, an Hibernian Tale: Taken from Facts, and from the Manners of the Irish Squires, Before the Year 1782,* was published by Joseph Johnson in London. *Castle Rackrent* was the first major, popularly successful, fully Irish novel or novella. After reading it King George III claimed, "I rubbed my hands and said what what—I know something now of my Irish subjects" (quoted in Butler 1972, 359). This novella introduced several of the most distinctive features of the Irish novel: a colloquial narrative voice (an innovation without which *Huckleberry Finn,* as well as *Ulysses* or many another Irish novel, would have been unimaginable), along with what the novelist and critic Anthony Cronin has described as its "curious stancelessness" and "absence of plot" (1982, 25). As he describes the successive, disastrous generations of Rackrents, Thady Quirk, humble steward and narrator, laments the lost pseudofeudal world in which reputedly faithful servants such as himself supposedly lived happily ever after on the estates of their good-hearted, incompetent landlords, in this first widely celebrated "Big House" novel. (The "Big House" novel, a distinguished and persistent subgenre, focuses on the degeneration of the Anglo-Irish family, centered on an imposing ascendancy house and estate.) At story's end, however, Jason, Thady's son, takes over the Rackrent properties. *Castle Rackrent* was a title that conjured up gothic expectations but delivered pointed social realism, generating huge sales and establishing Edgeworth as the most popular fiction writer in the British Isles until Sir Walter Scott (influenced by *Castle Rackrent*) published *Waverley* in 1814. Edgeworth later explained to a friend the origin of Thady's narrative in John Langan, her own family's steward: "I heard him when I first came to Ireland, and his dialect struck me, and his character; and I became so acquainted with it, that I could think and speak in it without effort: so that when, for mere amusement, without any idea of publishing, I began to write a family history as Thady would tell it, he seemed to stand beside me and dictate; and I wrote as fast as my pen could go" (Barry 1931, 243).

Poetry

Eibhlín Dubh Ní Chonaill (b. circa 1745) died. She was best known for her great Gaelic poem "Caoineadh Airt Uí Laoghaire" (The lament for Art O'Leary, circa 1770), an elegy for her husband, a retired officer who was murdered by a man with whom he had a bitter dispute over a horse (de Breffny 1983, 196).

1803

Protestant nationalist idealist Robert Emmet (b. 1778) attempted an abortive rebellion in July and was executed (after delivering his famous "Speech from the Dock") in September. He ended his speech with the words "When my country takes her place among the nations of the earth, then, and not till then, let my epitaph be written."

1805

Periodicals

John Magee (1780–1814) began a liberal and pro-Catholic newspaper called the *Evening Herald,* no relation to today's evening edition of the *Irish Independent* (which goes by the same title). It changed its name to the *Sentinel* in 1814 and closed in 1815 (Hickey and Doherty 1987, 158).

1806

Fiction

Sydney Owenson's (1777–1859) third novel, *The Wild Irish Girl,* made her name (which became "Lady Morgan" when Owenson married Sir Charles Morgan in 1812) as it went through seven editions in two years; by 1807 its author was playing the role of Glorvina, her cape-wearing, harp-bearing heroine, in literary salons and for the popular press. Daughter of a journeyman Irish actor, Lady Morgan became one of the most successful popular novelists of the first half of the nineteenth century and a determined supporter of Daniel O'Connell (1775–1847) and champion of women's accomplishments and rights. *The Wild Irish Girl,* originally commissioned as a travel book, was instead a highly romantic novel narrating how a profligate Ascendancy hero falls in love with a brave, bold heroine in the west of Ireland. Like the hero, readers of this potboiler fell in love not only with Glorvina but also with the new version of Ireland she embodied: a shadowy, Celtic, and above all romantic place.

1808

Fiction

Charles Maturin's (1782–1824) second novel, *The Wild Irish Boy,* was obviously meant to capitalize on Owenson's success. In it Lady Montrevor appears at a ball actually dressed as Glorvina, the Wild Irish Girl. Its twist in the love story—that the hero really loves the mother of the woman he marries—recurs in Maturin's later Irish novel *Women; or, Pour et Contre: A Tale* (1818).

Poetry

The first installment of the *Irish Melodies* of Thomas Moore, which continued to appear until 1834, introduced what would become the most popular body of Irish, romantic, nationalist verse in the nineteenth century. "The Harp that Once through Tara's Halls" is typical of these verses: "The harp that once through Tara's halls / The soul of music shed, / Now hangs as mute on Tara's walls / As if that soul were fled." Moore's *Melodies* reverberated even during the Literary Revival and later, as in the works of James Joyce (who grew up hearing his father sing them).

1809

Fiction

Ennui, Maria Edgeworth's second Irish tale, was a novel centered on the Earl of Glenthorn, who overcomes his natural indolence by returning to Ireland to become a responsible landlord under the moral guidance of Ellinor O'Donoghue (who turns out to be his mother, who switched him at birth with the true heir to an estate so that he could inherit it instead) and the noble land agent McLeod, who runs a progressive school. Like most of Edgeworth's subsequent works, *Ennui* reflects the strongly utilitarian educational philosophy of her father, the landlord and reformer Richard Lovell Edgeworth. It was also notable for helping to introduce a narrative perspective that became typical in the nineteenth-century Irish novel: the traveler from England who functions as a narrative "lens" on Ireland for English readers, who far outnumbered Irish ones during the nineteenth century.

1810

Periodicals

William Corbet (1779–1842) founded the *Patriot* newspaper in support of the government and the Protestant Ascendancy. It remained small and later switched support to Daniel O'Connell's Catholic Emancipation movement—at which point, in 1828, it changed its name to the *Statesman and Patriot,* lost government support, and folded a year later (Hickey and Doherty 1987, 466).

1811

Poetry

Armagh writer and editor James Stuart's (1764–1842) *Poems on Various Subjects* employed the conventions of eighteenth-century English narrative verse with assurance, particularly in "Morna's Hill" (Deane et al. 1991, 2: 10–11).

1812

Fiction

Edgeworth's novel *The Absentee* told a story very similar to that of *Ennui:* Lord Colambre leaves behind decadent amusements in London and visits the family estate in Ireland anonymously; there he observes a good land agent, Burke, and a bad land agent, Garraghty, and then not only becomes a good landlord himself but even convinces his absentee parents to return home to their estate. Didactically countering the growing problem of absenteeism, *The Absentee* ends with its stated moral: "It's the growing fashion not to be an absentee."

Charles Maturin's *The Milesian Chief* revised the typical Englishman-goes-to-Ireland plot by sending a *heroine* to the wilds of Connacht, where she abandons her English fiancé and falls in love with the grandson of an Irish chieftain.

1814

The position of resident magistrate (R.M.) was established by law. Throughout the century R.M.s were appointed to oversee "disturbed areas" in rural Ireland. R.M.s became virtually extinct by the end of the nineteenth century, but were made famous in Somerville and Ross's celebrated "Irish R.M." stories at the turn of the century (see 1899 entry).

Fiction

O'Donnel by Sydney Owenson (Lady Morgan) had been planned as a historical novel but became instead a romantic tale about how a modern hero (the first *Catholic* gentleman hero in an Irish novel) falls in love with a brilliant governess employed by a landlord with liberal Edgeworthian principles whose name, Glentworth, sounds suspiciously like that of the protagonist of Edgeworth's *Ennui*. Richard Lovell Edgeworth had written to Owenson congratulating her on *The Wild Irish Girl,* but her next novel, *Florence Macarthy* (1818), was detested by Maria Edgeworth, even though (or perhaps because) it ended with the Edgeworthian sentence, "Ireland can best be served in Ireland."

1815

Architecture

Building commenced on St. Mary's Pro-Cathedral, the Catholic cathedral in Dublin (de Breffny 1983, 27).

1817

Fiction

In Edgeworth's last Irish novel, *Ormond,* the protagonist learns to have a passion for the land from Corney O'Shane ("King Corney") and a progressive knowledge about how to manage an estate from Sir Herbert Annaly (an Englishman clearly modeled on Edgeworth's father), marrying Sir Herbert's daughter Florence at the end, and moving onto the estate of the dead "King Corney." Like Edgeworth's other heroes, Ormond spends time in England

and Paris but can find his true identity only in Ireland. This time, however, it is a specifically identified *part* of Ireland, near Lough Rea in the midlands, rather than the more generic "Ireland" of *Ennui* and *The Absentee*—a change reflecting an increasing attention to regionalism in the Irish novel.

1818

Irish Language and Literature

The Irish Society was founded by Church of Ireland leaders for the purpose of trying to convert Gaelic speakers to Protestantism (Hickey and Doherty 1987, 262).

1820

Fiction

Charles Maturin's masterpiece, *Melmoth the Wanderer,* contained enough gothicism to establish that theme as the chief focus of subsequent criticism, but it also followed and extended several central features of the Irish novel. The bizarre narrative of the unfortunate, subjugated, wandering, exiled Melmoth looks back to Swift, and forward to Joyce and Flann O'Brien, among others. Most of the novel is a series of meandering, diverse "tales" unified more by theme than by storyline—a method evident in other Irish novels running from *Castle Rackrent* to *Ulysses.*

1823

The Catholic Association was founded by Daniel O'Connell— "the Liberator," "the Counsellor," the most popular and important Catholic leader of his (or perhaps any) era—and later reconstituted to avoid prosecution. The O'Connells were Catholic landowners in county Kerry who had managed to hold onto their lands during the Penal Age due to an oversight, and O'Connell became an attorney after the relaxation of the Penal Laws in 1793. O'Connell's Catholic Association was the organizing touchstone of his mass movement for Catholic Emancipation as well as an important service association.

Cultural Institutions

An Irish association of painters and artists, the Royal Hibernian Academy, was incorporated, with William Ashford as its first president, and instituted annual exhibitions three years later. Architects were also members; one of them, Francis Johnston (1761–1829), constructed a building for the academy in the following year that looked ahead to Victorian architectural styles (de Breffny 1983, 182, 27).

Periodicals

On 1 December appeared the first issue of the *Irish Times,* which was to develop into today's most prestigious Irish newspaper. The first issues were evening editions, cost five pence, and were only four pages long. At this stage the paper was a weekly, and closed down because of problems with printers in 1825—and was not revived until 1859 (appearing daily since then). From its first issue, however, the *Irish Times* demonstrated the interest in and prescience about foreign affairs that are still evident today, predicting at that time that "should the Government of the United States carry its political views into futurity, should it extend them to centuries yet to come, it would not lend its aid to the establishment of powerful republics on the American continent, republics which might in a short time become her rival both in war and commerce." This first issue also carried a report, closer to home, of a meeting of the Catholic Association, at which the remarks of Daniel O'Connell were met by "loud applause."

The *Dublin Evening Mail* was launched and remained "a venerable and much-loved institution in the city" until it closed down operations in 1962 (Oram 1983, 48).

1824

Periodicals

Michael Staunton founded the *Dublin Morning Register,* a liberal newspaper, unusual in that it focused on Irish rather than foreign affairs. It supported Daniel O'Connell and his Catholic Emancipation campaign, and later its reporters and editors included

Thomas Davis (1814–45), Charles Gavan Duffy (1816–1903), and John Blake Dillon. In direct counterpoint, Joseph Haydn (1786–1856) began the *Dublin Morning Star,* in the same year, as a bitterly anti-Catholic paper (Hickey and Doherty, 1987, 137–38).

Prose Nonfiction

Later proclaimed the "first Irish socialist" by James Connolly, William Thompson (1775–1833) of county Cork published a long treatise entitled *An Inquiry into the Principles of Distribution of Wealth Conducive to Human Happiness; Applied to the New Proposed System of Voluntary Equality of Wealth.* Thompson had studied the utilitarian Bentham and the economist Ricardo, and became convinced that laborers were entitled to the full value of their labor; according to P. Berresford Ellis in his *History of the Irish Working Class,* "it is this that made Thompson the founding figure of scientific socialism. The concept of surplus value is the fundamental principle of Marxist socialism" (1973, 87).

1825

Architecture

Cavan Courthouse was built by William Farrell (de Breffny 1983, 29).

Fiction

Beginning in this year, John (1798–1842) and Michael (1796–1874) Banim, middle-class Catholic brothers from Kilkenny, published several volumes of *Tales by the O'Hara Family* about Irish peasant life. The first three-volume set contained three relatively short novels: *Crohoore of the Bill-Hook, The Fetches,* and *John Doe. The Fetches,* saturated in gothicism and folklore, suggests the influence of Charles Maturin; *John Doe,* describing faction-fighting and rural violence in general, looks ahead to the more celebrated fiction of William Carleton. The most interesting of the three novels is Michael's *Crohoore,* concerning a misunderstood peasant, accused of the murder of his reputedly adoptive parents, but finally absolved of the crime and revealed to be their natural son. *Crohoore* sought to explode the old anti-Irish stereotype of the subhuman, violent Irishman. The Banims were the first truly middle-class, regional Irish novelists; in our own century middle-class backgrounds and attention to local details would become increasingly common among Irish writers.

Meanwhile, Maria Edgeworth had stopped writing Irish fiction, convinced that "it is impossible to draw Ireland as she now is in the book of fiction—realities are too strong, party passions too violent, to bear to see, or to care to look at their faces in a looking glass. The people would only break the glass and curse the fool who held the mirror up to nature" (quoted in Lubbers 1985, 63).

Folklore

Beginning in this year and continuing to 1828, Thomas Crofton Croker's (1798–1854) *Fairy Tales and Legends of the South of Ireland* were published. These were tales based on Irish folklore, and served to help cultivate a taste for such works in Irish and English readers.

Periodicals

The *Dublin Journal* folded and its interest was bought by the owners of the *Irish Times*—which had been founded two years earlier but also closed in this year (Oram 1983, 48).

The *Christian Examiner* was founded by Caesar Otway (1780–1842) as the first religious magazine associated with the Protestant Church of Ireland (Hickey and Doherty 1987, 456). Otway was a fanatically anti-Catholic publishing entrepreneur. This magazine would be best remembered as the place where William Carleton's earliest stories were published.

Prose Nonfiction

The socialist William Thompson (see 1824 entry) was also a strong advocate of women's emancipation. In this year he published *An Appeal of One Half of the Human Race, Women, against the Pretensions of the Other Half, Men, to Retain Them in Political and Thence in Civil and Domestic Slavery.* He was a close friend and fellow activist in the cooperative movement with Anna Wheeler, who wrote to Robert Owen (founder of the utopian community of New Harmony, Indiana): "Shall man be free and woman a slave . . . never say I!" (quoted in Ellis 1973, 88).

1826

The first Ribbon Society appeared (Hickey and Doherty 1987, 506). Along with the earlier Whiteboys and other groups, the Ribbonmen were involved in often secret agrarian agitation and terrorism against landlords. The Ribbonmen were Catholics and most active during the winter months, in central Ireland.

Fiction

This was the year in which both of John Banim's two best novels, *The Nowlans* and *The Boyne Water,* appeared. In its despairing near-naturalism, gritty Dublin scenes, and focus on the struggles of a Catholic priest, *The Nowlans* was an entirely new kind of Irish novel and a long way from the Ascendancy novels of Edgeworth and others. It focuses on the conflicting demands of spirit and flesh in John Nowlan, a pious young priest who commits the ultimate "sin" by going off to live with a cultured Protestant woman, Letty Adams, who shares his poverty in Dublin, before eventually dying in childbirth. *The Boyne Water* was the best Irish historical novel of the nineteenth century. Closely modeled on Scott and based on careful historical research on the Jacobite-Williamite War (1689–91), this novel uses as its fictive "lens" the Protestant brother and sister Robert and Esther Evelyn, who wander into the glens of Antrim in the north of Ireland where they survive a tornado, fall in love with Catholic Eva and Edmund O'Donnell, learn to be tolerant of Ireland and Catholicism, and emerge as emblems of how war ruins love as well as examples of how Protestants can learn to understand and love Irish Catholics. Written at the height of Daniel O'Connell's popularity, *The Boyne Water* was intended as a tract in favor of Catholic Emancipation.

1827

Fiction

Like the stories of the Banim brothers, *Holland-Tide* and *Tales of the Munster Festivals* by Gerald Griffin (1803–40)—a young, middle-class, Catholic writer from county Limerick whom John Banim helped start on his way as a writer in London—consisted of local color sketches focused on the peasantry. These were intended to be as realistic as possible in capturing rural folklore and customs but also were frequently melodramatic. One of the more interesting tales, "Half-Sir," critiqued Anglo-Irish values from the point of view of a peasant.

The *O'Briens and the O'Flahertys* was the last and best Irish novel by Sydney Owenson (Lady Morgan), more pessimistic and complex than her earlier ones. At story's end, Murrogh O'Brien, the hero, marries Beavoin O'Flaherty, the mysterious, beautiful ex-nun who has repeatedly saved Murrogh from various catastrophes in the course of the book. Beavoin tried to reform the Catholic institution of which she was a part, but then abandoned it; Owenson was sympathetic to the plight of Catholics in the Ireland of her time, but negative about Catholicism itself.

Prose Nonfiction

Sir Jonah Barrington's (1760–1834) *Personal Sketches,* like his subsequent *The Rise and Fall of the Irish Nation* (1833), contained memorable portraits of swashbuckling Ascendancy types (created by one of their number) similar to the "Rackrents" earlier described by Maria Edgeworth.

1828

Daniel O'Connell was elected in county Clare to serve (illegally, since he was a Catholic) as a member of Parliament. Something of O'Connell's election rhetoric and oratorical abilities were captured in the conclusion to a speech reprinted by W. J. Fitzpatrick: "Electors of the County Clare! Choose between me and Mr. Vesey Fitzgerald; choose between him who has so long cultivated his own interests, and one who seeks only to advance yours; choose between the sworn libeller of the Catholic faith, and one who has devoted his early life to your cause; who has consumed his manhood in a struggle for your liberties, and who has ever lived, and is ready to die for, the integrity, the honor, the purity, of the Catholic faith, and the promotion of Irish freedom and happiness" (quoted in Fitzpatrick 1888, 1:159).

Architecture

John Semple designed the Black Church in Dublin—one of many new Church of Ireland churches built during this period—with a distinctive parabolic vault (de Breffny 1983, 27).

Fiction

John Banim's *The Last Baron of Crana* and *The Conformists,* published together, were sequels to *The Boyne Water.* Both dealt with the eighteenth-century Penal Age, though not as effectively as *The Boyne Water* had with the Jacobite-Williamite War. Also published in this year was his *The Anglo-Irish of the Nineteenth Century,* which was much more pessimistic than *The Boyne Water* about the possibility of achieving true Irish-English rapprochement; its protagonist, Gerald Blount, listens to many of the nasty Catholic Emancipation debates that Banim himself heard in both London and Ireland.

Periodicals

Richard Barrett began the *Pilot* newspaper in support of O'Connell and his Catholic Emancipation campaign, continuing until 1849, two years after O'Connell's death (Hickey and Doherty 1987, 475).

The *Christian Examiner and Church of Ireland Gazette* was founded, with the Reverend Caesar Otway serving as its first editor until 1831, with the expressed purpose of combating "Popery and its errors and calumnies" and the "usages and superstitious observances of the now corrupt church of Rome" (quoted in Hayley 1987, 31). To Otway's credit, however, he discovered William Carleton, a brilliant young Irishman of peasant background who, following his failure to gain admission to the

Catholic Maynooth Seminary, had converted to Protestantism and now sought to become a gentleman. Under such headlines as "Popular Romish Legends," Otway published Carleton's remarkable stories set in rural Ireland, which would eventually be collected as his famous *Traits and Stories of the Irish Peasantry* (1830, 1833). Later praised by Yeats as "the historian of his class," Carleton was one of the first important Irish writers of Catholic background in English.

Irish newspapers and journals in general increased in number during these years, and often tended to divide along political and religious lines. The pro-O'Connell *Dublin Morning Register,* for example, had its bitter anti-Catholic counterpart in the *Dublin Morning Star;* the *Irish Protestant,* in the *Irish Catholic;* the *Union Magazine,* in the *Anti-Union Weekly Magazine* (Lubbers 1985, 49).

1829

Catholic Emancipation was legally granted, enabling Catholics to enter Parliament and hold civil and military offices, but voting qualifications required ten pounds rather than the previous forty shillings, thereby reducing county voters from 216,000 to 37,000 (Foster 1988, 302). Thus, it was specifically the small Irish Catholic middle class that was empowered. To his credit, Emancipation campaign leader Daniel O'Connell wrote to his friend James Sugrue, "How mistaken men are who suppose that the history of the world will be over as soon as we are emancipated! Oh! *That* will be the time to *commence* the struggle for popular rights" (quoted in Fitzpatrick 1888, 1:176).

Fiction

This was the annus mirabilis of Gerald Griffin. His best novel, *The Collegians,* appeared in this year, as did two other worthy ones, *The Rivals* and *Tracy's Ambition.* Based on an actual case in county Clare in 1809, *The Collegians* focuses on Hardress Cregan, a young Ascendancy Trinity College graduate who falls in love with a young Catholic woman, Eily O'Connor (the daughter of a rope-maker), secretly marries her, but then permits his demented servant, Danny Mann, to "remove" her because Cregan wants to marry the cultured, monied Anne Chute. The hero of the novel is Kyrle Daly, a middle-class Catholic friend of Cregan, who eventually marries Anne after Cregan is exiled. Beneath this novel's didactic surface lurk several compelling secondary characters, such as Myles na Coppaleen, Griffin's noble Gaelic horseman and "perfect Ulysses." Myles was subsequently transmogrified into both a major character in Dion Boucicault's phenominally popular play *The Colleen Bawn* (1860) and the pseudonym of Brian O'Nolan (Flann O'Brien) in his brilliant *Irish Times* satires commencing in 1939. *The Collegian*'s complexity of characterization and social scope were not matched by *The Rivals, Tracy's Ambition, The Christian Physiologist* (1830), *The Invasion* (1832), or *The Duke of Monmouth* (1836), and Griffin abandoned literature and joined the Christian Brothers a year-and-a-half before dying of typhus at age thirty-seven.

The first of Mrs. S. C. (Anna Maria Fielding) Hall's (1800–71) two series of *Sketches of Irish Character* (1829, 1831) appeared. Though written from her upper-class, Anglo-Irish perspective, Hall's stories evidenced an interest in the peasantry and their dialect that was taken up much more effectively by William Carleton, who wrote out of a native knowledge and understanding.

1830

Periodicals

The new *Dublin Literary Gazette; or, Weekly Chronicle of Criticism, Belles Lettres, and Fine Arts,* though short-lived, like most other Irish periodicals, reflected the growing interest in, and demand for, Irish writing. Within the same year it changed its name to the *National Magazine* and increasingly emphasized reviews of books by Irish authors such as Gerald Griffin, the Banims, and Anna Hall (Hayley 1987, 33).

Prose Nonfiction

Practical Directions for the Speedy and Economic Establishment of Communities was the culmination of Cork socialist William

Thompson's thinking and activism in the cooperative movement (Ellis 1973, 90).

1831

Fiction

Evaluating the Irish novel from Maria Edgeworth to Gerald Griffin, the *Edinburgh Review* asserted that English readers had become more informed about the Irish than they had been at the beginning of the century. This claim was true of only a small minority, for much ignorance remained. Worse, after Daniel O'Connell's immensely popular and successful Catholic Emancipation Campaign in the 1820s, a backlash in attitude occurred during the 1830s and 1840s, clearly reflected in the cartoon caricatures of the Irish in the English magazine *Punch,* where drawings of playful "Paddy" were replaced by those of dagger-bearing, simian monsters (Lubbers 1985, 184–85).

Folklore

Like Thomas Crofton Croker's earlier *Fairy Tales and Legends of the South of Ireland* (1825–28), Samuel Lover's (1797–1868) *Legends and Stories of Ireland* were based on Irish folklore and helped create an interest in these kinds of Irish materials.

Irish Language and Literature

James Hardiman (1782–1855) published his two-volume collection of *Irish Minstrelsy,* containing a sizeable body of Gaelic poetry with facing-page translations by various Irish scholars (Martin 1980, 28).

Periodicals

The *Dublin Penny Journal* was founded by Caesar Otway and included articles on Irish folklore, history, language, music, and other topics by such essayists as George Petrie. It was one of the earliest and perhaps the best known of several such inexpensive, popular "penny" journals and magazines published in Dublin during the mid–nineteenth century. Lasting until 1837, it published works by William Carleton and Samuel Lover. Otway's anti-Catholic stance provoked a *Catholic Penny Magazine* (1834–35) into existence—countered yet again and all too predictably by a *Protestant Penny Journal* (1834–36).

The publisher James Duffy (1809–71) brought out his first independent publication. Over the next forty years Duffy published more Irish books of nationalist interest than anyone else, including many works by Catholic authors, and as such was the first of his kind and arguably the father or forerunner of the Irish publishing industry as we know it today. His authors included Thomas Davis, John Mitchel (1815–75), James Clarence Mangan (1803–49), Charles Gavan Duffy, Thomas D'Arcy Magee, William Carleton, John Banim, Gerald Griffin, and Charles Kickham (Hickey and Doherty 1987, 138).

1832

Ireland was struck by a bad cholera epidemic, particularly in county Clare. Among those active in relief efforts were Charles Lever (1806–72)—a physician before he became a novelist—and Father Theobald Mathew (1790–1856), the famous temperance leader (see 1838 entry).

Irish Language and Literature

State-funded elementary education was introduced. Though strongly opposed by the Established (Protestant-dominated) Schools, the Church of Ireland, and the Presbyterian church, it was supported by a majority of the Roman Catholic hierarchy. The principle of the new National Schools was that individual religious beliefs were not to be violated, though this ideal was to be achieved only slowly. Since English was the sole language of instruction, these schools became a major factor in the decline of the Irish language; Douglas Hyde later attributed to them an "unrelenting determination to stamp out the Irish language" (quoted in Todd 1989, 14). In some cases students were made to wear sticks around their necks, and parents were instructed to make a notch in the stick when their children spoke Irish at home so that disciplinary measures could be exacted at school.

Periodicals

The Catholic *Irish Monthly Magazine of Politics and Literature,* until its demise two years later, carried some original fiction and poetry as well as lengthy articles on Irish literary and historical topics (Hayley 1987, 34).

1833

Fiction

By this date two volumes of William Carleton's *Traits and Stories of the Irish Peasantry* had been published. Carleton wrote vividly realistic, pioneering stories of peasant life, such as "Denis O'Shaughnessay Going to Maynooth" and "The Battle of the Factions." Perhaps his very best story is the riveting "Wildgoose Lodge," which describes the burning of an Ascendancy house and family by Ribbonmen in unsentimental, realistic detail and with a compactness much closer to the modern twentieth-century short story than to the typically rambling nineteenth-century tale.

Periodicals

The *Dublin University Magazine* was founded, soon establishing itself under one of its earliest editors, Isaac Butt (1813–79), as the most significant Anglo-Irish intellectual magazine of the period and, though politically pro-Unionist, the most important and long-lasting periodical publisher of Irish fiction until its cessation in 1877. An early editorial declared, "We must fight our battle now with a handful of types and a composing-stick, pages like this our field, and the reading public our arbiter of war" (quoted in Martin 1980, 28). Barbara Hayley called the *Dublin University Magazine* "the most familiar, long-running literary journal ever published in Ireland" (1987, 35). Its first article in its opening issue was an entertaining and incisive dialogue on "The Present Crisis" in which one speaker asks the other, "Is it true that you are about to undertake the management of a periodical, to be conducted on Tory principles?" The editorial voice confirms that this is the case and, when warned of the futility of the attempt, insists, "I would much rather lose ground by deserving to maintain it, than maintain, by deserving to lose it." (1, no. 1 [January 1833]: 1). The first issue also included a story by Samuel Lover and a review of Carleton's *Traits and Stories.*

1835

Architecture

The Pain brothers constructed the courthouse in Cork City (de Breffny 1983, 29).

Irish Language and Literature

Ancient Ireland—A Weekly Magazine was the first periodical with any focus on the Irish language, intended as "a cheap light periodical, to be devoted exclusively to literature, its main object being—to revive the cultivation of the Irish language, and to originate an earnest and vigorous inquiry into the Ancient history of Ireland" (quoted in Nic Pháidín 1988, 72).

The county Mayo Gaelic poet Anthony Raftery (b. 1784)— "blind Raftery"—died. His songs are still sung in the west of Ireland—for example, "An Pósae Glégeal" (The bright flower), a love song in praise of Mary Hynes, a local beauty. Later Raftery was much celebrated by Douglas Hyde, Yeats, and Lady Gregory; Lady Gregory arranged for a stone to mark his grave, which was dedicated in 1900 (Murphy and MacKillop 1987, 108).

Poetry

Dubliner George Darley (1795–1846) displayed considerable talent in his long poem *Nepenthe,* but as an Irishman writing in

English modes, he suffered from the lack of any clear, substantial audience (Deane et al. 1991, 2: 14).

1836

The Royal Irish Constabulary (RIC), the governmental police force, was formed (Hickey and Doherty 1987, 510).

Cultural Institutions

The earliest known Irish photographer, Francis S. Beatty of Belfast, used the daguerreotype process shortly after its initiation. He opened the first Belfast photography studio six years later (de Breffny 1983, 192).

Periodicals

The *Dublin Review* was founded and persisted in three separate series until 1969—a remarkably long life for a periodical. Despite its title, it was published in London, with an original intent to uphold Catholicism and with backing from Daniel O'Connell among others. Its development reflects the international appeal of Irish nationalism and writing (Hayley 1987, 37–38).

1837

Fiction

William Carleton's novel *Fardorougha, the Miser* was published serially in the *Dublin University Magazine* during the years 1837–38. *Fardorougha (fear dorcha,* "dark man" in Irish) incorporated vivid dialogue and strong characterizations in a story structurally focused on the protagonist's conflict between his destructive greed and his love for his son, Connor. Like Gerald Griffin's *The Collegians* (1829), this was a realistic account in a rural setting of a character ruined by pride—eschewing the more common fictional frame of the "English visitor to Ireland" and disquisitions on Irish politics in favor of a thoroughly Irish story that says more about the lust for money, land, and reputation than did earlier "textbook" novels.

Samuel Lover's novel *Rory O'More: A National Romance,* which had begun as a ballad and was later recast as a play, sought to demonstrate to English readers that any Irish excesses during the 1798 rebellions were the fault of a few fanatics and that many idealists were involved in the nationalist movement. In the end Lover avoids the risings altogether by removing his heroes—the foreign soldier Horace de Lacy and his eventual companion, the Irishman Rory O'More—to France, since he felt that the rebellions were "too fearful . . . for mortal pen to be trusted with" (quoted in Sloan 1982, 34).

Periodicals

Like Caesar Otway's *Christian Examiner,* which began twelve years earlier, the Reverend Edward Nagle's (1799–1883) *Achill Missionary Herald and Western Witness* was an anti-Catholic periodical that sought (according to its self-description) to "bear a faithful and uncompromising testimony against the superstition and idolatry of the Church of Rome" (quoted in Hickey and Doherty 1987, 3). It lasted into the early 1850s.

1838

In Cork, Father Theobald Mathew began his celebrated campaign against drinking. Father Mathew's temperance crusade became one of the most popular movements of the 1840s, extending throughout Ireland and even to the United States.

Education

A nondenominational teacher-training college was established in Dublin. At first it admitted only men, but beginning in 1845 women too could enroll (de Breffny 1983, 80).

Irish Language and Literature

A chair in Irish was established at Trinity College, Dublin, after a campaign supported by members of the Irish Society (see 1818 entry), which wanted future Church of Ireland ministers to learn Irish so that they could convert Gaelic speakers to Protestantism (Hickey and Doherty 1987, 263). Future beneficiaries of this requirement were to include Douglas Hyde and John Millington Synge, both of whom learned Irish as part of divinity studies at Trinity. Instead of proceeding to the ministry, however, both men became central leaders of the nationalist Literary Revival.

1839

Architecture

The Royal Institute of the Architects of Ireland was founded, reflecting the growth of architecture as a home-grown profession. Muckross House in county Kerry was designed by William Burn (de Breffny 1983, 27, 29).

Fiction

Charles Lever's first novel, *The Confessions of Harry Lorrequer,* was written serially for the *Dublin University Magazine.* The unabashed Lever described it as "little other than a notebook of absurd and laughable incidents." Surprised by the ease of composition and his success, Lever—a doctor by training and a colorful character—was thereby launched on his long and prosperous career as a novelist.

1840

Periodicals

Samuel Lover founded and illustrated the *Irish Penny Journal* (1840–41), its title suggesting the fact that Lover sought to hover above the sectarian lines earlier established by the *Catholic Penny Magazine* (1834–35) and the *Protestant Penny Journal* (1834–36). He published writers as different as Carleton and Anna Hall (Lubbers 1985, 133).

At this point the *Dublin Morning Register* was coedited by

Thomas Davis and John Blake Dillon (Hickey and Doherty 1987, 114).

1841

Fiction

Charles Lever's *Charles O'Malley, the Irish Dragoon* was a hilarious, episodic, in some respects almost aburdist novel recounting the adventures of a young Trinity College student and (subsequently) vagabond soldier. Lever was delighted and surprised by its success, noting in its preface: "My whole strength lay in the fact that I could not recognize anything like literary effort in the matter. If the world would only condescend to read that which I wrote precisely as I was in the habit of talking, nothing could be easier than for me to occupy them." Lever was lionized in England, but condemned in Ireland, as one of the reputedly anti-Irish Ascendancy school of "Lover and Lever." His early novels, however, reflect the Ascendancy laughing at itself.

Prose Nonfiction

Soon to become the short-lived leader of the "Young Ireland" movement, Thomas Davis (1814–45) argued in his essay "Udalism and Feudalism" that if its feudal economy could be discarded, Ireland would become a happy, prosperous county like similarly wet, mountainous Norway—which Davis imagined as controlled by a thoughtful and busy middle class with a landowning peasant proprietorship (M. Brown 1972, 47).

1842

Fiction

Samuel Lover's *Handy Andy* fixed the very popular (but in critical circles very negative) reputation that has been attached to Lover ever since. Yeats claimed that this novel "created the stage Irishman" (quoted in Lubbers 1985, 179), but really it only perpetuated this very old type. *Handy Andy* is a loose, episodic book filled with Andy's ludicrous exploits, but in spite of his idiocy Andy becomes a hero, finally getting married, becoming an aristocrat, and sitting down to dinner with the gentleman-poet Edward O'Connor. *Handy Andy* is also full of the worst exploits of degenerate landlords (rather in the vein of *Castle Rackrent*), but most commentators remember only stage-Irish Andy, not the Ascendancy characters lampooned much more harshly by Lover.

Periodicals

The *Nation* newspaper was founded by Thomas Davis and his fellow Young Irelanders John Mitchel, Charles Gavan Duffy, and William Smith O'Brien (1803–64). The first issue of 15 October declared that "the first duty of men who desire to foster Nationality is to teach the People not only the elevating influence but the intrinsic advantage of the principle . . . that National feelings, National habits, and National government are indispensable to individual prosperity." This sixteen-page weekly boasted in early issues, "This journal . . . is the LARGEST in IRELAND—as may be ascertained by measuring the sheet with any of the existing Newspapers—and . . . contains more Original Matter, and by more Distinguished Writers, than *any Newspaper in the Empire* (15 October, p. 16). The *Nation* was to publish not only Davis's heartfelt and popular though inferior verse—"A Nation Once Again," "The West's Asleep," "Lament for the Death of Owen Roe O'Neill," and numerous others—but also the far better poetry of James Clarence Mangan, such as his famous and influential "Dark Rosaleen." Samuel Ferguson (1810–86), also a better poet, is sometimes associated with the *Nation* even though he never actually published in it. It was the first nationally popular, nonsectarian, nationalist newspaper in Ireland, and was later cited by Yeats as a precursor of his own literary and cultural efforts: "Nor may I less be counted one / With Davis, Mangan, Ferguson" ("To Ireland in the Coming Times," 1893). The *Nation* was, however, flawed by an atavistic devotion to anything Irish and by a lack of critical acumen. Yeats knew this to be true: "My rhymes more than their rhyming tell / Of things discovered in the deep."

Meanwhile, Charles Lever took over as editor of the *Dublin University Magazine,* broadening its appeal and raising circulation to over 40,000 a month (including a good-sized readership in

England). Its next editor would be the equally well-known Irish novelist Joseph Sheridan Le Fanu (1814–73) (Hayley 1987, 35). At this time Lever was so identified with his earlier fictional work published in the magazine that the announcement of his appointment to its editorship identified him as "Mr. Lever (Harry Lorrequer)," thereby linking his name to that of his first fictional protagonist, and assured readers that he "will also contribute largely and exclusively to each number of the magazine" (19 [March]).

1843

Proclaimed by Daniel O'Connell as the "Repeal Year," after years of campaigning to repeal the Union of Ireland and England. Early pro-Repeal rallies were the largest in Irish history, with close to a million people on hand (in a country of perhaps eight million at the time) at the Hill of Tara in county Meath to hear O'Connell speak. But his pacifism and belief in the law caused O'Connell to honor the government's prohibition of his announced mass rally for Repeal at Clontarf (near Dublin) in October, after which many nationalists abandoned him in favor of the Young Ireland movement begun by Thomas Davis and other (mostly Protestant) nationalists surrounding the *Nation.* The ambiguous relationship of the *Nation* to O'Connell, as well as Young Ireland's growing impatience with him, can perhaps best (and most amusingly) be seen in verses by James Clarence Mangan:

> O'Connell's a tremendous ass-
> aulter of tyranny and Tories
> And we the *Nation,* are his ass-
> istants and share—hurrah—his glories.

> (quoted in M. Brown 1972, 63)

In anger O'Connell later turned against Young Ireland, whose leader, Davis, died in 1845. O'Connell himself died in 1847, in the midst of the Great Hunger. O'Connell's career ended in failure, but the Irish folk imagination selectively remembers only his early feats as "the Counsellor," an unbeatable lawyer; more stories about him are preserved in Irish folklore than about anyone else in modern Irish history.

Architecture

St. Mary's Cathedral in Kilkenny was designed by William Deane Butler (de Breffny 1983, 28).

Prose Nonfiction

The Spirit of the Nation was a very popular, influential collection of many of Thomas Davis's articles and poems from the *Nation* newspaper (Hickey and Doherty 1987, 115).

1844

Architecture

Amiens Street train station in Dublin was constructed by William Deane Butler (de Breffny 1983, 30).

Poetry

Edward Walsh's (1805–50) *Reliques of Irish Jacobite Poetry* appeared, with lively translations of Gaelic ballads: "Five guineas would price every tress of her golden hair, / Then think what a treasure her pillow at night to share!" (quoted in McHugh and Harmon 1982, 114).

1845

From September onward a fungus blight (*Phytophthora infestans*) attacked potato crops in Ireland, rotting the plants. It became worse in 1846 and returned in 1848. Because of the nearly complete dependence of the peasantry on the potato, a "Great Hunger" or "Famine" ensued. (Many prefer the former term to the latter since, literally, a famine involves starvation due to lack of food, whereas in Ireland cash grain crops, unaffected by the blight, were steadily exported during these years.) Population— 8.2 million in the early 1840s but only 4.4 million in 1911— declined by more than 2.2 million during the period 1845–51

(Foster 1988, 323). Public and private relief efforts were pursued, but a million people died (some estimates are lower, some higher) and as many emigrated, with many forced by poverty to make the journey to America on the infamous, dangerous "coffin ships." The effects of these events were long lasting, and their popular memory phenomenally persistent. People passed down "Famine" stories for many decades afterward, into recent times. The impact on the Irish language was devastating and massive, since a disproportionately high percentage of those who died or who emigrated were Irish speakers.

James Fintan Lalor (1807–49) founded a Tenant League in Tipperary, subsequently taking charge of the *Irish Felon* in 1848 and publishing broadsides focusing on the class nature of the land question. Lalor felt that it was time to "unmuzzle the wolf-dog. There is one at this moment in every cabin throughout the land, nearly fit already to be untied—and he will be savage by-and-by" (quoted in M. Brown 1972, 103). Lalor's ideas were to be influential on nationalist leaders such as John Mitchel.

Thomas Davis (b. 1814) died at age thirty-one, three days after the first report of the potato blight. William Smith O'Brien served as de facto leader of the Young Ireland movement following Davis's death.

Fiction

Written under the encouragement of Davis and the *Nation,* William Carleton's *Valentine McClutchy* was a bitter satire of the rural Irish economic way of life in which grasping middlemen oppressed poor laborers in the name of absentee landlords. "Humours" names were assigned to its villains: "McClutchy" or "Val the Vulture," the land agent or middleman in the tradition of Edgeworth's Jason Quirk; Darby O'Drive, McClutchy's enforcer; Solomon McSlime, an attorney who mixes evangelism and a corrupt administration of the law; and the Reverend Phineas Lucre, a prosperous preacher, a kind of earlier-day Elmer Gantry or TV evangelist.

Anna Fielding Hall's *The Whiteboy* was a typical nineteenth-century Irish novel. Edward Spencer, the hero, is traveling on a steamship to look after his estate in Cork. While onboard he is given a quick course in Irish politics and culture by two veterans of the country, in preparation for taking up his Edgeworthian duties. Responsibility and marriage naturally ensue.

Even the comic master Charles Lever, chastised two years earlier by William Carleton for his Irish "caricatures," joined the Irish novelists busy publishing "patriotic" novels: his *The O'Donoghue* and *St. Patrick's Eve,* both of which appeared in this year, took English policies to task and presented much more somber portraits of Ireland than did his earlier novels. The better of the two was *St. Patrick's Eve,* describing the cholera epidemic in county Clare in 1832, which Lever had witnessed during his term of service as a doctor working in the poor districts.

Yet another "patriot" novel by an Ascendancy author was Sheridan Le Fanu's *The Cock and Anchor,* celebrating the Irish nationalism of the period of the Battle of the Boyne (1690). This was Le Fanu's first novel. A lengthy, hyberbolic review in the *Dublin University Magazine* (which Le Fanu would subsequently edit and own) "rejoiced that to the literature of Ireland there has been made an addition, in every way so calculated to do it honour" (26 [November]: 625).

1846

At a meeting in July, Young Ireland, led by William Smith O'Brien, walked out on Daniel O'Connell, convinced that his nonviolent tactics were no longer the way to solve Ireland's grim problems.

Poetry

In the midst of (and in reaction to) the Great Hunger, James Clarence Mangan's poem "My Dark Rosaleen," a version of the traditional Irish verse "Róisín Dubh" (with its romantic identification of the dark rose with Ireland), made its original appearance in the *Nation:* "The Judgment Hour must first be nigh, / Ere you can fade, ere you can die, / My Dark Rosaleen!" Mangan's image of the suffering rose was to reverberate in the 1890s in the poems of W. B. Yeats. Mangan also prefigured the Literary Revival and furthered interest in the relevance of the native Irish poetic tradition by publishing, in the *Dublin University Magazine* in the

following year, two installments of "Anthologia Hibernica"—
some translations of Gaelic verse and commentaries on them.
Mangan had earlier published in this magazine some translations
from European poets; now he noted that "it has occasionally
occurred to us that we might perhaps be as gracefully, if not as
profitably, employed in 'looking at home,' and culling the simple
poetical wildflowers of our own dear Mother-land" (29 [February
1847]: 239).

1847

This was "black '47," the worst year of the Great Hunger, when
the potato blight and resulting starvation and emigration reached
their peaks. Even the normally conservative, detached *Dublin
University Magazine* published a forty-page exposé, "The Famine
in the Land": "Little is there in [Ireland's] present condition on
which the mind can dwell with any feeling but that of the most
intense pain. And gloomy as is the retrospect, and appalling as is
the spectacle around us, we grieve to add that in the prospect there
seems nothing to vary the monotony of horror" (29 [1847]: 501).

In May Daniel O'Connell (b. 1775) died in Genoa on his way
to Rome, traveling to Italy on the advice of his physicians.
According to his own wishes, his heart was extracted and buried in
Rome. His body was returned to Ireland and buried in Glasnevin
Cemetery in Dublin.

Fiction

In his novel *The Black Prophet* William Carleton vividly captured
the suffering of the Great Hunger, then at its height, and ironically
"dedicated" his tale to the English prime minister, Lord John
Russell (1792–1878). However, Carleton's polemical position and
ability to write gripping realistic dialogue were undermined by his
plot, which focused on an obscure murder story involving events
twenty years earlier than the main action of this novel.

The Fortunes of Colonel Torlogh O'Brien, Sheridan Le Fanu's
second novel, celebrated the early eighteenth-century version of
Irish nationalism. Le Fanu's class bias, at the same time, is clear:
his upper-class Catholic hero has to defeat the evil lower-class

Catholic villain in order to marry into the Protestant Ascendancy at the end. This novel also contains some grisly gothic strains that look ahead to the kind of writing that would make Le Fanu's name.

Charles Lever resettled to Florence, Italy.

Periodicals

James Duffy began *Duffy's Irish Catholic Magazine,* the first of many periodicals he was to publish during the period, including *Duffy's Fireside Magazine,* the *Catholic Guardian or the Christian Family Library,* the *Catholic University Gazette, Duffy's Hibernian Magazine,* the *Illustrated Dublin Journal,* and *Duffy's Hibernian Sixpenny Magazine* (which ceased publication in 1864). As suggested by the plethora of titles, Duffy was a one-man business, an entrepeneur of "cosy family Catholicism" (Hayley 1987, 42). He published, in both periodical and book form, the fiction of Carleton and several other Irish writers.

The *Cork Magazine* began, and ended in the following year, but in its short life published fiction by such writers as Fitz-James O'Brien (Kilroy 1984, 11).

Poetry

Jeremiah Joseph Callanan's (1795–1829) *Poems,* originally published in periodicals in the 1820s and finally collected in book form, are now mostly forgotten, but are interesting in how they look back to the Gaelic tradition and ahead to the romanticism of poets such as Yeats:

> 'Tis down by the lake where the wild tree fringes its sides,
> The maid of my heart, my fair one of Heaven resides;
> I think, as at eve she wanders its mazes along,
> The birds go to sleep by the sweet wild twist of her song."
>
> (quoted in McHugh and Harmon 1982, 114)

1848

John Mitchel—temporarily expelled from the Young Ireland movement because of the extreme nature of his nationalist views, as influenced by James Fintan Lalor—started the newspaper the *United Irishman* in February and was tried in May under the new Treason-Felony Act (which gave the government almost unlimited powers to take action against Fenians), was found guilty by a stacked jury, and was sentenced to exile in Van Diemen's Land (Tasmania). Author of the famous *Jail Journal* (see 1854 entry), Mitchel subsequently settled in the United States, where (paradoxically) he became a defender of slavery.

In July William Smith O'Brien organized an abortive rising in county Tipperary (called the "Young Ireland" rising, parallel to other European rebellions of this year) and was sentenced to death but then transported for life to Van Diemen's Land, like Mitchel.

After Thomas Francis Meagher (1822–67) returned from France with a French tricolor flag as a gift to Irish citizens, John Mitchel remarked, "I hope to see that flag one day waving as our national banner" (quoted in Hickey and Doherty 1987, 571). He would have his wish in 1922, when the Irish Free State adopted an Irish tricolor—with the colors changed to green and orange with white in the middle to symbolize peace between Catholics and Protestants—after this flag had been first flown during the 1916 Easter Rising.

Fiction

William Carleton tackled the crucial problem of emigration in *The Emigrants of Ahadarra,* but this novel is flawed by digressions on politics and a melodramatic plot. In the same year he also published *The Tithe Proctor,* in which he went on the offensive against Irish nationalists and sought to expose Catholic militants who, in the 1830s, had attacked collectors of tithes (taxes forced on Catholics, since the time of King Henry II, to raise money to support the Protestant clergy in Ireland). Carleton unfairly linked Daniel O'Connell to the perpetrators of violence.

Music

The senior Irish institute for the teaching of music, the Royal Irish Academy of Music, was founded at a location in Westland Row, Dublin. Now examining about 18,000 students annually at all levels, this academy is partially funded by the Department of Education (de Breffny 1983, 208).

1849

James Fintan Lalor attempted another rebellion in Tipperary and Waterford that turned out to be merely a skirmish, though several constables and attackers were killed. Thomas Clarke Luby (1821–1901) and John O'Leary (1830–1907), both subsequently to be leading Fenians, participated. Lalor was arrested, jailed, and died soon after his release from prison, in Dublin (M. Brown 1972, 115).

Having traveled around Ireland to observe the effects of the Great Hunger, Thomas Carlyle noted in the *Nation*, "No words printed in a newspaper or elsewhere will give a man who had not seen it a conception of the fallen condition of the West and South" (quoted in M. Brown 1972, 120).

Fiction

Years after she had despaired of writing any more of Ireland, Maria Edgeworth (b. 1767) died.

1850

With the support of Archbishop MacHale and the leadership of Charles Gavan Duffy (who now pursued a probably ill-advised effort to attract the support of the Catholic church), the Irish Tenant League was founded in August at a meeting in Dublin. Demands that would continue to be made in ensuing decades were formulated, in particular the "Three Fs": free sale of improvements made by the tenant to the property (already a practice in Ulster), fixity of tenure, and fair rent. Any possibility of early fulfillment of these aims, however, was squashed when two opportunistic members of the Tenant League, John Sadleir (1815–56) and William Keogh (1817–78), used the league's electoral triumph in 1851 as the ticket to cabinet jobs in the newly formed British government (rather than as a mandate for the Three Fs)—and when Duffy, the league's founder, left Ireland in disgust in 1855 and resettled in Australia (M. Brown 1972, 121, 131–32). Sadleir and Keogh were notoriously remembered as "the Pope's brass band" because of their efforts to win special favors for the clergy, which succeeded in alienating the Tenant League's Protestant supporters.

The Reform or Franchise Act quadrupled the Irish county electorate by shifting to a system of qualification based on land occupation.

Anti-English and antilandlord sentiment ran strong during and after the Great Hunger; in this year a priest in county Clare told his congregation, "My advice to you is to throw over altogether the legal rights of landlords and seek for your just rights and not your legal rights. I would not give anything for the landlords' legal rights but to tell you to throw them over altogether" (quoted in Foster 1988, 343).

Poetry

Ballads, Poems and Lyrics, Original and Translated by Denis Florence MacCarthy (1817–82) included such verses as "The Pillar Towers of Ireland," concerning the round towers of early Christian Ireland (Deane et al. 1991, 2: 59).

1851

Fiction

Sheridan Le Fanu's *Ghost Stories and Tales of Mystery* appeared. Mostly set in England, these stories launched Le Fanu's reputation as author of gothic short fiction, the most celebrated aspect of his career.

Irish Language and Literature

The census estimated that 23 percent of the population spoke Irish as their first language (Todd 1989, 15). This reflected a large decline since before the Great Hunger, and the figure would continue to decline throughout the late nineteenth century as a disproportionately high percentage of Irish speakers continued to emigrate.

1853

The *New York Tribune* carried "a closely reasoned article on Tenant Right by Karl Marx. In his articles both in German and American newspapers, Marx was making known the plight of Ireland to the world. Expounding the cause of Tenant Right, Marx pointed out that the process by which landlords increased rents after the tenant had made an improvement to their farm amounted to the tenant paying interest on his own money. . . . Marx argued that only the expropriation of the landlords by nationalisation of the land would solve the Irish agrarian question" (Ellis 1973, 126–27).

Folklore

In his *Irish Popular Superstitions* Sir William Wilde (1815–76), Oscar Wilde's father, noted the decline of Irish folk tradition as a result of the Great Hunger and described rural desolation: "The old forms and customs, too, are becoming obliterated; the festivals are unobserved, and the rustic festivities neglected or forgotten; the bowlings, the cakes and the prinkums (the peasants' balls and routs), do not often take place when starvation and pestilence stalk over a country, many parts of which appear as if a destroying army had but recently passed through it" (quoted in T. Brown 1985, 41).

1854

Cultural Institutions

The Dublin Photographic Society, renamed the Photographic Society of Ireland four years later, was founded by a group including John J. Coghill and James Robinson (de Breffny 1983, 192).

Drama

In Westland Row in Dublin, adjacent to Trinity College, was born Oscar Fingal O'Flahertie Wills Wilde (d. 1900), son of the leading eye surgeon Sir William Wilde and the colorful, patriotic, versatile Irish Renaissance woman, Lady Wilde (1826–96) or "Speranza," her literary-cultural pseudonym. Like George Bernard Shaw, born two years later, Wilde spent the first twenty years of his life in Dublin and, when he achieved great success later as a comic dramatist for the London stage, he did so aided by his critical outsider status as an Irishman examining English society.

Education

The Catholic University (later to become University College, Dublin) was established in Dublin, with Cardinal John Henry Newman (1801–90) as its first rector.

Prose Nonfiction

The *Jail Journal* of John Mitchel, the former Young Irelander, was published. This book is at least as interesting for its depiction of a double-minded, victimized prisoner psyche as it is for any of its political insights. It opens with a meditation on suicide, and takes up Mitchel's assertion elswhere that "Every man holds chained up within him a madman" (quoted in M. Brown 1972, 135). Mitchel later lived out his notion of the doppelgänger by continuing to argue for Irish independence while at the same time writing in support of slavery in the United States.

1855

Discouraged by events in Ireland, the Young Ireland and Tenant League leader Charles Gavan Duffy emigrated to Australia, where he was also to become a notable figure in Australian history.

Sir Benjamin Guinness (1798–1868) assumed control of the Guinness Brewery; under his guidance the company developed a huge export trade and he became the richest man in Ireland (Hickey and Doherty 1987, 213). He served as lord mayor of Dublin and made famous a family tradition of philanthropy, which was continued by his son Sir Arthur Guinness and subsequent owners of Ireland's most famous brewery.

Poetry

The *Poems* of Aubrey de Vere (1814–1902) appeared; poems such as "The March to Kinsale" and "The Dirge of Rory O'Moore" influenced Yeats and other writers of the later Literary Revival (McHugh and Harmon 1982, 115).

1856

Friedrich Engels toured Ireland with his Irish wife, Mary Burns, and described, in a letter to his friend and collaborator Karl Marx, "gendarmes, priests, lawyers, bureaucrats, squires in pleasing profusion, and a total absence of any and every industry, so that it would be hard to understand what these parasitic growths live on if the misery of the peasants didn't supply the other half of the picture. . . . Ireland can be regarded as the first English colony, and as one which, because of its proximity, is still ruled directly in the old way. Here it can be clearly seen that the so-called liberty of the English citizens is based on the oppression of the colonies" (quoted in Ellis 1973, 129).

Architecture

The University Church next to St. Stephen's Green, Dublin, designed by J. Hungerford Pollen, was built in an early Christian style that broke with the more typical classical and gothic styles (de Breffny 1983, 28).

Drama

George Bernard Shaw (d. 1950) was born at 33 Synge Street in Dublin on 26 July. Though Shaw spent the first twenty years of his life in Dublin, commented often on Irish affairs during his long and distinguished career, and left a fortune to the National Gallery, only in 1991 (forty-one years after Shaw's death) when it was reminded of Shaw's massive support did the National Gallery board agree to help finance the restoration of the 33 Synge Street house in commemoration of Shaw.

Fiction

Charles Lever's novel *The Martins of Cro Martin* was written in the spirit of his friend Maria Edgeworth. Its heroine is Mary Martin (modeled on Edgeworth), who insists on taking care of the peasants on her family estate even after her elders sell their properties. Lever draws on his own experiences working as a doctor with county Clare cholera victims in describing Mary's efforts in county Galway in the 1830s. A number of experiences— the cholera epidemic, the criticisms of his early comic novels by William Carleton and others, the Great Hunger and the course of Irish politics afterward, his own exiled posture living in Italy— now influenced Lever to write more somber novels than his earlier ones.

1858

James Stephens (1825–1901), encouraged by John O'Mahony (1816–77), founded the Irish Republican Brotherhood (IRB), more popularly known as the "Fenians" after the warrior band the Fianna, celebrated in the medieval saga of Fionn MacCumhail. This became the most popular Irish nationalist movement of the nineteenth century, recapturing much of the romanticism of earlier underground groups such as the Ribbonmen and Whiteboys and involving such other notable leaders and writers as Jeremiah O'Donovan Rossa, Thomas Clarke Luby, Charles Kickham, Yeats's future mentor John O'Leary, and John Devoy. It also produced Michael Davitt (1846–1906), founder of the Land League in the late 1870s—thus forming an important link to the land struggle. The Fenians engendered an avowedly violent brand of Irish nationalism that rejected the nonviolent politics earlier practiced by Daniel O'Connell. In his *Recollections of Fenians and*

Fenianism (1896), John O'Leary was to recall Thomas Luby insisting, "Far better it were, in a struggle for freedom, to have but 300 true men, on whom you could rely for support to the last drop of their blood—who, if called upon, would conquer or die with you. . . . Better a thousand times such a small band than 50,000 doubters or shams" or "tea-table revolutionists, who join a cause while danger is remote, who love at once to frighten and fascinate weak girls by tall talk, but who sing small when danger drops on them" (quoted in M. Brown 1972, 155).

1859

Architecture

Kilmore Cathedral in county Cavan was designed by William Slater in a thirteenth-century English style (de Breffny 1983, 28).

Periodicals

The *Irish Times,* which had first appeared during the years 1823–25, was revived by Major Lawrence Knox and published initially three times a week and thereafter daily—the second penny newspaper in Ireland (Oram 1983, 68). For many years a conservative, Unionist newspaper, the *Irish Times* eventually developed into the chief liberal paper in the country and also the most culturally erudite and detailed in literary terms—today's "highbrow" paper.

1860

Drama

The Colleen Bawn, the first Irish play by Dion Boucicault (1820–90), was a popular melodrama drawing on Gerald Griffin's novel *The Collegians* (1829). Boucicault created the nineteenth century's most popular stage Irishmen, and was virtually the only nineteenth-century Irish playwright (before the celebrated dramatists of the 1890s) who is still remembered and whose plays are still performed. It is a measure of the poverty of the nineteenth-century Irish stage that Boucicault had to emigrate first to London and then to New York in order to succeed as a playwright. His plays were comedies and melodramas written for huge theaters such as Covent Garden and Drury Lane in London, with histrionic speeches written in colorful language, full of dialect, and meant to be projected to the distant rafters of these theaters.

1861

Periodicals

Sheridan Le Fanu bought the *Dublin University Magazine,* became its editor, and wrote and serialized nine novels (an average of one per year) before selling the magazine in 1869.

Poetry

The Sisters, Inisfail and Other Poems by Aubrey Thomas de Vere presented a series of events from Irish history in poetic form (Deane et al. 1991, 2: 55).

Prose Nonfiction

Leaders of Public Opinion in Ireland, Trinity College historian W. E. H. Lecky's (1838–1903) first book, appeared. Lecky, whose statue now stands in the middle of the Trinity College courtyard, was a pioneer of modern Irish historiography.

1862

The Irish Language and Literature

The periodical *Fíor-Éirionnach* (True Irish) was attempted by Richard D'Alton as "the first move to the restoration of the Irish language, to be printed in weekly numbers, containing Catholic

prayers and selections from the poetry and history of our country"
(quoted in Nic Pháidín 1987, 72). It lasted only a short time.

1863

Architecture

Sir Thomas Deane (1828–99) designed Tuam Cathedral in a
thirteenth-century Irish style.

Cultural Institutions

The still-thriving porcelain factory in Belleek, county Fermanagh,
began production (de Breffny 1983, 28, 43).

Fiction

The House by the Churchyard, later a source for James Joyce, was
Sheridan Le Fanu's best Irish novel. This gothic, Big House tale of
mystery and intrigue, set in eighteenth-century Chapelizod, a
village just outside Dublin (and also the "scene" of *Finnegans
Wake*), interweaves several plots: the quest of the melancholy
Mervyn to clear his name, make a fortune, and satisfy his desire
for romance; the mysterious disappearance and reappearance of
Charles Nutter; the guilt and eventual apprehension of the murderer Charles Archer (alias Paul Dangerfield); and several other
smaller but equally vivid plots or subplots.

During this year William Carleton wrote, "Banim and Griffin
are gone, and I will soon follow them. . . . After that will come a
lull, an obscurity of perhaps half a century" (Wolff 1980, 127).
Carleton's assessment was fairly accurate, not only about his own
declining powers but also about this increasingly dark age in the
fortunes of Irish literature, lasting until the rise of Yeats and the
Literary Revival movement at the end of the century. Carleton
died six years later.

Periodicals

In November appeared the first issue of the *Irish People,* founded
by James Stephens (with John O'Leary, O'Donovan Rossa [1831–

1915], Thomas Luby, and Charles Kickham [1828-82] on the staff) to further the Fenian cause. It was hoped that this newspaper would be as popular as Young Ireland's the *Nation* had been in the 1840s, but it never achieved similar success. Two years later a police spy infiltrated the staff, and Luby, O'Leary, and Rossa were tried, convicted of treason, and received lengthy prison sentences (life imprisonment in Rossa's case).

1864

Cultural Institutions

The National Gallery opened in Merrion Square, Dublin; the original building, enlarged and extended in 1968, was designed by Francis Fowke (1823-65). Chief benefactors were later to include Sir Hugh Lane and George Bernard Shaw. One of the larger European galleries, it contains fine collections of paintings by Dutch masters and the seventeenth-century French, Italian, and Spanish schools, together with a representative collection of Irish works (de Breffny 1983, 165).

Poetry

William Allingham (1824-89) published his novel in verse about land evictions, *Laurence Bloomfield in Ireland.*

1865

By this date the Fenians or Irish Republicans numbered an alleged 80,000 in the United Kingdom, and the allied National Brotherhood of St. Patrick was publishing the newspaper the *Irish Liberator* and running fifteen branches (Foster 1988, 366), much as the Clan na Gael (see 1867 entry) would became a very popular support organization in the United States.

Drama

Boucicault's *Arrah-na-Pogue* drew on Samuel Lover's novel *Rory O'Moore* (1837).

Poetry

Samuel Ferguson's volume *Lays of the Western Gael,* which treated Irish heroic themes, appeared. William Butler Yeats (d. 1939), Ireland's greatest poet, was born in this year.

1866

Architecture

William Hague designed the town hall in Sligo, one of the earliest of a spate of new town halls constructed in Ireland during the latter part of the nineteenth century (de Breffny 1983, 30).

1867

In March a Fenian rebellion, planned more than two years earlier, was a military flop though in part a successful publicity stunt. After short-lived local successes in counties Limerick, Clare, Louth, and Waterford, this "rising" collapsed in defeat within forty-eight hours, after considerable confusion (with intercepted countermanding orders) about the precise date it was to occur and in the face of the largest snowfall in memory the night before the planned date (5 March). Many participants (though not the Fenian chief, James Stephens) were imprisoned, and after a subsequent gunrunning attempt in Sligo Bay, three men—William Allen, Michael Larkin, and Michael O'Brien—were hanged in Manchester, England, in November (M. Brown 1972, 203–4, 208). Karl Marx wrote, "Fenianism has entered a new phase. It has been baptised in blood by the English government. The political executions at Manchester remind us of the fate of John Brown at Harper's Ferry. They open a new period in the struggle between Ireland and England" (quoted in Ellis 1973, 140).

Three weeks after the Manchester hangings, London Fenians engineered an explosion at the Clerkenwell House of Detention in an attempt to liberate some Fenian prisoners. Instead, the explosion demolished a block of tenements across the street, killing twelve and injuring many others. This act initiated the lengthy tradition of Irish nationalist sabotage and violence directed against targets in England, especially London. Joseph Casey, one of the Fenian prisoners in Clerkenwell, later turned up as "Kevin Egan" (repeatedly called to mind by Stephen Dedalus) in James Joyce's *Ulysses.* During his first trip to Paris in 1902, Joyce paid a visit to Casey (M. Brown 1972, 223–24).

Jerome Collins founded the Clan na Gael in New York City as a Fenian support organization. This organization would be a gathering point for many Fenians subsequently exiled to the United States, such as Jeremiah O'Donovan Rossa and John Devoy, and later played a significant role in preparations for the 1916 Easter Rising (Hickey and Doherty 1987, 74–75).

Fiction

Lord Derby conferred on Charles Lever the British consulship in Trieste, Italy, remarking, "Here are 600 pounds a year for doing nothing, and you, Lever, are just the man to do it."

Literary Criticism

Matthew Arnold's essay "On the Study of Celtic Literature" encouraged the study of Irish literature in the English-speaking world along with a somewhat stereotyped view of the subject as reacting "against the despotism of fact" in favor of magic, sensuousness, and other antirational qualities. It seems almost appropriate that this essay appeared in the year of the Fenian rebellion: Arnold viewed the Teutonic-Saxon and Celtic temperaments as polarities, though he attempted to idealize a romantic union of the two. Whatever their degree of accuracy (or lack thereof), Arnold's notions remained very influential on many writers, including W. B. Yeats.

1868

William Gladstone (1809–98) replaced Benjamin Disraeli (1804–81) as British prime minister. Gladstone was to be involved in late-nineteenth-century land reform and Irish attempts to enact Home Rule.

Education

The Irish National Teacher's Organisation (INTO), the oldest and largest teachers' union in Ireland, was founded (Hickey and Doherty 1987, 250).

Prose Nonfiction

George Sigerson's (1836–1925) *Modern Ireland: Its Vital Questions, Secret Societies, and Government* incorporated a valuable analysis of Fenianism. Sigerson sympathized with Fenian aims, disagreed with their violent means, and argued that reforms needed to be made that would reduce the Fenians' support and divert nationalist activity to constitutional means (Deane et al. 1991, 2: 238–39).

1869

An Irish Amnesty Association, with the liberal Tory Protestant Isaac Butt as president, was formed on behalf of Fenian political prisoners. Butt was the chief leader of parliamentary Irish nationalism until he was eclipsed by Charles Stewart Parnell eight years later.

Fiction

His writing and his reputation having been in decline for a number of years, William Carleton (b. 1794) died in relative poverty.

1870

Gladstone's Land Act legalized where it already existed the "Ulster Custom" of recognizing a tenant's investment in his holding, called for compensation for improvements made by tenants and for eviction for reasons other than nonpayment, and encouraged (though ineffectually) the idea of land purchase by tenants.

In May Isaac Butt founded the Home Government Association to advocate Home Rule for Ireland. It was replaced by the Home Rule League three years later (Hickey and Doherty 1987, 228).

Though he never finished it, by this date Friedrich Engels, who visited Ireland twice, had planned to write a history of Ireland; he filled fifteen notebooks, learned some Irish (even writing to Marx to send him a grammar), and wrote one chapter and part of a second before events on the Continent changed his plans. (An English translation of the unfinished history was to appear much later in the *Irish Democrat,* between 1950 and 1953, and the original German version in 1962 in the *Works of Marx and Engels,* vol. 16.) (Ellis 1973, 142).

Drama

Dion Boucicault's play *The Flying Scud* was a great success at the Walnut Street Theater in Philadelphia. Boucicault's "scud" was a horse and the play, written in 1866, concerned a horserace—and reverberated in the popular press as late as 1991, when an Associated Press story remarked on the semantic connection between Boucicault's "scud" and the missiles launched by Iraq's Saddam Hussein during the Gulf War.

Periodicals

The *Belfast Telegraph* newspaper, still prominent today, began publishing (Oram 1983, 72–73).

Galway-born Patrick Ford (1837–1913) founded the *Irish World* newspaper in New York and published it until his death in 1913 (Hickey and Doherty 1987, 268). It was to be an important support mechanism for the Fenian movement as well as the Land League.

1871

Drama

John and Michael Gunn opened the new Gaiety Theatre in South King Street in Dublin, with Goldsmith's *She Stoops to Conquer* as its first production (Hickey and Doherty 1787, 185). This handsome, double-balconied Victorian theater endures today as a center for classic and popular plays.

Oscar Wilde began his studies at Trinity College, Dublin, where he read classics under Professor Mahaffy and won several awards. It was at Trinity that Wilde became convinced of the opinion that he later expressed to Yeats: "We Irish are all dismal failures, but we are the greatest talkers since the Greeks." No one would better illustrate this maxim than Wilde himself.

John Millington Synge (d. 1909) was born on 16 April in Rathfarnham, Dublin.

Periodicals

Lamented the pseudonymous "Dublinienis" in the *Dublin Builder* in October, "With a purely native literature at the lowest ebb—with our native-born *litterateurs* and journalists in foreign fields working for a foreign market—with our country deluged for the most part with foreign literary publications of a demoralizing, effeminate, and denationalizing tendency—with a Press that gives indiscriminate praise to works bad, good, and indifferent—with public spirit dead, and public representatives and professional men leaping at each other's throats—how can an able and honest art, literary, and theatrical criticism be supposed to have an existence in this island?" (1871, 250).

1872

The Ballot Act introduced the secret ballot to Ireland, finally enabling tenant farmers to vote against the interests of their landlords (Hickey and Doherty 1987, 25).

Fiction

Lord Kilgobbin, Charles Lever's last novel, was carefully plotted, as if this author of episodic novels wanted to prove that he actually could write one with a tight plot. Half-Irish and half-Greek, the orphaned Nina Kostalergi comes from the Continent to live with her relatives at the home of the kindhearted Mathew Kearney, who is regarded as the true "Lord Kilgobbin" by the peasants and whose son Richard wants to rackrent the tenants in order to support his Trinity College life-style. The beautiful Nina rejects the crafty politicians who woo her, including the familiar trickster type Joe Atlee, in favor of the good Fenian rebel Dan Donogan, running off with him to America at the end. Championing an Irish rebel and positioning a heroic woman at the center of his novel, Lever showed how much he had changed since the days of his early comic novels. He died in Italy this same year, and a long obituary appeared in the *Dublin University Magazine,* recognizing that "since the last issue of this Magazine there has passed away a man who for some years controlled its course" (1872, 104). Its review of his career concluded, "In the more recent of his works he has somewhat changed his *venue:* he has transported us from the rollicking gaiety of Irish dragoons. . . . But the verdict is the same. There is the same unfettered and unflagging vivacity" (1872, 109).

Poetry

Samuel Ferguson's mythic, epic *Congal* was published. It explored the conflict between paganism and Christianity, and was to influence Yeats. A lengthy review in the *Dublin University Magazine* concluded, "We are not aware of any requisite quality of a great heroic poem which it does not possess. . . . Ireland has at last been presented with a noble national epic by one of her sons" (1872, 400). It cannot be said, however, that a large number of people took the poem to their hearts.

1873

A Home Rule conference in Dublin led to no clearly focused course of action, despite Belfast M. P. Joseph Biggar's (1828–90) argument that all Irish members of Parliament ought to vote as a block at Westminster on Home Rule and indeed all other matters (M. Brown 1972, 237–38).

Periodicals

Father Matthew Russell (1834–1912) launched the *Irish Monthly,* which he edited until 1912. It began as a religious magazine but also became a literary one, with later contributions from W. B. Yeats, Aubrey de Vere, and others (Hickey and Doherty 1987, 249).

1874

Drama

The Shaughraun was Dion Boucicault's most successful Irish play, containing his best Irish rogue-hero and generating huge profits in New York. Later Seán O'Casey grew up acting *The Shaughraun* and Shakespeare.

1875

Political exile John Mitchel, recently returned to Ireland, was elected to Parliament, but the House of Commons refused him his seat (and Mitchel would have boycotted it anyway). Shortly thereafter Mitchel died, and his brother-in-law John Martin (b. 1812), member of Parliament for Meath, caught pneumonia at his funeral and died himself a few days later. A by-election to fill Martin's seat was won by Charles Stewart Parnell (1846–91), the future "uncrowned king of Ireland." Upon taking his seat Parnell joined Joseph Biggar in hours of filibustering during debate on an Irish coercion bill—and similar, unsuccessful, but memorable obstruction efforts on several other items of legislation.

The Dublin's Women Suffrage Association, the first such organization in Ireland, was formed. It subsequently grew into the Irishwomen's Suffrage and Local Government Association (Hickey and Doherty 1987, 267).

Cultural Institutions

The earl of Charlemont founded the Royal Irish Academy, a learned institution divided into sections for the humanities and the sciences.

Poetry

At Oxford University, Oscar Wilde won the prize for poetry for "Ravenna." At Oxford Wilde studied under and was greatly influenced by John Ruskin and Walter Pater (who contributed to Wilde's developing notions of aestheticism and "art for art's sake"). He graduated with honors three years later.

Prose Nonfiction

Isaac Butt's speech "The Parliamentary Policy of Home Rule" advanced the central argument of the Irish Parliamentary party. Butt would subsequently be supplanted as the party's leader by Parnell.

1876

While the typical landlord in Ireland owned about 2,000 acres, by this date "less than 800 landlords owned half the country" (Foster 1988, 375). This was the case in the midst of growing interest in land reform and tenants' rights: "the Three Fs"—free sale, fair rent, and fixity of tenure—all implying the Irish tenant farmer's natural moral right to the land that he farmed.

Drama

George Bernard Shaw moved from Dublin to London, where at first he worked for the Edison Telephone Company and then wrote a series of unsuccessful novels.

Irish Language and Literature

The Society for the Preservation of the Irish Language was formed to try to counteract the decline of the language (MacEoin 1969, 57).

1877

In August the Home Rule Confederation elected Parnell as president in place of an angry Isaac Butt (who died two years later).

Cultural Institutions

An act of Parliament founded both the National Museum and the National Library of Ireland, eventually to occupy impressive adjoining sites in Kildare Street in Dublin.

1878

Architecture

J. J. McCarthy designed the chapel at Glasnevin in a Hiberno-Romanesque style tied to the rise of Irish nationalism (de Breffny 1983, 28)—appropriately enough, since many of the best-known Irish patriots were buried nearby in Glasnevin Cemetery.

Prose Nonfiction

The first volume of Standish James O'Grady's (1846–1928) *History of Ireland* appeared (see 1880 entry).

1879

The Land League was organized at meetings and rallies in county Mayo. It was to become, in the words of its organizer Michael Davitt, "the most formidable movement that had confronted the English rulers of Ireland in the century" (quoted in M. Brown 1972, 256). In the midst of a "New Departure" emphasizing Fenian and parliamentary cooperation, the Land League adopted the Anglo-Irish Charles Stewart Parnell—rather than its founder, the working-class Fenian, labor organizer, and social theorist Davitt—as its central popular hero. "Keep a firm grip of your homesteads and lands," Parnell told tenants at a Land League rally in Westport, county Mayo, in June. Henceforth he served the

Home Rule movement and Irish nationalism in general as "the uncrowned king of Ireland," the most popular leader since Daniel O'Connell. "We created Parnell," reflected his parliamentary lieutenant Tim Healy (1855–1931) later, "and Parnell created us. We seized very early in the movement the idea of this man with his superb silences, his historic name, his determination, his self-control, his aloofness—we seized that as the canvas of a great national hero" (quoted in Foster 1988, 401). He also served Yeats, Joyce, and other twentieth-Irish writers as a symbol of both nobility and futility.

Architecture

J. L. Robinson built the town hall at Dun Laoghaire (then Kingstown) near Dublin (de Breffny 1983, 30).

Cultural Institutions

Fifteen people reported seeing the Virgin Mary next to a church in Knock, county Mayo. As a result, Knock has been the major site of Irish Catholic pilgrimage ever since—an Irish Lourdes. A Knock Shrine Society would be founded in 1935, and an Irish Folk Museum established at Knock in 1973 (Hickey and Doherty 1987, 281).

Education

The University Education Act established the Royal University of Ireland, with University College, Dublin (originally Catholic University), as one of its constituent parts.

Fiction

Charles Kickham's *Knocknagow* was, in Malcolm Brown's words, "the most important literary work ever written by a leading Irish revolutionist" (quoted in Wolff 1979, ix), and became one of the most popular of Irish novels. Narrated through the fictive lens of

Henry Lowe, an upper-class English visitor, *Knocknagow* is a repository of small-town customs and nineteenth-century folkways. Even people who had never read it could repeat some its sayings, such as "The world is only a blue rag. . . . Have yer squeeze of it." *Knocknagow* is a sentimental tribute to Kickham's hometown of Mullinahone, county Tipperary. Irish historians mention it as often as do literary critics, with the revisionist historian F.S.L. Lyons stressing Kickham's fundamental conservatism, despite his Fenian activities.

Irish Language and Literature

At earlier levels of the national school system, Irish was (for the first time) permitted to be taught, but only as an "extra subject" offered after ordinary school hours (Akenson 1975, 41).

1880

Agricultural conditions were now abysmal after a series of poor crops, which redoubled popular determination to change the system by which farmlands were controlled in Ireland. An essay on "Ireland in 1880" in the upper-class and typically cautious and conservative *Dublin University Magazine* began, "From three of the four provinces of Ireland, a cry has arisen that in intensity of sound and vehemence of language has no parallel since the fatal famine period of 1846. That a catastrophe such as then overtook the inhabitants of the island should again happen to them is a simple impossibility, for, in Ireland, the last thirty years have done the ordinary work of a century, and the whole structure of society has undergone alteration" (1880, 77).

"It is a very curious thing," remarked a witness at the government's Bessborough Commission hearings on agricultural conditions, "that what the people call a good landlord is a man who lets them alone" (quoted in Foster 1988, 377). In autumn Land League activists ostracized and waged a nonviolent campaign against Lord Erne's land agent in Mayo, Charles Boycott, thereby giving birth to the word *boycott*. "Boycott is gone," Thomas Brennan (1842–1915) wrote in the *Irish World* on 11

December, "but Boycotting remains" (quoted in Ellis 1973, 159). To illustrate that the word *boycott* need not necessarily have caught on to the point where it is an unremarked part of our vocabulary today, it can be noted that at this time the word *girlcott* was put into use in a more transitory way. When a young woman was warned against consorting with or marrying a boycotted landlord, this was a "girlcott" (Hickey and Doherty 1987, 191).

Drama

John Casey (Seán O'Casey, d. 1964) was born in Dublin.

Irish Language and Literature

Reporting on the foundation of the Society for the Preservation of the Irish Language four years earlier, the French scholar Henri Gaidoz understandably lamented that "Irish literature would seem to be dead, at least in the old language, and will not revive again in spite of the efforts of the Society" (quoted in MacEoin 1969, 57).

Periodicals

The *Leinster Leader* newspaper first appeared. By this time there were seventeen daily newspapers in Ireland (Oram 1983, 78).

Prose Nonfiction

The second volume of *History of Ireland* by Standish James O'Grady, often called (because of Yeats's claim to this effect) the "father of the Literary Revival," was published, two years after the first volume. Far from a modern, factual account, it lionized particularly the ancient, misty world of Cúchulain and his fellow Ulster heroes of the old sagas.

The Land League's boycott activities and the publication of O'Grady's *History* were connected by the public activities of O'Grady, who served as secretary in an autumn conference of landlords. O'Grady was to argue repeatedly, in such books as *The Crisis in Ireland* (1881) and *Toryism and the Tory Democracy*

(1886), that the Ascendancy should be maintained by active, conscientious landlords, in sharp contrast to the established pattern of absenteeism and neglect, at the same time that he stressed that such a supposedly enlightened Ascendancy should have nothing to do with the Land League, socialists such as Michael Davitt, or peasant leaders in general. His pleas for more active and productive landlords fell on deaf ears, though O'Grady was very influential on the writings of Yeats.

1881

Belfast's population had increased from 80,000 to 200,000 during the preceding thirty years, "largely because of the growth in the twin trades of linen making and shipbuilding" (Todd 1989, 46). It had become the only large primarily industrial city in Ireland, and its population continued to grow until World War I.

In a country still dominated by farming, Gladstone's new Land Act completed the enactment of the "Three Fs": free sale, fixity of tenure, and fair rent. Eviction without just cause was banned, and it was mandated that tenants' improvements to the property could not be added to valuation and therefore increase their rent (as had been a common practice earlier). The Land League was divided over whether to accept the new act as a sufficient improvement, so Parnell suggested that the league ignore the act until test cases determined what it would mean in practice, and this proposal was adopted.

At Michael Davitt's urging, Anna and Fanny Parnell, Charles's sisters, organized the Ladies' Land League as the women's auxiliary of the Land League.

In October the Land League was outlawed and Parnell was arrested and held in Kilmainham Jail in Dublin until May 1882. He issued an unsuccessful "No-Rent Manifesto" from Kilmainham. Antilandlord violence increased during Parnell's imprisonment, probably with his tacit approval since it provided useful political leverage. In prison, Parnell cagily and privately wrote, "Politically it is a fortunate thing for me that I have been arrested, as the movement is breaking fast, and all will be quiet in a few months, when I shall be released" (quoted in M. Brown 1972, 290).

Irish Language and Literature

Later the great fiction writer Máirtín Ó Cadhain was to write,
"One can say that modern Irish writing began with the founding of
the monthly *An Gaodhal* in Brooklyn . . . by a West of Ireland
emigrant, Micheál Ó Lócháin, in 1881" (1971, 139).

Periodicals

Early in the year Charles Stewart Parnell cabled to the *Irish World*
(the New York organ of the sizeable Irish-American world of
support), as reported in its 12 February issue, "The fight the Irish
members are making for the liberties of the people is inspiriting
and strengthening every Irishman. We are now in the thick of the
conflict. The present struggle against coercion will, please God, be
such as never has been seen within the walls of Parliament." One
could find much more news about the Land League struggle in the
Irish World in New York than in the *Irish Times* in Dublin, whose
pages during these years were dominated by the doings of British
parliamentary leaders and the British military overseas.

1882

Symbolically enthroned in his Irish prison while his followers
carried on the struggle, Parnell emerged from Kilmainham Jail on
2 May under the terms of a quiet working arrangement with
English Liberal members of Parliament (the "Kilmainham Treaty"), moderating his nationalist (and especially his land) campaign in practice, and accepting the previous year's land
legislation. Yet Parnell continued to be lionized more than ever by
Irish nationalists and land activists.

Shortly after Parnell's release the British chief secretary, Lord
Frederick Cavendish (1836–82), and the undersecretary, Thomas
Burke (1829–82), were assassinated in Phoenix Park, Dublin. The
"Phoenix Park murders" were at first attributed to the Irish
Republican Brotherhood, but quickly disclaimed by IRB leaders
Charles Kickham and John O'Leary. Parnell offered to Gladstone
to resign as leader of the Irish party (his offer was declined), and he
published a letter "To the Irish People" condemning the murders.

Members of a group who called themselves "the Invincibles" were tried for the murders in the following year; five were hanged and several more imprisoned. The government's chief informant, James Carey (1845–83)—who was subsequently shot dead by another Irishman while sailing to South Africa with his family under an assumed name—was to be called to mind several times by Leopold Bloom in Joyce's *Ulysses* as an emblem of betrayal. In Joyce's "Cyclops" chapter, the hanged Invincible Joe Brady also makes an appearance (M. Brown 1972, 278–83). These Phoenix Park murders were to haunt Parnell five years later when a forged letter praising the deed appeared over his name in the London *Times* (see 1887 entry).

In autumn as a result of meetings at Parnell's home, Avondale in county Wicklow, the Land League was replaced by the National League—the change of adjectives reflecting Parnell's determination to close down the land war and shift his efforts to a parliamentary campaign for Home Rule.

Architecture

Sir Thomas Newenham built the town hall at Bray, county Wicklow (de Breffny 1983, 30).

Drama

Having achieved notoriety via Gilbert and Sullivan's operetta *Patience* (1881), which lampooned the aesthetic movement and contained a colorfully dressed character clearly based on Wilde (by now a well-known London bon vivant), Oscar Wilde was sent by the play's producers to America on a celebrated lecture tour. Asked by the customs officials in New York if he had anything to declare, Wilde replied, "I have nothing to declare except my genius."

Fiction

James Joyce (d. 1941) was born in this year, on 2 February, which the writer James Stephens (d. 1950), with dubious reliability, also claimed as his birthdate.

Irish Language and Literature

Irisleabhar na Gaeilge (the *Gaelic Journal)* was begun in Dublin. Devoted entirely to Irish language and literature, this journal provided a crucial forum and means of publication for writers in Irish during the revival years. It continued until 1909. Its first editor was David Comyn, but "he soon yielded place to the fiery old man, Seán Pléimeann, a native speaker of Irish from Waterford whose long life bridged the gap between the old literary tradition and the new awakening" (MacEoin 1969, 57).

1883

By this time Parnell was truly "the uncrowned king of Ireland," and had appeared to set into effect "the fall of feudalism in Ireland." He was described even by the typically hostile London *Times* as apparently invincible: "The Irishman has played his cards well, and is making a golden harvest. He has beaten a legion of landlords, lawyers, and encumbrances of all sorts out of the field, driving them into workhouses. He has baffled the greatest of legislators, and outflanked the largest of British armies in getting what he thinks his due" (quoted in M. Brown 1973, 301). No one anticipated the struggles that lay ahead for Parnell.

Periodicals

Parnell started his own newspaper, *United Ireland,* edited very successfully by William O'Brien.

1884

Cultural Institutions

The Gaelic Athletic Association (GAA) was founded, stressing the organization of traditional native Irish sports such as hurling (a more violent version of field hockey). Its principal founder was Michael Cusack (1847–1907), a strident cultural nationalist who was later lampooned by James Joyce as "The Citizen" in the "Cyclops" chapter of *Ulysses.* Often linked to the Fenians, the

GAA developed into a pervasive social (and partly political) network in the countryside.

Drama

Oscar Wilde married Constance Lloyd (1858–98), daughter of an Irish attorney. They would have two children and remain married, despite Wilde's subsequent homosexual affairs that led to his downfall (see 1895 entry) and his predilection for living beyond his means. Early during his marriage, Wilde remarked, "It is only by not paying one's bills that one can hope to live in the memory of the commercial classes" (quoted in Ellmann 1988, 255).

1885

The British parliamentary elections left Gladstone's Liberal party ahead of the Tories 334 to 250, but lacking a majority—and leaving Parnell's Irish party (with 86 seats) with pivotal "swing" votes. Gladstone's son then announced that his father might be willing to support Irish Home Rule, stirring up great excitement. In opposition, Ulster leader Lord Randolph Churchill insisted, famously or notoriously, that "Ulster will fight and Ulster will be right"—thereby introducing the "Ulster problem" into the Irish struggle at an early date.

The Unionist movement that later grew into the Unionist party began, however, not in the North as one might expect, but in the South in the form of the Irish Loyal and Patriotic Union (founded in this year), which eventually became the Unionist party (Hickey and Doherty 1987, 585).

Drama

Oscar Wilde began writing reviews for London's *Pall Mall Gazette,* for which Shaw also later reviewed.

Poetry

Young W. B. Yeats met the Fenian and former nationalist exile John O'Leary at a Dublin club, where O'Leary startled the assembled members by declaring that the then twenty-year-old poet was the only person in the room "who will ever be reckoned a genius" (quoted in M. Brown 1972, 314). Thus began a friendship that many identify as pivotal to Yeats's own developing sense of Irishness and thus crucial to the future Irish Literary Revival. Frank O'Connor characteristically exaggerated but nonetheless tellingly registered O'Leary's influence, in his remark in his *Short History of Irish Literature,* that "but for an accidental meeting with the old Fenian leader John O'Leary, Yeats might easily have ended as a fine minor poet like Walter de la Mare" (1967, 165). O'Leary lent Yeats books and money, impressed him with his impassioned nationalism, yet did not defend inferior nationalist verse—even that of Thomas Davis, the mid-nineteenth-century Young Irelander who had originally inspired O'Leary.

In this same year, the Dublin Hermetic Society was formed, with Yeats presiding, and his first published poems appeared in the *Dublin University Magazine.*

Prose Nonfiction

Michael Davitt's *Leaves from a Prison Diary* was written during his confinement in jail earlier in the decade, and contained meditations on land nationalization, a concept that marked Davitt as an unusually progressive thinker for his time and made him unpopular among the mass of Irish nationalists, for whom "the land for Ireland" meant simply "the land for me." It also included literary flourishes reflecting the increasingly imaginative cast of Davitt's mind (see Cahalan 1976).

1886

In February William Gladstone replaced the Tory Robert Salisbury as British prime minister. But in the following month, Joseph Chamberlain (1836–1914) resigned from Gladstone's cabinet, declared war on Irish Home Rule, and divided the Liberal party over this issue. And on 7 June Gladstone's Irish Home Rule Act—supported by an alliance of Gladstone's Liberals and

Parnell's Irish party members—was defeated in the House of Commons, 343 to 313.

William O'Brien (1852–1928) and John Dillon (1851–1927) organized a "Plan of Campaign" to fix specific rent controls on selected rural estates. It continued until 1891.

Fiction

Emily Lawless's (1845–1913) *Hurrish* was the story of a family feud set amid the Land League struggles in county Clare. In its focus on a big hearted peasant who eventually clears himself of a murder charge, this novel recalls Michael Banim's *Crohoore of the Bill-Hook* (1825). Its original book blurb cited English reviewers who praised it as "a picture of the Irish peasant as he really is." Gladstone praised *Hurrish* as he prepared his arguments for Home Rule, stating that Lawless had presented to her readers "not as an abstract proposition, but as a living reality, the estrangement of the people of Ireland from the law." Yet the *Nation* accused Lawless of exaggerating peasant violence and called *Hurrish* "slanderous" (quoted in Brewer 1983, 121–22).

The cousins Edith Somerville (1858–1949) and Violet Martin (1862–1915)—who as "Somerville and Ross" were to form the closest, most successful collaboration in modern Irish literature—met for the first time at Drishane, the Somerville family estate in county Cork.

George Moore's (1852–1933) first Irish novel, *A Drama in Muslin,* was released. Telling the tale of the sordid expeditions of young, rural Ascendancy women led by their mothers to the Dublin "marriage market" centered on the Shelbourne Hotel in Dublin, Moore painted small-minded characters in grim Dublin scenes—nearly thirty years before "A Mother," "The Boarding House," and the other stories of Joyce's *Dubliners* (1914). Moore focused his story on an exceptional woman: Alice Barton, the sole escapee from the prison of rigid roles staked out for women of her social caste. Alice marries a hard-working doctor and leaves Ireland (in a scene reminiscent of the conclusion to Joyce's *A Portrait of the Artist as a Young Man)* for London with her husband to write and to raise a family, after having been encouraged in this independent, artistic direction by a Dublin writer resembling

Moore himself. Moore looked back on *A Drama in Muslin* as "the turning point of his career" (quoted in Becker 1986, 149).

Literary Criticism

Meanwhile, Yeats published a lengthy essay on "The Poetry of Sir Samuel Ferguson" in the November issue of the *Dublin University Review,* following Ferguson's death. He concluded by insisting that "of all the many things the poet bequeaths to the future, the greatest are great legends; they are the mothers of nations. I hold it the duty of every Irish reader to study those of his own country till they are familiar as his own hands, for in them is the Celtic heart" (1886, 941). Yeats felt that Ferguson was "the greatest poet Ireland has produced" (quoted in M. Brown 1973, 317).

Periodicals

Following the failure of the Home Rule Bill, *Notes from Ireland* was a Conservative-Unionist bulletin that reported the continuing Home Rule campaign of the Irish Parliamentary party, and which appeared until 1914 when the third Home Rule Bill became law (Hickey and Doherty 1987, 409–10).

Prose Nonfiction

John O'Leary's pamphlet *What Irishmen Should Know* expressed opinions that influenced and would be repeated by Yeats: that Irish was no longer a viable language but that much could be learned from Irish legends and poems in translation, that Irish folklore and mythology were precious national possessions, and that James Clarence Mangan was a better poet than Thomas Davis but still not as good as Ireland deserved (M. Brown 1972, 15).

1887

In April the London *Times* published a letter linking Parnell to the Phoenix Park murders of 1882, but two years later Richard Pigott (1828–89), former publisher of the Fenian newspaper the *Irish-*

man, was exposed (in the hearings of a special commission) as the forger of the letter and eventually committed suicide. In the cultural mythos, Pigott (like Timothy Healy soon thereafter) is an instance of the "Judas" theme of Irish history according to which it seemed as if some great leader or (in the words of one observer) "noble stag" was always being dragged down by the spiteful, revengeful masses.

Drama

A Fabian, socialist march in London protesting unemployment was broken up violently by the police—an experience that convinced Fabian activist George Bernard Shaw that intellectual and political means were preferable to physical ones. He increasingly turned to his writing.

Oscar Wilde became editor of the *Lady's World* in London, but resigned in boredom two years later.

Periodicals

The Gaelic Athletic Association began the *Gael,* and this newspaper ran weekly for two years. Contributors to its literary section, edited by John O'Leary, included W. B. Yeats, Douglas Hyde (1860–1947), and T. W. Rolleston (1857–1920) (Hickey and Doherty 1987, 183).

Poetry

Yeats moved to London and became active in spiritualist, theosophical circles.

Prose Nonfiction

George Moore wrote in *Parnell and His Island* that "I am an Irish landlord, I have done this, and I shall continue to do this, for it is as impossible for me as for the rest of my class to do otherwise; but that doesn't prevent me from recognizing the fact that it is a worn out system, no longer possible in the nineteenth century, and one whose end is nigh."

1888

Music

Patrick Weston Joyce's (1827–1914) collection *Irish Music and Song* appeared.

George Bernard Shaw became music critic for the *Star* newspaper in London, continuing until 1890.

Poetry

The anthology *Poems and Ballads of Young Ireland* was edited by Yeats and others.

1889

Poetry

William Butler Yeats's first volume, *Crossways* (a title he said he adopted because here he "tried many pathways"), was neoromantic, showing the influence of Blake and Shelley. He remarked that "many of the poems in *Crossways,* certainly those upon Indian subjects or upon shepherds and fauns, must have been written before I was twenty, for from the moment I began [the long poem] 'The Wanderings of Oisin,' which I did at that age, I believe, my subject matter became Irish." "The Wanderings of Oisin," published in this same year, placed him in the tradition of the eighteenth-century poet James Macpherson and others who had published poetry couched in the mode of ancient Celtic saga and mythology. Yeats's Oisin enjoys Tir na nOg (the Land of Youth) at the expense of the loss of his own contemporary place in the world. In January Yeats met Maud Gonne (1866–1953), his famous unrequited love and subject for poetry, for the first time, later recalling, "She seemed a classical impersonation of the Spring, the Virgilian commendation 'She walks like a goddess' made for her alone. Her complexion was luminous, like that of apple-blossom through which the light falls, and I remember her standing that first day by a great heap of such blossoms in the window" (quoted in Kelly and Domville, 1986, 1:134). The image of apple blossoms recurred in such notable later poems as "The Song of Wandering Aengus" and several others.

1890

Parnell's ten-year liaison with Kitty O'Shea (1845–1921), the wife of an acquiescent follower, was revealed. Next came an infamously bitter campaign dividing Ireland between Parnellites (loyalists and many Fenians) and anti-Parnellites—the latter group involving a loose and unusual coalition of people including Michael Davitt, the Catholic hierarchy, and politicians willing to sacrifice Parnell in order to win Home Rule from Gladstone. Parnell met his opponents in Committee Room 15, urging them to be sure to get the promise of Home Rule in writing as the price for their abandonment of their support for him. The conclusion was Parnell's electoral defeat and his death in October 1891, followed by a massive funeral in Dublin. Irish nationalists were left divided and leaderless, without Parnell and without Home Rule, and years of depression and lack of direction ensued. Yet Yeats wrote later: "The modern literature of Ireland, and indeed all that stir of thought which prepared for the Anglo-Irish war, began when Parnell fell from power in 1891. A disillusioned and embittered Ireland turned from parliamentary politics; an event was conceived" (quoted in Foster 1988, 431). For example, the reputedly apolitical James Joyce's first known work, written not long after Parnell's fall, was a lost boyhood poem called "Et Tu, Healy?" attacking the role of Timothy Healy, Parnell's former lieutenant and future Free State minister, in the campaign against Parnell. Malcolm Brown notes of Healy, " 'Tiger Tim' he had been in the land war. After the Split he was 'Healy the Hound' " (1972, 339). In the political world, Parnell would remain dead and gone, but in the literary imagination he remained vividly alive, provoking what Malcolm Brown calls "literary Parnellism." As Standish James O'Grady accurately predicted in 1894, "Posterity will easily forgive Parnell and like him probably all the better for his weakness" (quoted in M. Brown 1972, 374).

Cultural Institutions

Enabled by an 1877 act and begun in 1884, the National Library finally opened in new premises in Kildare Street in Dublin. It contains the most comprehensive collection of Irish books, periodicals, and manuscripts in existence (de Breffny 1983, 165).

Fiction

Emily Lawless's historical novel *With Essex in Ireland* was published. Along with her historical romance *Maelcho* (1894), this was included by Yeats in his 1895 list of the "Best Irish Books."

Irish Language and Literature

Douglas Hyde—the noted translator, folklorist, playwright, and later president of Ireland—published *Beside the Fire,* consisting of English translations of fifteen Irish tales with Irish and English positioned on facing pages. These were very literal translations that helped forge a new "Irish English" or "Anglo-Irish" way of writing, which reached its apogee in the plays of John M. Synge.

Music

George Bernard Shaw became music critic, under the pseudonym of Corno di Bassetto, for the *World* newspaper in London, until 1894.

Periodicals

Michael Davitt founded a short-lived newspaper in London, the *Labour World.* In the same year, he founded the Irish Federated Trade and Labour Union in Cork as an attempt to organize agricultural laborers (Hickey and Doherty 1987, 245). Both efforts folded in the midst of the disastrous campaign against Parnell.

Poetry

Yeats's "The Lake Isle of Innisfree" was published for the first time, in the *National Observer* in December (Kain 1962, 185).

1891

Fiction

Early on Yeats left his mark on the nascent canon of Irish fiction (as well as poetry and drama), publishing in this same year his collection of *Representative Irish Tales,* which included works by Maria Edgeworth, William Carleton, John Banim, and others. This was the first anthology of nineteenth-century Irish fiction. However, Yeats's own novel, *John Sherman* (also published this year), was much less successful than the fictional works of his predecessors despite the fact that he insisted that it was "as much an Irish novel as anything by Banim or Griffin" (quoted in Marcus 1970, 40). Its wooden opposites, the dreamer John Sherman and the intellectual John Howard, are generally cited by Yeatsians as early examples of the poet's idea of antithesis.

Oscar Wilde published *The Picture of Dorian Gray,* a novel that became a bible of the aesthetic movement but was condemned by the authorities as obscene. Wilde commented, "I am afraid it is rather like my own life—all conversation and no action. . . . I can't describe action: my people sit in chairs and chatter" (quoted in Ellmann 1988, 314).

Irish Language and Literature

The Purchase of Land Act established the Congested Districts Board, as instructed by British chief secretary Arthur Balfour, to oversee those areas of Ireland identified as too poor in natural resources to support their population. All of the Gaeltacht or Irish-speaking areas of counties Donegal, Mayo, Galway, Kerry, Cork, and Waterford were included in these districts (Ó Danachair 1969, 113).

Literary Criticism

Shaw published *The Quintessence of Ibsenism,* championing Ibsen's brand of critical social realism and outlining ideas that would be central to his own plays. Like James Joyce, Shaw was profoundly influenced and inspired by the great Norwegian playwright.

Periodicals

In December, two months after Parnell's death in October, the newspaper that he had founded in the previous year early in his final campaign, the *Irish Daily Independent,* finally published its first issue, along with its evening edition called the *Evening Herald.* It became the *Irish Independent* (one of today's three major Dublin dailies) in 1905 (Hickey and Doherty 1987, 247).

Poetry

Having helped begin the Rhymers' Club earlier in the year, Yeats founded the Irish Literary Society at a meeting in London in December. Yeats's rhetoric during the 1890s was reminiscent of Thomas Davis's in the 1840s. Yeats wrote: "Amid the clash of party against party we have tried to put forward a nationality that is above party, and . . . we have tried to assert those everlasting principles of love of truth and love of country that speak to men in solitude and in the silence of the night" (quoted in M. Brown 1972, 355–56). Yet when Charles Gavan Duffy—returned from Australia and now accepting Yeats's invitation to serve as the new society's first president—tried to dominate the society, wrapping himself in the flag of Young Ireland, Yeats attacked the poetry of Davis and Young Ireland. With the support of John O'Leary, Lionel Johnson, and others, Yeats eclipsed Duffy and gradually emerged as the major figure in the new movement.

1892

Drama

Wilde's *Lady Windermere's Fan,* an extreme version of the "well-made play," was a big commercial success in London, as was *A Woman of No Importance* in the following year.

Fiction

Grania (The Story of an Island) was Emily Lawless's best novel. It tells the tragic story of a victimized woman living on Inis Meáin in the Aran Islands, who struggles to survive married life as a peasant and take care of her invalid sister. Grania ends up dying while traveling by boat during a storm in a desperate attempt to get a doctor for her dying sister. Protagonist and place—the rocky, water-swept island—are fused in the narration as well as the title of this work, an early feminist or protofeminist Irish novel.

Jane Barlow (1857–1917) published *Irish Idylls,* also descriptive of Irish rural life.

Irish Language and Literature

Douglas Hyde lectured in November "On the Necessity for De-Anglicizing the Irish People," arguing against the mimicking of "materialist" English ways and in favor of the revival of Irish Gaelic. This lecture was one of the opening programs of the Irish National Literary Society in Dublin, which was founded in this year by Yeats and others.

Poetry

William Larminie's (1850–1900) *Fand and Other Poems* was a volume overshadowed by the work of Yeats and other Irish writers of the Literary Revival period, but Larminie's assonantal verse was an important influence later on the work of Austin Clarke (McHugh and Harmon 1982, 115).

Prose Nonfiction

W. E. H. Lecky's *History of England in the Eighteenth Century,* more than half of which was devoted to Ireland, appeared.

1893

The second Irish Home Rule Bill narrowly passed the House of Commons, but was overwhelmingly defeated in the House of Lords. No Parnell was on the scene to carry the day or adequately continue the fight; his successor as leader of the Irish party, John Redmond (1856–1918), was a pallid facsimile not up to the task. In the popular view this result proved that Parnell had been sold down the river for nothing, that his earlier opponents had not gotten his proper "price" as he had urged them to do at their 1890 meeting in Committee Room 15 (see 1890 entry). Not long thereafter, the Irish-American nationalist support organization Clan na Gael disintegrated in the wake of a feud between its leader, the Fenian John Devoy (1842–1928), and the upstart Alexander Sullivan (1847–1913), and so the cause of Home Rule and Irish independence seemed more hopeless than it had in many years.

Folklore

Yeats's collection of tales entitled *The Celtic Twilight* borrowed from Irish folklore, putting a characteristically romantic cast on traditional stories and subjects.

Irish Language and Literature

Conradh na Gaeilge (the Gaelic League), led by Douglas Hyde and Eoin MacNeill (1867–1945), was established. It focused on the revival of Irish and an idealization of the Gaelic west of Ireland, and grew markedly after the turn of the century (from 107 branches in 1899, for example, to nearly 400 by 1902) (Foster 1988, 456). It was originally nonpolitical and nonsectarian in its stated aims, but became linked to the advanced nationalist movement after the turn of the century. At the time of its founding, 99 percent of the people of Ireland could speak English and 85 percent could not speak Irish (Ó Cuív 1969, 128).

Douglas Hyde published his collection of popular *Love Songs of Connacht,* with Irish and translated English facing pages, in an idiom that was even more of an influence on Synge and other Anglo-Irish writers than was Hyde's earlier prose collection of 1890, *Beside the Fire.*

Literary Criticism

In May Yeats lectured on "Nationality and Literature" to the National Literary Society in Dublin. Arguing that English literature was in the last, decadent, lyric phase of literature while Irish literature was still in the midst of the first, vibrant, epic phase, he urged Irish writers to write on Irish subjects and work to perfect their styles.

Periodicals

The *New Ireland Review* replaced the *Lyceum,* a literary review founded in 1887 by Father Thomas Finlay at the Royal University (later University College, Dublin) (Hickey and Doherty 1987, 319). It lasted until 1911.

Poetry

Yeats's first major Irish volume, *The Rose,* contained such memorable early lyrics as "To the Rose Upon the Rood of Time," "The Lake Isle of Innisfree," and "To Ireland in the Coming Times." This banner Yeatsian year also included his edition with Edwin Ellis of *The Works of William Blake.*

1894

The Irish Trades Union Congress (ITUC) was formed in Dublin. After the turn of the century, the great labor leaders James Larkin (1876–1947) and James Connolly (1868–1916) brought it to prominence.

The Irish Agricultural Organisation Society was established. Horace Plunkett (1854–1932) played a leading role in the movement for cooperative creameries and agricultural reform in general, as did George Russell (1870–1935) or "Æ" (a mystical poet but also a very pragmatic man), who edited the movement's journal, the *Irish Homestead,* and "envisioned a new society in Ireland based upon rural communes" (Ellis 1973, 172).

Cultural Institutions

The Arts and Crafts Society of Ireland was founded by Lord Mayo to support the work of groups like the Fivemiletown Art Metal Workers and individuals such as the bookbinder Sir Edward Sullivan (1852–1928) (de Breffny 1983, 36).

Drama

Funded by the rich English theater patron Annie Horniman, George Bernard Shaw's play *Arms and the Man* and Yeats's *The*

Land of Heart's Desire shared the same bill in London, with Yeats's play ignored amid the great acclaim for Shaw's eloquent comedy of ideas. Yeats's biographer Joseph Hone "described the first night as 'a complete disaster,' but also remarked that 'Yeats was in the theatre almost every night for several weeks, noting in the light of the performances the changes he might make in the monosyllabic verse, in which his interpreters were ill at ease'" (quoted in Hogan and Kilroy 1975, 1:25). As for Shaw, *Arms and the Man* was his first play to make any real impression on the public, and launched him on the longest major career in modern drama. His play, an unromantic analysis of militarism, could not have been more different than Yeats's play. Yeats remarked that to him, Shaw's dialogue sounded like continually clicking knitting needles. For Shaw's response to Yeats and his movement, see the 1905 entry below.

Fiction

Somerville and Ross's *The Real Charlotte,* one of the best two or three Irish novels of the nineteenth century, was the first since Gerald Griffin's *The Collegians* (1829) to capture so extensively and effectively a panorama of Irish society—including in this case a paralytic Ascendancy embodied in the Dysart family and also the oafish soldier, Hawkins; people trapped in the middle of a class conflict, especially Charlotte Mullen, who chats pleasantly with the Dysarts but is privately driven by a desire for money as well as marriage; and the peasants from whom Charlotte collects rents and with whom she can drive a hard bargain, even when they start speaking Irish in her presence. *The Real Charlotte* is much more than merely a social "slice of life" novel, however; it focuses unforgettably on the tragic Charlotte and her beautiful but doomed niece, Francie Fitzgerald.

Folklore

Standish James O'Grady's *The Coming of Cuculain* [*sic*]— extended into a trilogy in *In the Gates of the North* (1901) and *The Triumph and Passing of Cuculain* (1920)—was essentially an extended rewrite of his *History of Ireland* (1878, 1880) as romance, seeking to be more entertaining and more popular while at the same time perpetuating his own romanticized view of ancient Irish mythology.

Irish Language and Literature

Although it did not appear in completed book form for another ten years, in this year Father Peadar Ó Laoghaire (1839–1920) began serializing *Séadna* to great acclaim in the *Gaelic Journal*. *Séadna* (the name of the protagonist) is an extended version of an international folktale following the Faust theme. Told beside the fireplace by a young girl to her even younger listeners, it recounts the story of a shoemaker who sells his soul to the devil, but eventually regains it. *Séadna* is a thin work but crucially encouraged in others the notion that one might profitably write modern fiction in idiomatic Irish.

Ó Laoghaire's *Ar nDóthain Araon* (Enough for both of us) was the first short story collection in Irish (Hickey and Doherty 1987, 441).

Irisleabhar na Gaeilge (the *Gaelic Journal*) shifted to the editorship of Eoin MacNeill.

Literary Criticism

W. P. Ryan's (1867–1942) book *The Irish Literary Revival* helped coin this phrase, encapsulating the developing sense of a movement.

Music

Eoin MacNeill cofounded the Feis Ceoil (music festival) (Hickey and Doherty 1987, 343).

Poetry

Homeward: Songs by the Way, a volume by Æ (George Russell), was published. Æ was not himself a great writer but he was tremendously influential on his friend Yeats and on many younger writers; Oliver St. John Gogarty (1878–1957) called him "the poet-maker."

Appearing nearly thirty years after her death, *Songs, Poems and Verses* by Lady Dufferin (1807–67) contained such folk-styled ballads as "The Irish Emigrant" (Deane et al. 1991, 2: 103).

1895

Drama

This was the year of Oscar Wilde's greatest success and of his tragic downfall. His masterful farce *The Importance of Being Earnest* opened in London on 4 February, just two months before the beginning of his libel suit against the marquis of Queensbury (the father of Lord Alfred Douglas, his lover), which provoked Queensbury's countersuit against Wilde and Wilde's conviction for homosexuality. Subtitled *A Trivial Comedy for Serious People, The Importance of Being Earnest* hilariously lampooned Victorian conventions (with the Dublin-bred Wilde casting a cold eye on English values, as Shaw also did) and brilliantly prefigured twentieth-century absurdism. Wilde would spend two years in prison and the rest of his short life, until his death in 1900, in misery. Earlier the most humorous, in the end Wilde's career became certainly the most tragic one in modern literature. The same English Victorian society that he had so brilliantly satirized exacted its revenge by destroying Wilde, with his own hubris (the vanity that led him to sue Queensbury) contributing as a crucial mistake.

Meanwhile, in Dublin, previous to the founding of the Irish Literary Theatre a few years later, the quality of popular theater was suggested in a review by Joseph Holloway (1861–1944)—an intermittent architect and indefatigable playgoer and diarykeeper —of a production at the Queen's Royal Theatre: *The Bandit King* was "a drama written round four trained horses. Mr. J. H. Wallick took the part of 'Jesse James,' the outlaw, and although he has been playing it for fifteen years he struck me as not being up to much as a melodramatic actor. . . . The other parts were indifferently filled. The piece was rot. The house was full. There was . . . much shooting during the unfolding of the incidents" (quoted in Hogan and Kilroy 1975, 1: 14).

Literary Criticism

W. B. Yeats published a list in the *Irish Bookman* of the "Best Irish Books," giving top ratings to works by William Carleton, Standish James O'Grady, Maria Edgeworth, Gerald Griffin, and John Banim. As part of his series of articles on "Irish National Literature" in the *Bookman,* such Yeatsian pronouncements were decidedly idiosyncractic but definitely contributed to the development of a distinctively Irish literary canon. A review of Yeats's list in the April 1895 issue of the *New Ireland Review* noted that "we are thankful" for the list, but added that "it was too short. Only thirty moving, thought-kindling Irish books! There were extraordinary omissions" (122). During this time Yeats was indeed concerned with the formation of an Irish literary canon. On 3 November he wrote to T. Fisher Unwin, the London publisher, "I have only just found time to find & tare [*sic*] out the articles on Irish literature which I want you to publish in a pamphlet under the title 'What to Read in Irish Literature'" (Kelly and Domville 1986, 1: 475). The pamphlet did not come into being, but Yeats's suggested title is illustrative of his didactic, canon-making streak.

Periodicals

The *Irish Homestead* began in this year, continuing under the editorship of Æ until 1923. As in his later journal the *Irish Statesman,* the successor to the *Homestead,* Æ's voice and influence were enlightened and progressive. The first issue (9 March 1895) of the *Irish Homestead* was dominated by advice and information about cooperative farming on behalf of the Irish Agricultural Organisation Society, in which Æ was very active working with its founder, Horace Plunkett. This pragmatic side of Æ is often forgotten in the emphasis on him as mystical poet— which was another side of him. Following the articles about livestock and such, however, was Æ's obituary notice for Christina Rossetti. Perhaps only Æ could have combined dairy farming and the pre-Raphaelite imagination in a single periodical. The Rossetti article appeared in the "Fireside Section," a literary segment that later included James Joyce's first stories (in 1903) and provided the basis for the *Irish Statesman* (which began in 1923).

1896

In March James Connolly (1868–1916) founded, in Dublin, the
Irish Socialist Republican party, which later became the Socialist
party of Ireland under William O'Brien (Hickey and Doherty
1987, 262).

Drama

Yeats's crucial first meetings with Lady Augusta Gregory (1859–
1932) and John Synge occurred. Together they would found the
movement that would become the Abbey Theatre.

Fiction

Standish James O'Grady's *Ulrick the Ready* was a historical novel
written in the mode of Sir Walter Scott and dealing with the period
surrounding the Battle of Kinsale (1601).
　　　Liam O'Flaherty (d. 1984) was born on Inis Mór in the Aran
Islands near mainland counties Galway and Clare.

Film

The first public projection of a film occurred at the Star Theatre of
Varieties in Dublin, less than seven years after the first projections
in England and the United States. Two years later Dr. R. A.
Mitchel of Belfast became the first Irishman to make a film (of a
yacht race in Belfast Lough) (de Breffny 1983, 64).

Periodicals

Alice Milligan (1866–1953) and Ethna Carbery (1866–1902)
edited *The Shan Van Vocht,* a nationalist newspaper later taken
over by Arthur Griffith's (1871–1922) the *United Irishman* (Hickey and Doherty 1987, 528).

1897

Art

Jack B. Yeats (1871–1957), the poet's younger brother, had his first public exhibition in London (de Breffny 1983, 250). Son and namesake of the painter John Butler Yeats, he was to develop into one of modern Ireland's most important painters. He is especially well known for his impressionistic paintings of Irish peasants, which can be found today in such galleries as the Hugh Lane Municipal Gallery of Modern Art and the National Gallery, both in Dublin, and the Yeats Museum in Sligo.

Drama

The Dublin theater movement was planned at a summer meeting at Coole Park, Lady Gregory's estate in county Galway. Full of Yeatsian rhetoric, a letter was drafted that declared, "We propose to have performed in Dublin, in the spring of every year certain Celtic and Irish plays, which whatever be their degree of excellence will be written with a high ambition, and so to build up a Celtic and Irish school of dramatic literature. . . . We will show that Ireland is not the home of buffoonery and of easy sentiment, as it has been represented, but the home of an ancient idealism" (quoted in Hogan and Kilroy 1975, 1: 25).

Fiction

Yeat's volume of stories *The Secret Rose* appeared. In such tales as "Rosa Alchemica" and "The Adoration of the Magi" he combined the symbolism of the occult Order of the Golden Dawn in London with the iconography of Irish nationalism and his own personal vision of the conflict between the real world and the spiritual world.

Standish James O'Grady's *The Flight of the Eagle* was a popular but tedious historical romance about the Elizabethan Gaelic chieftain Red Hugh O'Donnell.

Irish Language and Literature

The Gaelic League held its first Oireachtas (gathering), a one-day affair at which "competitions were few in number and all literary, except one for a song or anthem for the Gaelic League which could be sung at their meetings. The Oireachtas was held on the day before the Feis Ceoil [music festival] in order that people could more easily attend both" (MacEoin 1969, 58–59).

Prose Nonfiction

By now Yeats was writing and in general operating very much independently of his mentor John O'Leary, to whose book *Recollections of Fenians and Fenianism* he gave a mixed review in the *Bookman*. Instead Yeats now turned to his fellow occultists and to Lady Augusta Gregory for imaginative nourishment.

1898

The Local Government Act gave women the right to vote in local (though not national) elections (Hickey and Doherty 1987, 267).

Drama

Preparation for the flourishing of drama during the Irish Literary Revival could be found in the productions of Boucicault's melodramas, as reflected in a description by Joseph Holloway recorded during this year: "A typical Queen's [Theatre] audience, noisy and full of suggestions to the players, filled the cosy little theatre to see Dion Boucicault's admirably constructed and most interesting Irish drama, *Arrah-na-Pogue* [1865], acted by Kennedy Miller's Favourite Company of Irish Players. The Queen's is the home of Irish drama. There you may always reckon to see this form of piece well played by genuinely Irish actors; and, as the audience knows every line of the text and every bit of by-play in the various parts, it sees that it gets the full value for its money, or lets those on the stage know why" (quoted in Hogan and Kilroy 1975, 1: 19).

In London, Shaw married Charlotte Payne-Townshend, showing up for the ceremony bedraggled, outdressed by most others present, injured, and on crutches, looking like "the inevitable beggar who completes all wedding processions" (Shenfield 1962, 55). In this year's preface to *Plays Pleasant and Unpleasant,* Shaw remarked: "As an Irishman I could pretend to patriotism neither for the country I had abandoned nor the country that had ruined it" (quoted in Dietrich 1987, 74).

John Synge made his historic first trip to the Aran Islands; he spent parts of the summers of 1898–1902 on the islands of Inis Meáin and Inis Mór. The self-translations from Irish into English (both oral and written) that the islanders did to help Synge clearly constituted a significant source for the language of his subsequent plays (see entry on "A Story from Inishmaan," just below).

Fiction

Just four years after Somerville and Ross's heroine, Francie Fitzgerald, had died from a fall from a horse in their novel *The Real Charlotte* (1894), Violet Martin ("Martin Ross") suffered a bad riding accident herself. Her health would never be good thereafter; she would eventually die from a brain tumor, in 1915. No one ever seemed to question whether her accident was linked to the fact that like other women during this era, she was forced by repressive Victorian convention to ride side-saddle, with her right leg extended all the way across the saddle to its left side, a much more difficult and dangerous way to ride.

Irish Language and Literature

For the Gaelic League's second annual Oireachtas, the *Weekly Freeman* sponsored a short story competition. The prizewinner was "Pádraig Ó Séaghdha (who wrote under the pseudonym 'Conán Maol') and the four short stories, though no major works of literature, marked a new departure in Irish. They had the form and style of the modern short story, combined with correct idiomatic Irish" (MacEoin 1969, 59).

Synge published "A Story from Inishmaan" in the November issue of the *New Ireland Review,* prefacing it with the note that "the following story and others were told to me in Inishmaan, middle island of the Aran group, by an old man who came every day and sat with me by the kitchen fire, in the cottage where I lodged. As the stories went on, the family would draw round on their stools. Some of the near neighbours came in to listen also, while the mother or her daughter, in their wonderful red garments, sat at their wheel by the door. The old man had some knowledge of English, and translated for my convenience, as my Celtic would not carry me through extended tales. I have kept closely to his language" (1898, 153). Synge followed "A Story from Inishmaan" with an analysis, much in the manner of a professional folklorist, of its folk motifs as found also in Shakespeare and other places.

Fainne an Lae (The break of day) was founded by Conradh na Gaeilge (the Gaelic League) as a bilingual newspaper fostering Irish language and literature. The English version of the first editorial, which appeared in both languages, asserted (with an allusion to the 1798 rebellions): "Our appearance at the opening of this Centennial year of 1898 is significant of the brighter days for the old tongue which Thomas Davis predicted would surely come. The propaganda of the Gaelic League for the past few years is bearing fruit, and Irishmen of all classes are beginning to realise that the disappearance of the Irish language would probably be the most serious loss the Irish nation could suffer" (8 January, 4).

Periodicals

In August James Connolly, the great leader of the labor movement and the 1916 Easter Rising, founded the *Workers' Republic,* a socialist newspaper whose presses were smashed by the police in 1900, but which Connolly later revived from time to time whenever he could, up until 1916.

T. P. Gill (1858–1931) served as editor of the Dublin *Daily Express* until December 1899 (Kain 1962, 187).

Poetry

Poems by Eva Gore-Booth (1870–1926)—also a dramatist, women's rights and union activist, and sister of Countess Constance Markievicz (1868–1927)—was praised by Yeats as a work of "poetic feeling . . . and great promise" (quoted in Hickey and Doherty 1987, 195).

Oscar Wilde's "The Ballad of Reading Gaol" was a melancholy poem penned in prison—a sharp contrast to his witty plays.

Prose Nonfiction

Michael Davitt's *Life and Progress in Australasia* was based on Davitt's trip to Australia and New Zealand three years earlier, and was evidence of the international range of his interests during his neglected later years.

R. Barry O'Brien's (1847–1918) *The Life of Charles Stewart Parnell* was a very sympathetic biography.

1899

In southern Africa, John MacBride (1865–1916), Maud Gonne's future husband, formed an Irish Brigade that fought with the Boers against England.

The Catholic Truth Society of Ireland was founded "to combat," according to its own description, "the pernicious influence of infidel and immoral publications by the circulation of good, cheap and popular Catholic literature" (quoted in T. Brown 1985, 69).

Architecture

St. Anne's church in Belfast, designed in a conservative style, was begun by Sir Thomas Drew (de Breffny 1983, 29).

Drama

As planned nearly two years earlier at a meeting at Lady Gregory's estate, Coole Park, the Dublin theater movement began in full force in May with a double bill at the Ancient Concert Rooms, sponsored by the Irish Literary Theatre, pairing Yeats's *The Countess Cathleen* and Edward Martyn's (1859–1923) *The Heather Field*. In the same month Yeats began publishing *Beltaine,* a magazine devoted to the Irish theater. He noted in his introductory article on "Plans and Methods": "The Irish Literary Theatre will attempt to do in Dublin something of what has been done in London and Paris; and, if it has even a small welcome, it will produce, somewhere about the old festival of Beltaine, at the beginning of every spring, a play founded upon an Irish subject. The plays will differ from those produced by associations of men of letters in London and in Paris, because times have changed, and because the intellect of Ireland is romantic and spiritual rather than scientific and analytical" (1899, 6). It appears that Yeats thought little of the literary abilities of Martyn, a wealthy Catholic landowner and cousin of George Moore (who directed the plays). Yeats was anxious, however, to ensure Martyn's financial backing at this early stage of the theater movement and therefore willing to accommodate his Ibsenesque play, which was in fact a greater popular success at the time than Yeats's symbolic morality play. Something of the tenor of the most negative vein of popular response to Yeats's play was suggested in a pamphlet by F. Hugh O'Donnell: "Mr. W. B. Yeats introduces a Celtic peasant woman who is false to her marriage vows. How very Irish. . . . Mr. W. B. Yeats seems to see nothing in the Ireland of old days but an unmanly, an impious and renegade people, crouched in degraded awe before demons, and goblins, and sprites . . . just like a sordid tribe of black devil-worshippers and fetish-worshippers on the Congo or the Niger" (quoted in Hogan and Kilroy 1975, 1: 32).

Seamus O'Sullivan (1879–1958) described the debut of *The Countess Cathleen:* "I was, by chance, in the gallery, and at the fall of the curtain a storm of booing and hissing broke out around the seats in which I and a few enthusiasts were attempting to express our appreciation of the magnificent performance. . . . But close to me, at the time unknown to me, was a lad who vigorously contributed his share to the applause. It was James Joyce." Meanwhile, the *Evening Herald* reviewer felt that "the whole performance was weird" (quoted in Hogan and Kilroy 1975, 1: 40, 43).

Fiction

The first volume of Somerville and Ross's *Some Experiences of an Irish R.M.*—later to include *Further Experiences of an Irish R.M.* (1908) and *In Mr. Knox's Country* (1915)—was published. These wonderful comic stories—such as "Lisheen Races, Second-hand"

and "Poisson d'Avril"—focused on Major Yeates, an Anglo-Irish resident magistrate (similar to a justice of the peace) who often makes a fool of himself while trying to understand the natives of the rural Irish area where he is stationed. Here we observe the Anglo-Irish Ascendancy laughing at itself—or more specifically, we see two Anglo-Irish women laughing at the Anglo-Irish male. By having Flurry Knox always outsmart Yeates, Somerville and Ross reversed the positions of Samuel Lover's Handy Andy and his masters.

My New Curate by Canon Sheehan (1852–1913) contained sketches of the lives of rural Irish priests typical of the popular, moralistic fiction of this county Cork priest.

Irish Language and Literature

The Irish Texts Society was founded by Douglas Hyde, Eleanor Hull (1860–1935), Robin Flower (1881–1946), and others. It published a number of bilingual books. One of its biggest projects was to be Father Patrick Dineen's (1860–1943) revised 1927 Irish-English dictionary (Hickey and Doherty 1987, 263).

An Claidheamh Soluis (The sword of light), the weekly newspaper of the Gaelic League, which was later edited by Pádraic Pearse (1879–1916), published its first issues. It was an important organ encouraging bilingualism and the revival of the Irish language. Edited by Eoin MacNeill, it ran until 1918.

Literary Criticism

Douglas Hyde's *A Literary History of Ireland* appeared.

The compilation *Literary Ideals in Ireland* included essays by John Eglinton (1868–1961), Yeats, Æ, and William Larminie that had appeared in the literary columns of the Dublin *Daily Express* (Kain 1962, 53).

Periodicals

Arthur Griffith founded the nationalist newspaper the *United Irishman,* published weekly until April 1906. As editor, Griffith was the most outspoken popular voice for Irish independence.

Poetry

Yeats's volume *The Wind among the Reeds* included such poems as "The Song of Wandering Aengus" and "The Cap and Bells." He commented that he had so meditated upon "images from Irish folklore that they had become true symbols," and that he had moments of vision "when these images took upon themselves what seemed an independent life and became part of a mystic language, which seemed always as if it would bring me some strange revelation."

1900

Having returned from the Boer War in South Africa, John MacBride stood for election in South Mayo, but was defeated.

Arthur Griffith and William Rooney (1873–1901) founded Cumann na nGaedheal (Society of the Gaels), not to be confused with W. T. Cosgrave's (1880–1965) political party organized in 1923. Griffith and Rooney's nationalist organization numbered Maud Gonne, John MacBride, Thomas Clarke (1858–1916), and John O'Leary among its members (Hickey and Doherty 1987, 107).

Maud Gonne founded Inghinidhe na Éireann (Daughters of Ireland) with the assistance of Countess Constance Markievicz and Francis Sheehy-Skeffington (1878–1916) as a more strongly separatist alternative to the Irish Parliamentary party. This organization subsequently published the magazine *Bean na hÉireann* (Woman of Ireland) and in 1913 was absorbed into Cumann na mBan (Society of women) (Hickey and Doherty 1987, 236–37). Its feminist as well as nationalist focus is suggested by its title and leadership.

Drama

Not long before his death in Paris in this year, Oscar Wilde remarked, "I am dying, as I have lived, beyond my means." In France he had begun using the name of Sebastian Melmoth— from Charles Maturin's 1820 novel about the outcast Irish wanderer.

The Irish Literary Theatre's second season, at the Gaiety Theatre, included George Moore's *The Bending of the Bough*, his cousin Edward Martyn's *Maeve*, and Alice Milligan's *The Last Feast of the Fianna*. In an essay in *Beltaine* entitled "Plans and Methods," Yeats wrote that Moore's and Martyn's plays symbolized "Ireland's choice between English materialism and her own natural idealism," helping "to bring Ireland from under the ruins" of commercialism and materialism (quoted in Hogan and Kilroy 1975, 1: 65).

Education

By this date only 35.6 percent of Irish primary schools served both Catholic and Protestant students, whereas 53.6 percent of the schools had been mixed in 1862 (Akenson 1975, 4).

Fiction

John Whelan (d. 1991)—Seán O'Faoláin, as he later Gaelicized himself—was born in Cork. He became one of the most important writers and editors of the century.

Irish Language and Literature

The census suggested that there were only 210,000 monoglot speakers of Irish—those who spoke solely Irish (Todd 1989, 15). This number would continue to decrease; today virtually all native Irish speakers can also speak English. At this earlier point, school managers were permitted to teach Irish "during ordinary school hours as an optional subject, provided the other instruction did not suffer" (Akenson 1975, 41).

The Gaelic League was moving into high gear, but by no means was there unanimous popular Irish support for revival or continuance of the Irish language. For example, the Trinity College classicist (and earlier teacher of Oscar Wilde) Professor Mahaffy (1839–1919) testified, "during an inquiry into secondary education, that the revival of Gaelic was 'a retrograde step, a return to the dark ages,' " and added in a February Dublin *Daily*

Express interview "the sneering suggestion that Home Rulers plead in Irish at Westminster, which 'would not only be logical, but would save the House of Commons from a good deal of incompetent oratory' " (Kain 1962, 45). Enthusiasm for the language was too often left to the likes of the brilliant and eccentric George Moore, who rather pathetically wrote, in an essay on "The Irish Literary Renaissance and the Irish Language" in the *New Ireland Review,* "I have no children, and am too old to learn the language, but I shall at once arrange that my brother's children shall learn Irish. I have written to my sister-in-law, telling her that I will undertake this essential part of her children's education. They shall have a nurse straight from Aran" (1900, 72).

A year before Douglas Hyde's *Casadh an tSúgáin* (The twisting of the rope) at the Abbey, Peadar Ó Laoghaire's *Tadhg Saor* (Independent Tadgh)—staged in Macroom, county Cork— was the first play produced in Irish (Hickey and Doherty 1987, 441).

Literary Criticism

On 1 April eighteen-year-old second-year university student James Joyce's review of *When We Dead Awaken* by his hero, Henrik Ibsen, appeared in London's *Fortnightly Review.* When Ibsen sent him a note of thanks soon thereafter, the awestruck Joyce resolved to learn Norwegian and other languages and transform himself into an Irish European.

Periodicals

Standish O'Grady's *All-Ireland Review* was founded, lasted until 1907, and published a good deal of short fiction (Kilroy 1984, 11).

D. P. Moran (1871–1936) founded the *Leader,* a narrowly nationalist newspaper.

Poetry

T. W. Rolleston and Stopford Brooke (1832–1916) brought out their popular and influential *Treasury of Irish Poetry,* with intro-

ductory notes by Yeats, Hyde, Lionel Johnson (1867–1902), and
George Sigerson (1836–1925) (Hickey and Doherty 1987, 565).

Prose Nonfiction

Shaw's socialist critique *Fabianism and the Empire* appeared.

1901

Belfast's population reached 350,000 (Todd 1989, 46), thereby
exceeding Dublin's until later in the century (see 1936 entry).

Art

Sir Hugh Lane (1875–1915), who was to become the most
important early twentieth-century patron of Irish painting, was
introduced to Irish art at an exhibition of the works of Nathaniel
Hone (1831–1917) and John Butler Yeats (the poet's father) in
Dublin. Soon thereafter Lane began commissioning works by
Yeats and other Irish painters (de Breffny 1983, 185).

Drama

In October Yeats and Moore's *Diarmuid and Grania* and Douglas
Hyde's *Casadh an tSúgáin* (The twisting of the rope) were staged
together by the Irish Literary Theatre at the Gaiety Theatre in
Dublin. *Diarmuid and Grania* left its audience cold, and many left
without seeing Hyde's play. Moore suggested the difficulty of his
collaboration with Yeats in a letter to him written when they were
working on the play: "I do not think much of writing across the
table at each other, it results in superficial thinking and is only
useful occasionally" (Finneran, Harper, and Murphy 1977, 1: 71).
Casadh an tSúgáin was the first play put on in Irish at the Abbey
(and therefore the first to employ an entirely Irish cast), featuring
Hyde in the lead role, reenacting the folktale about the poet who is
tricked by a young woman's mother into helping her as she works
on a rope, the task backing the poet out of the house away from the

object of his desire until the mother can slam the door in his face. Joseph Holloway noted in his journal that Hyde, "though villainously made up, made love very persuasively, and rated those who would deprive him of the young maiden with delightful glibness and sincerely expressed abuse. I have always been told that Irish is a splendid language to make love in or abuse, and having heard Dr. Hyde I can well believe it. . . . The applause was great at the end" (Hogan and O'Neill 1967, 14). Moore directed *Diarmuid and Grania* but found it necessary to call on William Fay (1872–1947) to direct Hyde's play in Irish, thus bringing this important director-actor into the Literary Theatre. Yeats's theater magazine *Beltaine* (for Bealtaine or "May") was now renamed *Samhain* ("November" or "Winter"), and contained the text of Hyde's play and essays by Yeats and Moore. Yeats noted that "I have called this little collection of writings *Samhain,* the old name for the beginning of winter, because our plays this year are in October, and because our Theatre is coming to an end in its present shape. The profits on the sale of *Samhain* will be given to the Gaelic League" (October 1901, p. 10). "Let us learn construction from the masters and dialogue from ourselves" (7), Yeats advised his fellow Irish playwrights. In an essay on "The Irish Literary Theatre," George Moore wrote: "The Irish Literary Theatre is the centre of a literary movement, and our three years have shown that an endowed theatre may be of more intellectual service to a community than a university or a public library" (13).

Irish Language and Literature

Pádraig Ó Duinnín's (1860–1934) *Cormac Ó Conaill* was the first novel in Irish ever published in book form (Ó Háinle, 198), before Ó Laoghaire's better known *Séadna* (serialized earlier) appeared as a book.

Literary Criticism

Young James Joyce's "The Day of the Rabblement" was an essay printed in a pamphlet entitled *Two Essays* (with his university friend Francis Sheehy-Skeffington's plea for women's rights as the other). In it Joyce attacked the Irish dramatic movement for selling out to the mob by doing only Irish plays and ignoring continental masters such as Ibsen. Frank Fay (1870–1931) replied in the *United Irishman,* "One would be glad to know in what way the Irish Literary Theatre has pandered to popularity. Is it by producing a play in Irish? I ask this because Mr. Joyce speaks of 'sodden enthusiasm and clever insinuation and every flattering influence of vanity and low ambition.' But I have yet to learn that either the Irish Literary Theatre or the Irish Language movement is popular. Surely they both represent the fight of the minority against the 'damned compact majority'" (quoted in Hogan and Kilroy 1975, 1: 112–13). Arthur Griffith added in the *United Irishman,* "Patience, Mr. Joyce, and your desires for the masterpieces may have fulfillment" (quoted in Kain 1962, 53).

1902

Art

At the suggestion of Sir Hugh Lane, the poet's father, John Butler Yeats, left London, resettled in Dublin, and "undertook an extensive series of portraits in oil and crayon. Most of literary and artistic Dublin sat for him. Years later Susan Mitchell (1866–1926), a poet and one of his subjects, recalled his manner of painting: 'The brave, tall figure, brush in hand, advancing on his canvas with great strides . . . putting on touches with the ardour of one who would storm a fortress,' and, of course, 'talking enchantingly all the time, his whole nature in movement'" (quoted in Kain 1962, 61). John Butler Yeats moved to New York in 1907, remaining there for the rest of his life.

Drama

In April Yeats's *Cathleen ni Hoolihan* and Æ's *Deirdre* were produced by William Fay's newly founded Irish National Dramatic Society at St. Theresa's Hall in Clarendon Street, with Maud Gonne in the lead role of Yeats's play (in her only role on this stage) and William and Frank Fay and their dedicated Irish amateur cast (rather than English professionals as in previous Irish plays) as the driving theatrical force. By now George Moore

had withdrawn from the Literary Theatre and Yeats was working
with the Fays instead. In straightforward fashion, using folk
dialogue with which Lady Gregory helped Yeats, *Cathleen ni
Hoolihan* focuses on an old woman (the mythical *sean bhean
bhocht,* the poor old woman who personifies Ireland) who comes
to a peasant home in 1798 and convinces a young man, on the eve
of his wedding, to leave with her. With several future leaders and
participants in the 1916 Easter Rising in the audience, this play
had a powerful impact. Yeats noted in *Samhain* that "the performances of *Deirdre* and *Cathleen ni Hoolihan* . . . drew so many to
hear them that great numbers were turned away" (1902, 5).
Cathleen ni Hoolihan was the work concerning which Yeats asked
himself years later (in his poem "The Man and the Echo"), "Did
that play of mine send out / Certain men the English shot?" Máire
Nic Shiubhlaigh (Mary Walker, an actress) wrote in her memoirs,
"How many who were there that night will forget the Kathleeen ni
Houlihan of Maud Gonne, her rich golden hair, willow-like figure,
pale sensitive face, and burning eyes, as she spoke the closing lines
of the Old Woman turning out through the cottage door. . . .
Watching her, one could readily understand the reputation she
enjoyed as the most beautiful woman in Ireland, the inspiration of
the whole revolutionary movement. . . . Yeats wrote *Kathleen ni
Houlihan* specially for her, and there were few in the audience who
did not see why. . . . She was the very personification of the figure
she portrayed on the stage" (quoted in Hogan and Kilroy 1976, 2:
14).

Fay's Irish National Dramatic Society also staged Æ's
Deirdre, James Cousins's (1873–1956) *The Sleep of the King* and
The Racing Lug, Fred Ryan's *The Laying of the Foundations,*
Yeats and Lady Gregory's *The Pot of Broth,* and P. T. McGinley's
Éilís agus an Bhean Deirce (Lizzy and the tinker).

In London Shaw's bold critique of prostitution, *Mrs. Warren's
Profession* (originally written in 1893–94), was first performed.

Folklore

Lady Gregory's *Cúchulain of Muirtheimne,* subsequently assessed
by Yeats as "the greatest book to come out of Ireland in our time,"
appeared. It cast the ancient Ulster stories of Cúchulain and the

Red Branch, from the Ulster cycle, in the dialect of rural Galway, called "Kiltartanese" after the area around Coole Park, Lady Gregory's estate.

Irish Language and Literature

George Moore was delighted to have his collection of stories *The Untilled Field*—even before its publication the following year in retranslated English—translated into Irish by Pádraig Ó Súilleabháin and published as *An tUr Ghort*. Moore remarked that he was convinced that his stories were much improved by their "bath in Irish."

Literary Criticism

"The De-Davisasation of Irish Literature," an essay by John Eglinton (W. K. Magee), appeared in the *United Irishman* on 31 March, supporting Yeats's thesis that an Irish national literature needed to separate itself from simplistic nationalism (Maxwell 1984, ix).

James Joyce read an essay on the nineteenth-century poet James Clarence Mangan to the Literary and Historical Society at the Royal University (later University College, Dublin). It was published in the May issue of *St. Stephen's,* the university magazine. He defended the poet who was attacked because of his personal life and habits. "Mangan, however, is not without some consolation," Joyce noted, "for his sufferings have cost him inwards, where for many ages the sad and the wise have elected to be" (1902, 116). In the summer he met Yeats (telling him as they parted, "I have met you too late"), and in November left for London and Paris, returning to Dublin in April of the following year.

Periodicals

Edward O'Cullen founded *Ireland's Own,* a fashionable weekly magazine drawing on folk culture and filled with popular features. It grew steadily throughout the century (Hickey and Doherty 1987, 239).

Prose Nonfiction

Michael Davitt, who had visited the war region in southern Africa as a reporter, published *The Boer Fight for Freedom.*

1903

The Wyndham Land Act permitted tenants to buy their farms with the aid of long-term mortgages, thereby legislating a peasant proprietorship and eventually helping shift the political dominance of rural Ireland from the Anglo-Irish Ascendancy to the "strong farmers"—middle-class Catholics.

Art

The sculptor John Hughes (1865–1941) finished his figures of soldiers on the Victoria Memorial in Dublin, which were influenced by Rodin (de Breffny 1983, 215).

Drama

Replacing their Dramatic Society founded the previous year, the Fay brothers formed the Irish National Theatre Society, with Yeats as president, William Fay as manager, and Maud Gonne, Douglas Hyde, and Æ as vice-presidents.

John M. Synge's one-act folk play *In the Shadow of the Glen,* concerning a peasant woman who leaves her husband to go wandering the countryside with a tinker, created quite a stir. It introduced Synge's marvelous use of Irish-English dialect— inspired by the translations of Douglas Hyde and based on Synge's own knowledge of the Irish language as learned at Trinity College and developed during visits to the Aran Islands. The production of this play also served to settle the controversy in the dramatic movement between the artists (Yeats, Synge, and the Fays) and those who felt the theater should be an instrument of political propaganda, including Maud Gonne and others, in favor of the artists. Maud Gonne resigned from the Irish National Theatre Society, and *In the Shadow of the Glen* alienated many other nationalists (such as Arthur Griffith), thereby foreshadowing the *Playboy* riots of 1907.

Other early productions of the Irish National Theatre Society, in its first season at the Molesworth Hall, included Yeats's *The Hour Glass* and *The King's Threshold,* Lady Gregory's *Twenty-Five,* and Padraic Colum's (1881–1972) *Broken Soil* (Maxwell 1984, x). This was also a notable year in the history of the Irish theater movement because it marked its first performances in London, which were a great success. The international reputation of Yeats's theater was growing.

Fiction

George Moore's *The Untilled Field,* the first truly modern or modernist collection of Irish stories, was inspired by Turgenev and other Europeans, and in turn greatly influenced Joyce and other younger writers. In such stories as "Julia Cahill's Curse" and "Home Sickness," Moore examined unflinchingly the repressive aspects of life in rural Ireland.

The northerner Shan Bullock's (1865–1935) *The Squireen* was a novel critiquing the loveless, rural, arranged marriage— ultimately rewarded here by the husband's death and the wife's return to her father's farm.

The Cork writer William Buckley (so obscure that his dates are unknown) published *Croppies Lie Down,* a little-known but pivotal historical novel about the Wexford rebellion of 1798. Buckley abandoned the escapist romance formula and happy ending typical of the nineteenth-century Irish historical novel, in favor of a bleak, realistic story of the bloodbath in Wexford, thereby representing a significant turning point in the Irish historical novel (see Cahalan 1983, 103–8).

The master of the short story Frank O'Connor (Michael O'Donovan, d. 1966) was born in Cork.

Irish Language and Literature

Pádraic Pearse began his term as editor of *An Claidheamh Soluis* (The sword of light), the weekly newspaper of the Gaelic League. In its pages he published his own story "Iosagán," marked by a radically new *pléascach,* or explosive opening, and a series of essays arguing that writers in Irish needed to embrace European innovations in order to keep Irish language and literature alive. Pearse was as pivotal in the developmental of modern fiction in Irish as he was in the formation of twentieth-century Irish nationalism.

Literary Criticism

Horatio Sheafe Krans's *Irish Life in Irish Fiction* was the first attempt at a comprehensive survey of Irish fiction up to that time. Krans was heavily influenced by Yeats's critical pronouncements —especially in Yeats's introduction to *Representative Irish Tales* (1891). Krans followed Yeats's lead, for example, in dividing novelists into "peasants" and "gentry."

Music

A Chicago Irishman, Francis O'Neill (1849–1936), published *The Music of Ireland,* a pioneering collection of 1,850 traditional Irish dance tunes and slow airs. O'Neill's collections (see also 1907 entry) remained a major source for and influence on traditional Irish musicians in both Ireland and America.

Poetry

Yeats's *In the Seven Woods* contained such bold new poems as "Adam's Curse," marking a sharp shift in mood and style. There was a new directness and bleakness in "Adam's Curse," a conversation poem about his relationship with Maud Gonne and addressed to her. This poem culminates in the strikingly new image of the "hollow moon" as emblematic of their love, now grown "weary-hearted." In this year Gonne married the Irish soldier and rebel John MacBride—an event that Yeats combined imagistically with a big storm at Coole Park (Lady Gregory's home), noting that he composed many of these poems while "walking about among the Seven Woods, before the big wind of 1903 blew down so many trees, and troubled the wild creatures, and changed the look of things." In October he embarked on a speaking tour of America, thereby extending his growing international reputation.

Prose Nonfiction

Within the Pale: The True Story of Anti-Semitic Persecutions in Russia was based on Michael Davitt's trip to Russia, where he met Tolstoy. Several Irish writers during this period, including George Moore and Pádraic Ó Conaire (1883–1928), were similarly struck by the many parallels between Russia and Ireland, two agrarian, peasant-populated, traditionally oppressed, and increasingly revolutionary countries.

1904

Drama

Synge's *Riders to the Sea,* often acclaimed as the best one-act tragedy in English, was produced. Combining realistic folk and Greek tragic elements, this play concerns a brave woman of the Aran Islands who loses her husband and all of her sons to the tumultuous sea surrounding the islands. Later the publisher George Roberts recalled, "The rehearsals were intensely interesting. The scene, which was laid in the Aran Islands, required different treatment from any of our other peasant plays. Synge was very particular that every detail of the properties and costumes should be correct" (quoted in Hogan and Kilroy 1976, 2: 114). Joseph Holloway added in his journal that "the thoroughly in-earnest playing of the company made the terribly depressing wake episode so realistic and weirdly doleful that some of the audience could not stand the painful horror of the scene, and had to leave the hall during its progress. . . . The audience was so deeply moved by the tragic gloom of the terrible scene on which the curtains close in, that it could not applaud" (Hogan and O'Neill 1967, 35). Yeats praised the play in *Samhain* previous to its production, noting that Synge "has gone every summer for some years past to the Arran [sic] Islands, and lived there in the houses of the fishers, speaking their language and living their lives, and his play seems to me the finest piece of tragic work done in Ireland of late years. One finds in it, from first to last, the presence of the sea, and a sorrow that has majesty as in the work of some ancient past" (1903, 7).

Other productions of the Irish National Theatre Society at the Molesworth Hall included Yeats's *The Shadowy Waters* and Séamus MacManus's (1869–1960) *The Townland of Tamney* (Maxwell 1984, x).

In April, Annie Horniman, an Englishwoman who ironically was opposed to Irish nationalism but was much enamored of Yeats and very interested in drama, bought buildings in Dublin that, after renovation by Joseph Holloway, served as the site of the famous Abbey Theatre for more than forty years. At this point the Irish National Dramatic Society and the Irish Literary Theatre Society merged and formed the Abbey Theatre. The theater was deliberately small, with a stage only fifteen feet deep and a proscenium opening only twenty-one feet wide. Yeats's *On Baile's Strand* and Lady Gregory's *Spreading the News* premiered on 27 December, the night the Abbey opened. Holloway noted in his journal that "the opening of the Abbey Theatre was the most momentous event of the year in Dublin to my mind. History may come of it! Who can tell!" (Hogan and O'Neill 1967, 51). Yeats's play was the first of his Cúchulain cycle, concerning Cúchulain's killing of his son and his fight with the sea. The *Freeman's Journal* felt that *"On Baile's Strand* is one of the best acting plays that Mr. Yeats has written" (quoted in Hogan and Kilroy 1976, 2: 128). *Spreading the News* was a very popular folk comedy about the rapid-fire dissemination of a false rumor about a reputed murder committed by a man merely seen following someone with a pitchfork. The Abbey now centered around a professional group of actors including the Fay brothers and Sara Allgood. Horniman continued to subsidize the theater until 1910, when she and Yeats parted company.

Bulmer Hobson (1883–1969) was the leading founder of the Ulster Literary Theatre. Unlike the Abbey, its northern counterpart discovered no major dramatist, but some of the plays it produced were very popular. This company lasted until 1934.

The Cork National Theatre Society was also established in 1904, though it foundered early on and did not reemerge until 1908 (Maxwell 1984, 16, 64–65).

In London, the Royal Court Theatre in Sloane Square, run largely by Harley Granville-Barker, produced Shaw's play *Candida.* This theater remained closely identified with Shaw's major plays over the next few decades.

Fiction

At the end of a late-night drinking binge in Dublin, James Joyce was rescued by Alfred Hunter, a kind Dublin Jew whom he hardly knew. This event was to serve as one of the major epiphanies, or inspirations, for *Ulysses* (1922), in which Joyce immortalized 16 June 1904, the day he first met Nora Barnacle (1886–1951), as "Bloomsday." On 16 May he won a medal in a singing contest, and on 27 August sang on the same program as the great tenor John McCormack (Kain 1962, 190). In the fall he left Dublin for good with Nora, bound for the Continent. At the invitation of Æ, editor of the *Irish Homestead,* Joyce wrote what would be the first story of *Dubliners,* "The Sisters," and published it in the *Homestead.*

Film

Louis de Clerq's *Life on the Great Southern and Western Railway* was the first known Irish documentary film (de Breffny 1983, 64).

Folklore

Lady Gregory's *Gods and Fighting Men,* a sequel to *Cúchulain of Muirthemne* (1902), was published.

Irish Language and Literature

Irish school commissioners introduced a bilingual program for use "during ordinary school hours in Irish-speaking areas" (Akenson 1975, 41). This was the first official governmental introduction of bilingualism into the Gaeltacht.

Father P. S. Dineen's Irish-English dictionary *Foclóir Gaedhilge agus Béarla* was published; a revised edition appeared in 1927.

Literary Criticism

Emily Lawless published her biography of Maria Edgeworth, linking herself to her Ascendancy foremother; this book implicitly suggested a tradition of women's writing in Ireland.

Periodicals

Dana, founded and edited by Frederick Ryan (1874–1913) and John Eglinton, was Ireland's first modern "little magazine," appearing monthly for a little more than a year. During its short life *Dana* managed to publish Joyce (though it rejected his story "A Portrait of the Artist," which was not published until 1960 in the *Yale Review*), Æ, George Moore, Padraic Colum, Oliver St. John Gogarty, and Seamus O'Sullivan.

The monthly *Uladh: A Literary and Critical Magazine* was published in Belfast by the Ulster Literary Theatre, advocating Ulster literary regionalism (Denman 1987, 124–25, 127).

Poetry

New Songs, an anthology of poetry edited by Æ, included the work of young poets such as Padraic Colum and Seamus O'Sullivan. In his introduction Æ spoke of "a new mood in Irish verse," but many of the poems in this collection reflected the shadowy imagery of Yeats's 1890s "Celtic Twilight" (Garratt 1986, 51–52).

Prose Nonfiction

The Fall of Feudalism in Ireland was Michael Davitt's memoir and history of the Land War, Parnell's career, and related late-nineteenth-century matters. The founder of the Land League died two years later.

Arthur Griffith's *The Resurrection of Hungary* took events

following the 1848 uprising in Hungary as paradigmatic of what needed to happen in Ireland (Deane et al. 1991, 2: 354).

1905

Cumann na nGaedheal (Society of Gaels) began its reorganization (continuing through 1908) as Sinn Féin (We ourselves), with Arthur Griffith as a dominant figure. Sinn Féin later became the focus of nationalist activity following the 1916 Easter Rising, especially around 1918.

Drama

Padraic Colum's *The Land,* realistically focused on rural problems of land inheritance and emigration, premiered at the Abbey, as did William Boyle's (1853–1922) *The Building Fund. The Well of the Saints* became the first of Synge's plays to be produced there. This play depicted a peasant couple who rejects a holy man's cure for their blindness, believing that they are better off not being able to see each other and also better equipped to beg for alms; paganism thus vanquishes Christianity much as it had earlier in Yeats, and much as it would later in some of Liam O'Flaherty's stories. Joseph Holloway wrote in his journal, "I saw the entire play of *The Well of the Saints* gone through at the rehearsal at the Abbey Theatre and came to the conclusion that Mr. Synge is a complete master of picturesque strong language and sometimes brutal coarseness, not to say sheer repulsiveness" (quoted in Hogan and Kilroy 1978, 3: 15). Holloway accurately predicted that audiences would not take very well to Synge's play in 1905. Reviews were mostly negative, though George Moore defended Synge in the *Irish Times.*

Meanwhile, many patriots and language enthusiasts (including Maud Gonne and Arthur Griffith) had spun off into the National Players' Society, formed by the Keating Branch of the Gaelic League. The Keating Branch produced Thomas Hayes's *Seán na Scuab* (John the sweep) and the Irish dictionary compiler Father Dineen's *Creideamh agus Gorta* (Faith and famine) at the Abbey.

George Bernard Shaw's Irish comedy, *John Bull's Other*

Island, was turned down by the Abbey; Shaw later commented, "Like most people who have asked me to write plays, Mr. Yeats got rather more than he bargained for. . . . Good heavens! I have had to get all England and Ireland into three hours and a quarter." Yeats is said to have remarked later to Florence Farr, "Ah if he had but style, distinction, and was not such a barbarian of the barricades" (quoted in McHugh and Harmon 1982, 156). Meanwhile, however, London's Royal Court Theatre staged Shaw's masterful, epic, intellectual version of the Don Juan story, *Man and Superman. John Bull's Other Island* had already been successfully performed in London in the previous year; as in the case of King George III's enthusiasm over Edgeworth's *Castle Rackrent* (1800), *John Bull's Other Island* was performed for King Edward VII, and Prime Minister Balfour saw it five times. Shaw marvelously explained in the play's preface: "If I had gone to the hills nearby to look upon Dublin and to ponder upon myself, I too might have become a poet like Yeats, Synge, and the rest of them. But I prided myself on thinking clearly, and therefore could not stay. Whenever I took a problem or a state of life of which my Irish contemporaries sang sad songs, I always pursued it to its logical conclusion, and then inevitably it resolved itself into comedy. That is why I did not become an Irish poet. . . . I could not stay there dreaming my life away on the Irish hills. England had conquered Ireland; so there was nothing for it but to come over and conquer England." This situation, however, would be reversed in the case of *The Shewing-Up of Blanco Posnet* (see 1909 entry).

Fiction

George Moore's Irish masterpiece *The Lake* anticipated many of the strategies and themes of Joyce's *A Portrait of the Artist as a Young Man* (1916). It is framed as a series of letters between Father Oliver Gogarty and Rose Leicester (renamed Nora Glynn in Moore's 1921 revision of the novel), a young unmarried schoolteacher whom Gogarty denounced from the pulpit during her pregnancy. Rose's letters cause Gogarty to reexamine and repent his harsh action, and ultimately to abandon his parish in favor of a life of liberty such as the one Rose has found in England. He fakes a drowning and swims across a lake in order to escape anonymously to New York, where his final goal will be nothing less than the "full possession of his soul."

Irish Language and Literature

D. P. Moran, the editor of the *Leader* newspaper, argued in *The Philosophy of Irish Ireland* (in terms that would later be adopted by the Irish Free State and still later lampooned by Flann O'Brien / Myles na gCopaleen): "The foundation of Ireland is the Gael, and the Gael must be the element that absorbs. On no other basis can an Irish nation be reared" (quoted in T. Brown 1985, 56). He inaccurately pronounced Irish literature in English "defeated," declaring that henceforth the Gaelic League would control culture in Ireland and that writing in Irish would dominate the literary scene.

Periodicals

The *Nationalist*—a liberal, parliamentary-oriented newspaper influenced by Young Ireland—was edited by Thomas Kettle (1880–1916) and appeared weekly from September until April of the following year (Kain 1962, 191).

Out of the remains of a previous newspaper, the Parnellite *Irish Daily Independent,* the *Irish Independent* was launched as a major daily rival to the *Irish Times,* a status that it still maintains today (Oram 1983, 105). Its companion, the *Sunday Independent,* began publication in the following year (Hickey and Doherty 1987, 247).

Poetry

James Joyce's broadsheet poem "The Holy Office," composed in the previous year, was distributed in Dublin. It sharply satirized and ridiculed the writers of the Literary Revival, including Yeats. In the close of his satire of the poem "To Ireland in the Coming Times," in which Yeats had recorded his nationalist solidarity with earlier Irish poets, Joyce declared that he would "not accounted be" a part of their "mumming company," attacked Yeats and his movement for being overly sentimental, and claimed that Yeats "whinges" in poems with "Celtic fringes."

Now living in Trieste, Italy, with Nora Barnacle, Joyce was joined there by his brother Stanislaus in October.

1906

Architecture

The massive, imperial-style Belfast City Hall, designed by Sir Alfred Brumwell Thomas, was completed (de Breffny 1983, 30).

Drama

Yeats's *Deirdre,* with the traditional story cast rather in the mode of Greek tragedy, was produced at the Abbey, as was Lady Gregory's *The Gaol Gate,* a one-act tragedy about an innocent young man hanged in Galway for a murder after he refused to inform on his neighbors (as seen through the eyes of his wife and his mother). Reviewers set the tone for critics of Yeats's plays for years to come by declaring *Deirdre* lyrical but undramatic; they were equally imperceptive yet generally enthusiastic about *The Gaol Gate.* Also, the *Arrow* served as Yeats's Abbey Theatre magazine during the years 1906–9.

Samuel Beckett (d. 1989) was born near Dublin. His characteristic sense of irony and suffering should be kept in mind when it is noted that according to Beckett, he was born on Good Friday.

Irish Language and Literature

Pádraic Ó Conaire published "Nora Mhárcais Bhig" (Little Nora Marcus), his first story to appear in *An Claidheamh Soluis,* the Gaelic journal. Unlike anything previous in fiction in Irish, "Nora Mhárcais Bhig" concerns a young woman from Connemara who emigrates to London and becomes involved in prostitution and drinking. Following the advice of Pádraic Pearse, the editor of *An Claidheamh Soluis,* to turn to European models, Ó Conaire was busy writing stories in Irish that were the equivalent of the stories of Moore's *The Untilled Field* and Joyce's *Dubliners.* His tragedy was that writing in Irish, he was not able to reach the large audience that Moore and Joyce found in English; Ó Conaire eventually wasted his talent writing second-rate work for money, and his best stories in Irish were not collected until many years later.

Periodicals

Arthur Griffith edited *Sinn Féin* from May of this year until November 1914. Joseph Hone brought out the *Shanachie* during 1906–7 (Kain 1962, 191). The Catholic *Irish Theological Quarterly* was begun (Whyte 1971, 66).

Poetry

Joseph Campbell's (1879–1944) *The Rush Light* was a volume of folk verses.

1907

James Larkin, a thirty-one-year-old labor organizer from Liverpool, arrived in Belfast to organize dockers for the British National Dock Labourers' Union. Along with James Connolly and other organizers, Larkin was to revolutionize the labor movement throughout Ireland, especially in Dublin.

Drama

Lady Gregory's *The Rising of the Moon,* in which an Irish policeman allows a rebel to escape, made its successful debut at the Abbey; it was attacked by the Anglo-Irish *Irish Times* but dealt with more benignly by the nationalist papers such as the *Freeman's Journal.*

Infinitely more controversial was Synge's masterful tragicomedy *The Playboy of the Western World.* His play was based on a story he had heard on the island of Inis Meáin and actually toned down some racier sources in ancient Irish literature in presenting Christy Mahon, a young man who is lionized by a rural Irish community when he appears and gradually lets it be known that he has killed his father, but who later is rejected by the people and by Pegeen Mike (who had fallen in love with him) after his father arrives on the scene. Because of the play's portrait of a community taking a reputed murderer to its heart—and provoked by Christy's line, "What'd I care if you brought me a drift of chosen females, standing in their shifts itself?"—puritanical Irish nationalists of the Gaelic League organized riots that disrupted the play's performances, in the most notorious controversy in the history of the theater movement. On the first night Synge and Lady Gregory telegrammed Yeats (then in Scotland), "Audience broke up in disorder at the word shift." Yeats returned to defiantly help to defend Synge and his play against the many attacks, which included deliberate interruptions (verbal and otherwise) of the productions. The *Freeman's Journal* called the *Playboy* an "unmitigated, protracted libel upon Irish peasant men and, worse still, upon Irish peasant girlhood," and added, "It is quite plain that there is need for a censor at the Abbey Theatre." Even though Synge had drawn the premise and the language of the play from the west of Ireland, the *Evening Mail* review (entitled "A Dramatic Freak") claimed that it "smacks of the decadent ideas of the literary flaneurs of Paris rather than of simple Connaught" (quoted in Hogan and Kilroy 1978, 3: 125). Even the usually reasonable and supportive Joseph Holloway joined the attack, seeing red on the subject of Synge in his journal: *"The Playboy* is not a truthful or just picture of the Irish peasants, but simply the outpouring of a morbid, unhealthy mind ever seeking on the dunghill of life for the nastiness that lies concealed there. . . . Synge is the evil genius of the Abbey and Yeats his able lieutenant" (Hogan and O'Neill 1967, 81).

Much more popular at the time than Synge's *Playboy* was *The Country Dressmaker,* a comedy by George Fitzmaurice (1878–1963) which made good use of Kerry dialect. Yeats wrote to Synge, "How can we make [the audience] understand that *The Playboy* which they hate is fine art and *The Dressmaker* which they like is nothing?" (quoted in Maxwell 1984, 67).

Irish Language and Literature

Pádraic Peare's *Iosagán agus Scéalta Eile* (Little Jesus and other stories) appeared. These stories were subsequently much taught in Irish schools.

Father Peadar Ó Laoghaire published *Niamh,* a short novel based on mythology.

Music

Francis O'Neill of Chicago published his second collection, *Dance Music of Ireland,* containing 1,000 tunes divided into jigs, reels, hornpipes, set dances, and marches (Ó Canainn 1978, 21). This compendium was a major depository of traditional music played by musicians in Ireland as well as America. O'Neill's collections are the best known in this field and remain widely used today.

Peadar Kearney (1883–1942) and Patrick Heeney (1881–1911) collaborated on "The Soldier's Song," which later became Ireland's national anthem (Hickey and Doherty 1987, 275).

Poetry

Padraic Colum's volume *Wild Earth* appeared. Like Synge's plays, Colum's poems showed the influence of Hyde's translations (and a movement beyond Yeats's overweening influence) and embodied an elemental vision of life in the countryside.

James Joyce's first volume of poetry, *Chamber Music,* influenced by the cadences of Elizabethan lute songs, was published.

Prose Nonfiction

Much less controversial (and much less celebrated) than Synge's *Playboy* was *The Aran Islands,* his memoir and anthropological study of his several visits to the islands, which was published in this same year.

1908

Hanna Sheehy-Skeffington (1877–1946) and Francis Sheehy-Skeffington founded the Irish Women's Franchise League (Hickey and Doherty 1987, 532).

Art

Hugh Lane and the Dublin Corporation opened the Municipal Gallery of Modern Art in Dublin. Not long before the opening, Lane had remarked, "I hope that this Gallery will always fulfil the object for which it is intended, and—by ceding to the National Gallery those pictures which, having stood the test of time, are no longer modern—make room for good examples of the movements of the day." In the face of the rising and often conservative and puritanical middle class, however, Lane's task would not be an easy one. Shortly after the gallery's opening—faced by protests from artistic philistines over his exhibition of works by Renoir, Monet, Manet, Degas, and others—Lane felt compelled to remove some of the most important works of art to London (de Breffny 1983, 185–86).

The painter Sir William Orpen (1878–1931) was elected to the Royal Hibernian Academy. Orpen was "arguably the most important influence on the rise of the native tradition in early twentieth-century Irish painting" (de Breffny 1983, 176).

Drama

Yeats's *The Golden Helmet,* part of his Cúchulain cycle of plays, was staged at the Abbey. An eight-volume *Collected Works* appeared (more than thirty years before the end of his career), leading some to wonder if Yeats was about to retire. Also produced at the Abbey were ten other plays by seven different playwrights, including George Fitzmaurice's *The Pie-Dish,* Lennox Robinson's (1886–1958) *The Clancy Name,* and Thomas MacDonagh's (1878–1916) *When the Dawn is Come.* Especially since MacDonagh was to become one of the 1916 Easter Rising's rebel-martyrs, it is noteworthy that this play was (according to Joseph Holloway in his journal) "a peep into the future fifty years hence, when Ireland is having another dash for liberty with better success than in '98," though Holloway found it "dull and very talky" (Hogan and O'Neill 1967, 117).

William and Frank Fay, influential actors in the Irish dramatic movement who were unhappy with the diminishment of their importance in the Abbey Theatre as the result of Annie

Horniman's control, resigned from the theater. Willie had been "hardly even on snarling terms with Miss Horniman, and he was often at odds with the company. In his defense, it must be said that as the company's chief producer, chief comic actor, business manager and scene painter, he was monumentally overworked" (Hogan and Kilroy 1978, 3: 193).

Something of the tenor of Yeats's omnipresent persona in the theater movement is captured in Joseph Holloway's recollection of his remarks at a dinner following the revival of his play *Deirdre* in November: "Yeats commenced by saying that for once in his life he had nothing to say, and then went on to say it at some length, while he crucified himself with strange, weird, angular gestures many times. He said when he was a child he dreamed of a number of purple clouds in each of which beautiful white angels appeared. These were the passions. Tonight he thought of Mrs. Campbell as one of those angels as he saw her realise the passions of his *Deirdre* on the stage. It was worth writing to be so perfectly interpreted" (quoted in Hogan and Kilroy 1978, 3: 231).

Meanwhile, the Cork Dramatic Society reemerged to produce T. C. Murray's (1873–1959) *The Wheel of Fortune,* Daniel Corkery's (1878–1964) *The Hermit and the King,* and Lennox Robinson's *The Lesson of Life,* all one-act plays.

Education

According to the Irish Universities Act, higher education was reorganized by the government into the National University of Ireland (with constituent university colleges in Dublin, Cork, and Galway) and Queen's University, Belfast (replacing Queen's College, Belfast) (de Breffny 1983, 83).

Pádraic Pearse founded St. Enda's, his boys' school near Dublin, which was to serve as a hotbed of his brand of messianic nationalism. Five years later, for example, he would address himself "To the Boys of Ireland": "Two occasions are spoken of in ancient Irish story upon which Irish boys marched to the rescue of their country when it was sore beset—once when Cuchulainn and the boy-troop of Ulster held the frontier until the Ulster heroes rose, and again when the boys of Ireland kept the foreign invaders in check on the shores of Ventry until Fionn had rallied the Fianna: it may be that a similar tale shall be told of us, and that when men come to write the history of the freeing of Ireland they shall have to record that the boys of Na Fianna Éireann [see 1909 entry] stood in the battle-gap until the Volunteers armed" (1922, 111–12). Yet only three years before Pearse's leadership of the 1916 Easter Rising the editor of the *Irish Review* would still not recognize the future rebel in applauding "An Irish Educationalist —Mr. P. H. Pearse": "He is an educationalist who is incidently [*sic*] a poet and playwright" (1913, 608).

Irish Language and Literature

A playwriting contest sponsored by the Gaelic League was won by Pádraic Ó Conaire, then a young civil servant in London. His play *Bairbre Ruadh* (Red Barbara) had a plot slightly similar to that of a short story of the same title written nearly twenty years later by Liam O'Flaherty (who was to know Ó Conaire in the 1920s). As summarized by the *Freeman's Journal,* "It is a simple little play, dealing with an incident in the life of a young Galway girl, a farmer's daughter, who is in love with the servant boy, and for whom her brother, Máirtín, has made a match with a widower named An Brúnach, who has a publichouse in Galway. The action of the play takes place in the girl's house, and turns on the manner in which she elopes with her lover, Cuimin" (quoted in Hogan and Kilroy 1978, 3: 257).

Pádraic Ó Conaire's story "Páidín Mháire" focused on a fisherman who loses his sight, goes to the workhouse, becomes mad, and finally dies of tuberculosis.

Periodicals

Maud Gonne's organization, Inghinidhe na hÉireann (Daughters of Ireland), began publication of its magazine *Bean na hÉireann* (Woman of Ireland) (Hickey and Doherty 1987, 237).

Poetry

Susan Mitchell's *Aids to the Immortality of Certain Persons in Ireland: Charitably Administered* contained such verses as the satiric "Irish Council Bill": "Is it this you call Home Rule? / Says the Shan Van Vocht. / Do you take me for a fool? / Says the Shan Van Vocht" (Deane et al. 1991, 2: 740).

1909

In January the Irish Transport and General Workers' Union, led by James Larkin, was founded in Dublin. Countess Constance Markievcz and Bulmer Hobson founded Na Fianna Éireann (Soldiers of Ireland), a Republican youth organization (Hickey and Doherty 1987, 168).

Drama

Only thirty-eight years old and at the end of a creative burst of a few years of masterly plays, John Synge died of Hodgkins disease in March. Several newspapers previously hostile to his plays now eulogized him, and the *Evening Herald* reported the following remarks by Yeats: "He was a great dramatic genius, and one of the foremost prose writers of his time. . . . He was probably worse treated by his country than any writer, not even excepting Keats. The reviews of Keats's work in the *Quarterly* were infamous, and the treatment of Synge by a section of the Irish press will be equally infamous" (quoted in Hogan and Kilroy 1978, 3: 265–66). The previously hostile Joseph Holloway wrote in his journal, "Poor Synge, he was a gentle and lovable man personally and not at all like his works" (Hogan and O'Neill 1967, 125).

Shaw's *The Shewing-Up of Blanco Posnet*, whose production had been prevented in England, premiered at the Abbey. Undoubtedly recalling that Synge's *Playboy of the Western World* had earlier been received peacefully in London, Yeats explained in the *Irish Independent,* "You must remember that the Irish public and the English public are altogether different. A play objectionable in one country is not objectionable in the other. The religions of the countries are different, and the national characteristics of the countries are different." He remarked that a Shaw play would never be resented by an Irish audience because "he always has a clear argument," whereas "Synge's work . . . is precisely the work that is dangerous with an Irish audience. It is very hard to understand, and, therefore, the very desire to do so makes them impatient with it" (quoted in Hogan and Kilroy 1978, 3: 294, 295).

The Theatre of Ireland—a rival to the Abbey between 1906 and 1912, led by Edward Martyn, Padraic Colum, and Thomas Kettle—staged Séamus O'Kelly's play *The Shuiler's Child,* a tragedy about a wandering woman who gives up her child to a couple better able to provide for it. Nationalist reviewers praised the play and the Theatre of Ireland as a worthy (some said superior) rival to the Abbey, as in Susan Mitchell's essay "Dramatic Rivalry" in the newspaper *Sinn Féin.*

Fiction

James Stephens's volume *Insurrections* appeared, containing nature lyrics as well as poems protesting poverty in Dublin, yet at the same time lyrically portraying urban scenes there.

Film

On 20 December Ireland's first movie theater, the Volta, opened for business in Dublin. Its managing director was a young writer named James Joyce, who had acquired backers in Trieste and then journeyed to Dublin where he worked indefatigably between late October and late December acquiring and furnishing premises as well as advertising for and interviewing staff, and so forth. After a promising start and good reviews, however, the Volta was sold at a loss (Ellmann 1982, 301–3, 311).

1910

Drama

Birthright by T. C. Murray, which focused on a family conflict, premiered at the Abbey, as did the late John Synge's tragedy *Deirdre of the Sorrows,* a rendition in beautiful folk dialogue of the traditional, tragic story—very poignant with Máire O'Neill (Molly Allgood, Synge's beloved) playing Deirdre, who witnesses the death of her lover before she takes her own life.

The Abbey Theatre was dropped by its largest sponsor, the

patriotic Englishwoman Annie Horniman, when it remained open on the occasion of the death of King Edward VII; Yeats was away and left the decision to Lady Gregory, but her telegram to the new manager, Lennox Robinson, telling him to close the theater, arrived too late. Subsequently, Yeats and his fellow managers successfully raised money (partly from England) to replace Horniman's subsidy and keep the theater going. Yeats was therefore able to abandon the conservative Horniman, who had been infatuated with Yeats; Yeats had been quite willing to accept her support earlier while mostly ignoring her ideology. (See Frazier 1990 and Hogan and Kilroy 1978 for a full account of Yeats's use of Horniman's patronage.)

It was understandable that Yeats registered his mounting frustration with the Abbey Theatre in his volume of poems *The Green Helmet* (as cited just below). Synge had died in the previous year and the gifted Fay brothers had left the Abbey Theatre, and with them a good deal of the life had gone out of the acting in the Abbey company. The best-known English critics complained of this decline in their reviews of the 1910 Abbey tour. Max Beerbohm complained that "none of the players, in any of the strict sense of the word, acts. . . . They just talk on in their quick, soft, matter-of-fact undertone, expressing nothing through their faces except a melancholy to which they have long since grown accustomed." Added William Archer, "There is no crispness, no accent in their movements. . . . They tend to speak in one cadence. Speech will follow speech in the same set rhythm, each character unconsciously repeating the tune sung by his predecessor" (quoted in Cole 1962, 49).

Irish Language and Literature

Pádraic Ó Conaire's remarkable short novel, *Deoraíocht* (Exile), appeared. It was the most innovative, forward-looking Irish novel in either language during this period before the arrival of Joyce as a novelist, rivaled in this respect perhaps only by James Stephens's *The Charwoman's Daughter* (1912), which bears some similarities to it. Ó Conaire's protagonist and narrator, Micil, lost an arm and a leg in an accident and was presented with a few pieces of gold in compensation. In London he is loved and mothered by The Big Redheaded Woman and exploited by Alf Trott (The Little Yellow

Man), who signs him on as a freak for a circus sideshow and takes him to Galway, where he is temporarily married to The Fat Woman before returning to London. Somewhat as in Flann O'Brien's later novel *The Third Policeman,* only at the end of the book do we learn that Micil has already died—while lying in a park in London, in this case. Tomás Ó Broin emphasizes that *Deoraíocht* was the first and perhaps the only truly expressionistic novel in *any* language.

Periodicals

Seán MacDiarmada (1884–1916), Bulmer Hobson, and P. S. O'Hegarty (1879–1955) of the Irish Republican Brotherhood brought out a newspaper, *Irish Freedom,* until the government suppressed it in 1914. Pádraic Pearse and Thomas MacDonagh contributed to it (Hickey and Doherty 1987, 246).

Poetry

Yeats's slender volume *The Green Helmet* reflected his preoccupation with the struggles of the theater: "The fascination of what's difficult / Has dried the sap out of my veins, and rent / Spontaneous joy and natural content / Out of my heart." The title of the volume reflected Yeats's new combativeness; and its poems, his newly hard, classical imagery. Concerning Maud Gonne, "No Second Troy" was more detached (if also more bitter): "Why should I blame her that she filled my days / With misery, or that she would of late / Have taught to ignorant men most violent ways . . . ?"

Prose Nonfiction

The Irish socialist labor leader James Connolly argued in his book *Labour in Irish History* that Irish ills were to be laid at the feet of capitalism, closely identified with England (and thus linking Irish socialism and nationalism), but also crucially engineered by large-scale Irish employers, "the master class." He concluded with the hope that "Irish Socialists are wiser today. In their movement the North and the South will again clasp hands; again it will be demonstrated, as in '98, that the pressure of a common exploitation can make enthusiastic rebels out of a Protestant working class, earnest champions of civil and religious liberty out of Catholics, and out of both a united social democracy" (1910, 215–16).

1911

The census showed that in the twenty-six counties that would become the Republic of Ireland ten years later, 89.6 percent of the population was Roman Catholic. This figure would gradually but steadily rise, as reflected in subsequent census counts: 92.6 percent in 1926, 93.4 percent in 1936, 94.3 percent in 1946, 94.9 percent in 1961.

The Irish Women's Suffrage Federation replaced the previous Irishwomen's Suffrage and Local Government Association. Mary Hayden (1862–1942) was president and Æ a vice-president (Hickey and Doherty 1987, 267–68). Edith Somerville, coauthor of *The Real Charlotte* (1894) and the *Irish R.M.* stories, was to serve as president of the allied Munster Women's Franchise League.

Æ advanced an early warning about the dissatisfaction of Irishwomen: "Today the starved soul of womanhood is crying out over the world for an intellectual life and for more chance of earning a living. If Ireland will not listen to this cry, its daughters will go on slipping silently away to other countries, as they have been doing—all the best of them, all the bravest, all those most mentally alive" (quoted in Beale 1987, 36).

A Vigilance Association was founded to campaign against the importation of "immoral" literature from England (Whyte 1971, 27).

Drama

Yeats's earlier play *The Land of Heart's Desire* (1894) received its first production at the Abbey. Typically, the *Freeman's Journal* pronounced that "Mr. Yeats's material is suited to the creation of a poem, but not to the making of an acted play" (quoted in Hogan, Burnham, and Poteet 1979, 4: 118).

The Abbey undertook its first American tour, from September to March. There were protests over Synge's *Playboy* in Boston, New York, and Philadelphia, recalling the ones in Dublin four years earlier.

Fiction

Brian O'Nolan (d. 1966)—the novelist Flann O'Brien, later best known to Dublin readers of the *Irish Times* as Myles na gCopaleen—was born in Strabane, county Tyrone.

Periodicals

The *Irish Review* was begun with Pádraic Colum, Thomas MacDonagh, James Stephens, and David Houston as guiding forces. Though it lasted only until 1914, during its short life it served as an important forum for literary nationalism, attracting such writers as Yeats, Æ, George Moore, Standish O'Grady, John Eglinton, Seamus O'Sullivan, Pádraic Pearse, and Joseph Plunkett. An assessment in its pages of "The Revival in Letters" by T. Coulson noted, "It is interesting to examine the present position of Irish literature and to speculate upon its future course. Some critics will have us believe that the movement is in the full strength of manhood, whilst others contend that it still staggers upon infant limbs. That it has appealed more especially to the youth of the country (and the youth of other countries have not been deaf to the appeal) seems to indicate that is greatest measure of achievement has yet to be accomplished" (1 [June]: 174).

In May James Larkin founded the *Irish Worker* newspaper as a voice for the labor movement (Hickey and Doherty 1987, 268).

In 1911 the *Catholic Bulletin* was established with the original intent of warning the faithful about "immoral" literature, but it soon served to promote as well a narrow-minded, anti-Protestant, pro-Gaelic code (Whyle 1971, 3).

Poetry

The Circle and the Sword, a volume by Joseph Mary Plunkett (1887–1916), contained mystical and self-sacrificial themes calling to mind the poems and other writings of Plunkett's fellow 1916 Easter Rising leader, Pádraic Pearse.

Prose Nonfiction

George Moore left Ireland and published *Ave,* the first volume of his novelistic autobiographical trilogy *Hail and Farewell.*

1912

James Connolly and James Larkin founded the Labour party (Hickey and Doherty 1987, 283). Beginning as a forum for Connolly's vision of a workers' republic, the Labour party eventually developed into the more moderate, minority third party that it remains today.

Drama

At the Abbey, T. C. Murray's *Maurice Harte* examined the quintessentially Irish plight of the mother who pushes her unwilling son toward the priesthood. Other productions included Lennox Robinson's *Patriots,* St. John Ervine's (1883–1971) *The Magnanimous Lover,* and Yeats's *The Hour Glass* (Maxwell 1984, xi).

By this time, attempts at native Irish drama—in addition to the Dublin theaters and the Ulster and Cork societies—had spread well beyond the Abbey and Dublin: "Throughout 1912 in Ireland there was considerable activity among amateur theatre companies. Groups such as the Iona Players, the Pioneer Club, the Ringsend National Dramatic Association, the Aeolian Dramatic Club, the Leinster Stage Society, the Dublin University Dramatic Society, and the Metropolitan Players each managed to give at least one performance" (Hogan, Burnham, and Poteet 1979, 4: 223). Also, Count Casimir Markievicz's Independent Theatre Company staged Eva Gore-Booth's *Unseen Kings* at the Abbey (Lapisardi 1991, 216).

In London *Pygmalion,* later adapted as the musical *My Fair Lady,* further cemented Shaw's popularity.

Fiction

This was James Stephens's annus mirabilis: his two most cele-brated works of fiction, *The Charwoman's Daughter* and *The Crock of Gold,* were both released. *The Charwoman's Daughter* was a realistically based yet rather fantastic novella about a young, working-class Dublin woman who sensually comes of age, falls under the power of an imposing distant male (the Policeman), finds a truer and closer love (a young boarder, clerk, poet, and nationalist resembling Stephens himself), and approaches a higher consciousness by story's end. *The Crock of Gold,* his most cele-brated book, is an entertaining fantasy in which peasants and gods freely mingle and in which Caitilin MacMurrachu succeeds the charwoman's daughter as protagonist. This book ends with Aengus Og and Caitilin heading down to Dublin to free Stephens's Philosopher from jail and "the Intellect of Man . . . from the hands of the doctors and lawyers, from the sly priests, from the professors whose mouths are gorged with sawdust, and the mer-chants who sell blades of grass" (228). To finish off the year, Stephens also published his second volume of poems, *The Hill of Vision.* By the following year, the "Editor's Gossip" column in the *Irish Book Lover* indicated "on 28th November there was a crowded audience at the Royal Society of Literature when Mr. W. B. Yeats delivered an animating account of the literary awakening of Modern Ireland as personified in James Stephens, who was awarded the Edmond de Polignac prize by the Academic Commit-tee for his 'Crock of Gold' " (5 [January 1914]: 100).

Belfast novelist George Birmingham's (1865–1950) *The Red Hand of Ulster* depicted northern Unionists so opposed to Irish Home Rule that they demanded British withdrawal and staged their own revolt in order to prevent Home Rule. This was fiction not far from fact, for in this same year the Ulster Volunteers were formed in the North as a military organization in opposition to Home Rule, and almost 500,000 people in the North signed the "Ulster League and Covenant" against Home Rule (Darby 1976, xi).

Periodicals

Pádraic Pearse's short-lived *An Barr Buadh* (The peak of triumph) was the first avowedly political newspaper to be published in the Irish language (Ó Fiaich 1969, 110).

The Jesuit periodical *Studies* began publication (Whyte 1971, 64). It developed into a thoughtful journal of politics and literature, and has continued so until the present day.

Poetry

James Joyce's "Gas from a Burner" was written ostensibly in the voice of the Irish printer (of the Dublin publishing firm of Maunsel and Roberts) who was so offended by the contents of the text he was setting that he destroyed the galleys of what was to be published two years later as *Dubliners.*

In the poem, Joyce has the printer deliver a blowhard speech to "ladies and gents" about the "black and sinister arts" of an Irish writer "in foreign parts" who "sent me a book ten years ago." (Indeed, it did take Joyce a full decade, from 1904 to 1914, before *Dubliners* was published.) Joyce's printer explains that he has read the manuscript "a hundred times or so," from every angle, "backwards and forwards, down and up," before deciding (after looking at it once more "through both ends of a telescope"), that he is morally obligated to burn it, "so help me devil."

This was the year of Joyce's final visit to Dublin.

Prose Nonfiction

In Bulmer Hobson's IRB newspaper *Irish Freedom* during this year and the next, Thomas Clarke's (1857–1916) *Glimpses of an Irish Felon's Prison Life* appeared. Clarke had served more than fifteen years in prison beginning in 1883 (Deane et al. 1991, 2: 280). He was to be the oldest leader and martyr—the senior Fenian—of the 1916 Easter Rising.

1913

The Irish Volunteers, who would constitute the largest constituent nationalist force in the 1916 Easter Rising, were formed by Eoin MacNeill, leaders of the Irish Republican Brotherhood (IRB), and a number of other nationalists. At the same time the Cumann na mBan (Society of women) was formed as its women's auxiliary, replacing Maud Gonne's earlier Inghinidhe na hÉireann (Daughters of Ireland).

The Dublin Employers' Federation, led by William Martin Murphy (1844–1919), locked out thousands of members of the Irish Transport and General Workers' Union, led by James Larkin and James Connolly, after a period of mass mobilization by the union. In the short run, scabs were hired and the lockout was successful, but the strengthening of union leadership and membership boded well for the long run. During the lockout Larkin and the union were joined by many supporters, including such writers as Æ, Yeats, Joseph Plunkett, Thomas MacDonagh, Padraic Colum, Eamon Ceannt (1881–1916), Countess Markievicz, and others. Seán O'Casey was a member of the ITGWU and its Irish Citizen Army, and secretary of its Strikers' Relief Committee in 1913. The big lockout lived on in literature—in, for example, O'Casey's plays *The Star Turns Red* (1939) and *Red Roses for Me* (1942) and James Plunkett's novel *Strumpet City* (1969). James Larkin remained a most imposing, almost mythical figure, immortalized today in the heart of Dublin by a finger-pointing statue. Something of his stature as well as (in more general terms) the intermixture of the political and the literary in the Irish mythos is suggested in a journal entry written later by Joseph Holloway: "On my way to the Abbey I saw Jim Larkin holding forth to a meeting on Burgh Quay. On first seeing him standing up amid the crowd with his left hand on his hip and his right hand raised well above his head, I almost mistook him for W. B. Yeats" (Hogan and O'Neill 1967, 244). Yeats wrote "September 1913" largely in disgust over the lockout and more generally the mealy-minded, middle-class, "pence upon shivering pence" frame of mind he saw encapsulated in these events.

Art

Further evidence of the small-mindedness of the increasingly dominant middle-class power structure was the Dublin Corporation's ban on Yeats's friend and Lady Gregory's nephew Hugh Lane's proposed European art exhibition, prompting some angry verses from Yeats. Lane's 1908 exhibition of French impressionists had been met by protests from many of the same people.

Drama

A poor year in terms of new plays, but the Abbey continued to thrive: "1913 is not generally regarded as a remarkable year for the Abbey, but with extended tours to America and London, with a constantly varied schedule from the theatre's repertoire of favourites, and with fourteen new productions, the theatre had never performed the function of a repertory company so thoroughly and excitingly" (Hogan, Burnham, and Poteet 1979, 4: 240).

Fiction

James Stephens's collection of stories *Here Are Ladies* contained a series of character sketches set in Dublin.

When Emily Lawless (b. 1845) died in this year, Shan Bullock finished the novel that she had been working on, *The Race of Castlebar,* a historical novel about the 1798 Mayo rising, and it was published under both of their names.

Father Ralph was an autobiographical novel by Gerald O'Donovan (1871–1942), whose previous experiences in the priesthood may have provided an inspiration not only for this novel but also particularly for George Moore's *The Lake* (1905) and perhaps even for Joyce's *A Portrait of the Artist as a Young Man* (1916). O'Donovan's protagonist endures a manipulative mother and Maynooth, the famous seminary that rejected William Carleton. O'Donovan portrays the seminarians as possessing no loftier moral qualities than hangers-on at a racetrack. He extensively recounts the bishop's merciless suppression of the parish club that Father Ralph O'Brien idealistically begins, followed by his own mother's rejection of him, and his decision to leave the priesthood.

Poetry

Æ's *Collected Poems* were published.

Prose Nonfiction

Katharine Tynan (1861–1931) published *Twenty-Five Years,* a memoir of the Literary Revival. A close friend of Yeats since youth, Tynan was an extremely prolific writer who published 18 collections of poetry, no fewer than 105 novels, and 38 volumes in other genres (Murphy and MacKillop 1987, 164). The development of a retrospective view on the Literary Revival by those involved in it or close to it was also underscored by the publication of Lady Gregory's memoir *Our Irish Theatre* and the American scholar Cornelius Weygandt's pioneering study *Irish Plays and Playwrights.*

1914

It was estimated that in Dublin "229 persons per 1,000 were living in one-room tenements and 194 more per 1,000 in two-room tenements, as opposed to only 23 per 1,000 and 59 per 1,000 in one- and two-room tenements respectively in Birmingham. . . . In all, it was estimated that 74,000 people in Dublin lived in one-room tenements, and about 56,000 more in two-room tenements; and this 130,000 people represented 42 per cent of Dublin's citizens. It was small wonder that there was some resistance in Dublin to the British appeals to fight for the rights of small nations" (Hogan, Burnham, and Poteet 1979, 4: 361). Even the employers' apologist, Arnold Wright, admitted in his book *Disturbed Dublin* that conditions in the slums of Dublin were worse than those in Calcutta.

Exhausted after the events of the big lockout the year before, in October James Larkin left for the United States to raise money and organize Irish-American support for the Irish labor movement; he would not return until 1923. In his absence James Connolly became acting general secretary of the Irish Transport and General Workers' Union, commander of the Irish Citizen Army (which would join forces with the nationalist Irish Volunteers in the 1916 Easter Rising), and editor of the *Irish Worker* and the *Worker's Republic.*

An Irish Home Rule Bill (allowing for continuance within the United Kingdom of particular counties where a majority would prefer it) was passed in May, but its implementation was postponed because of the outbreak of World War I. By September, Irish Parliamentary party leader John Redmond—Parnell's nominal successor but a very faded copy in the view of strong nationalists—even urged Irishmen to enlist in the war on the British side and in defense of small, Catholic Belgium. This divided the nationalist Irish Volunteers between supporters of Redmond and opponents of enlistment, who believed that the war was England's war and that the focus should remain on Irish independence (arguing that "England's difficulty was Ireland's opportunity").

Irish Volunteers successfully landed guns at Howth near Dublin on 26 July, symbolically as well as practically demonstrating their preparedness for a rebellion. In response, government troops fired on a Dublin crowd shortly thereafter. By this time there were 132,000 members of the Irish Volunteers.

Drama

P. J. Bourke's (1882–1932) patriotic melodrama *In Dark '98* was presented at the Queen's Theatre, and "his advertising posters aroused the displeasure of the authorities for their anti-British bias" (Hogan, Burnham, and Poteet 1979, 4: 313; see also Herr 1991).

George Fitzmaurice's *The Dandy Doll,* a curious play about the supernatural in county Kerry, was published.

Fiction

James Joyce's collection of stories, *Dubliners,* which had been more than ten years in finding its way into print (earlier censored by Maunsel and Roberts but now published by B. W. Huebsch), unforgettably scrutinized the paralysis of a variety of people around the turn of the century in Joyce's native city. Written in a style of "scrupulous meanness," and viewed by their author as a kind of spiritual autobiography, this rather novelistic collection of fifteen stories moves from the impressionable young boys of "The Sisters," "Araby," and "An Encounter" to the older, disappointed protagonists of "A Little Cloud" and "Counterparts" and the entrapped women of "Eveline," "Clay," and "A Mother," toward the final, culminating masterpiece, "The Dead," in which Gabriel Conroy is drawn toward a terrifying but sympathetic vision of "all the living and the dead."

Periodicals

The *Irish Volunteer* was edited by Laurence de Lacey and Eoin MacNeill up until the time of the Easter Rising two years later (Kain 1962, 193).

Poetry

Yeats's volume *Responsibilities* was published, filled with poems such as "September 1913," which lamented that "Romantic Ireland's dead and gone, / It's with O'Leary in the grave." Increasingly he confronted the depressing and disturbed public world surrounding him. This volume was marked by a mood of haughty disappointment and reflected a new directness of style; as he declared in "A Coat," "there's more enterprise / In walking naked."

Prose Nonfiction

Vale—the final volume of George Moore's *Hail and Farewell,* which also included *Ave* (1911) and *Salve* (1912)—appeared. Half memoir and half novel, this long trilogy is Moore's portrait of the personalities of the Dublin Literary Revival, from which he exiled himself, resettling in London for the remaining twenty-two years of his life.

1915

During a time of more and more nationalist parades and maneuvers in Dublin, Pádraic Pearse delivered a much-quoted oration at the funeral of the old Fenian O'Donovan Rossa in August: "Life springs from death, and from the graves of patriotic men and women spring living nations." Pearse concluded with these stirring words: "They think that they have pacified Ireland. They think that they have purchased half of us and intimidated the other half. They think that they have foreseen everything, think that they have provided against everything; but the fools, the fools, the fools!—they have left us our Fenian dead, and while Ireland holds these graves, Ireland unfree shall never be at peace."

Art

Seán Keating (1889–1977) exhibited his painting *The Men of the West,* which struck a chord among Irish nationalists and art lovers (de Breffny 1983, 186).

Drama

St. John Ervine was appointed manager of the Abbey Theatre, following Lennox Robinson's resignation as play director in the previous year (Maxwell 1984, xi), and the Abbey had "a busy but undistinguished year" (Hogan, Burnham, and Poteet 1979, 4: 363). P. J. Bourke's patriotic melodrama *For the Land She Loved* was staged at the Abbey (see Herr 1991).

Fiction

After a long illness, Violet Martin ("Martin Ross") (b. 1862) died from a brain tumor. Edith Somerville continued to publish all of her work under the authorship of "Somerville and Ross" and believed that she could maintain psychic connection with her partner.

Irish Language and Literature

Douglas Hyde resigned his presidency of the Gaelic League in July because he felt it had become too militarized, and thereafter wrote to a friend: "My work for twenty-two years was to restore to Ireland her intellectual independence. I would have completed it, if I had been let. These people 'queered the pitch' on me, mixed the physical and the intellectual together, interpreted my teaching into terms of bullets and swords—*before the time,* and have reduced me to impotence" (quoted in Foster 1988, 476).

Father Peadar Ó Laoghaire's autobiography, *Mo Scéal Féin* (My own story), appeared. In itself it was an unremarkable book, but is worth noting because it was one of the earliest autobiographies in the modern Irish language, and this genre was to become an important one as practiced by later figures such as Tomás Ó Criomhthain, Peig Sayers, and others.

Periodicals

Nationality, a nationalist, antipartition journal edited by Arthur Griffith and Seumas O'Kelly, appeared until 1919 (Hickey and Doherty 1987, 939).

Denis Gwynn (1893–1971) and P. J. Little edited *New Ireland* until 1919 (Kain 1962, 194).

Prose Nonfiction

Yeats's *Reveries over Childhood and Youth* was the first of several autobiographical volumes eventually incorporated into his *Autobiographies.*

1916

In January James Connolly agreed with the Military Council of the Irish Republican Brotherhood to join their planned rebellion of the Irish Volunteers at Easter. Connolly's decision, in general terms, represented a linkage of Irish socialism and Irish national-ism, and in specific terms signified the culmination of the increas-ingly nationalist tenor of Connolly's socialism, though he had some reservations concerning the planned rebellion. On the one hand, he naively believed until just before the beginning of the Rising itself that action in Dublin would be joined by people throughout the country and that British imperialists would not want to destroy the city's capitalist buildings; on the other hand, it is said that as he entered the General Post Office (GPO) with his socialist Citizen Army at the beginning of the Rising, Connolly sagely told them, "If we should win, hold on to your rifles, because the Volunteers may have a different goal" (quoted in Foster 1988, 478).

April was the cruel month of the Easter Rising, which began on the 24th and lasted for six days. Germans had arranged with Roger Casement (1864–1916) to land arms in county Kerry by Easter Sunday, but their steamer was captured and the plan—and with it any chance for the success of the Rising—failed. Despite a countermanding order by the more moderate Eoin MacNeill, Pearse and Connolly led a Rising on Easter Monday, 24 April, instead of Sunday as originally planned, knowing by then that it must fail but nonetheless determined to rouse their countrymen according to Pearse's messianic notion of "blood-sacrifice." Pearse read a proclamation on behalf of "the Provisional Government of the Irish Republic" from the steps of the GPO, announcing that "in the name of God and of the dead generations from which she receives her old tradition of nationhood, Ireland, through us, summons her children to her flag and strikes for her freedom. . . . We declare the right of the people of Ireland to the ownership of Ireland, and to the unfettered control of Irish destinies, to be sovereign and indefeasible." Popular response in Dublin for the most part ranged from astonishment to indifference to derision; working-class Dubliners took advantage of the situation and looted the shops. British troops shelled the city center, 450 were killed and 2,614 wounded (compared to English losses of 130 out of a force of 2,000), and the rebels surrendered on Saturday, 29 April.

The pacifist and feminist Francis Sheehy-Skeffington (b. 1878)—who had gone through the streets urging soldiers to put down their arms—was murdered by a deranged British officer whose shooting of an unarmed boy had been witnessed by Sheehy-Skeffington. An obituary in the *Irish Book Lover* noted, "In 1908 his *Life of Michael Davitt* appeared, and in 1913 he took over the editorship of the *Irish Citizen*. He was arrested on the evening of 25 April, when returning home after attempts to stop looting, and on the next morning, at Portobello Barracks, he was shot without trial at the command of an officer subsequently found to be insane" (8, nos. 1–2 [August–September]: 20–21). Joint author with James Joyce of *Two Essays* (1901), a younger Sheehy-Skeffington was the original of Joyce's character McCann in *A Portrait of the Artist as a Young Man*.

Upper-class response to the Rising was encapsulated in the Easter Week issues of the *Irish Times*, which carried reassurances that the British "Home Forces" would prevail, and followed a 25 April column on the Rising (which ended with the advice that "those loyal citizens of Dublin who cannot actively help their country's cause at this moment may help it indirectly by refusing to give way to panic") with an article on "The Spring Show": "We are glad to learn that, in spite of the present troubles in Dublin, the Royal Dublin Society's Spring Show will be opened to-day" (4).

Between 3 May and 12 May, fifteen of the rebel leaders were executed, including Pearse, Connolly (shot sitting in a chair because he had gangrene in his legs), Pearse's fellow poets Joseph Mary Plunkett and Thomas MacDonagh, and Maud Gonne's husband John MacBride. Constance Markievicz was spared because of her gender, and future taoiseach (prime minister) and president of Ireland Eamon de Valera (1882–1975) because of his American citizenship. Later in the year, Roger Casement was executed despite a spirited defense by George Bernard Shaw, and large numbers of rebels were imprisoned in England.

News of the executions began to turn popular opinion in favor of the Rising and against the British; Shaw remarked that by executing the rebels, the brutal and foolish British leaders had canonized them. Though a pacifist himself, Shaw added that "an Irishman resorting to arms to achieve the independence of his country is doing only what Englishmen will do if it is their misfortune to be invaded and conquered by the Germans in the course of the present war" (quoted in Hickey and Doherty 1987, 529).

Drama

In the midst of these events, Lennox Robinson's comedy *The Whiteheaded Boy* was produced at the Abbey and Yeats's experimental Cúchulain play and first play for dancers, *At the Hawk's Well,* in London.

Fiction

Daniel Corkery's (1878–1964) realistic collection of stories *A Munster Twilight* appeared.

After many revisions—*Stephen Hero* was itself a promising and quite different earlier draft—and much delay, James Joyce's first novel, *A Portrait of the Artist as a Young Man,* was published. This brilliant autobiographical work employs an "embryonic" series of styles yet also achieves a classical unity. Each of its five sections ends with a sense of closure occasioned by an apparently climatic experience of the protagonist: at the end of book 1, Stephen Dedalus is cheered by his schoolmates because he has gone to the rector to complain about his unjust punishment in class; book 2 culminates in his sexual initiation with a Dublin prostitute; book 3, in the repenting Stephen's acceptance of Holy Communion; book 4, in his ecstatic, sensual, Dantesque vision of a beautiful girl wading in Dublin Bay; and book 5, in his first writings and the final diary entries dedicating himself to art and his imminent departure to Europe. Darcy O'Brien has remarked that "to say that *A Portrait* has influenced subsequent Irish writing is like saying that *A Preface to Lyrical Ballads* influenced the English romantic movement" (1976, 214).

Film

The Film Company of Ireland was founded by the Irish-American James Mark Sullivan, with John MacDonagh as its first director (de Breffny 1983, 64).

Irish Language and Literature

The original plates of Father Patrick Dineen's celebrated Irish-English dictionary, *Foclóir Gaedhilge agus Béarla* (1904), were destroyed during the Rising, necessitating a completely rewritten version that did not appear until 1927.

Literary Criticism

Ernest A. Boyd's critical study *Ireland's Literary Renaissance* appeared.
      Father Stephen Brown's (1881–1962) encyclopedic *Ireland in Fiction* was published. However, all of the copies of *Ireland in . Fiction*, housed at the General Post Office, were destroyed in the Rising, forcing a second (1919) edition.
      Thomas MacDonagh's *Literature in Ireland* was a pioneering critical study by this University College, Dublin, professor and Easter Rising leader, published following his execution in the same year, which advocated the use of Gaelic poetic techniques in

English. MacDonagh reportedly spent some time during Easter Week reading the galleys of this book, while also helping to lead the Rising.

Periodicals

The offices of the *Freeman's Journal* and its allied papers the *Evening Telegraph* and *Sport* were destroyed during the Rising (Oram 1983, 129).

Prose Nonfiction

In *The National Being* Æ advanced his co-operative, agrarian model for Irish society as earlier developed in his work with Sir Horace Plunkett.

1917

By October there were about 1,200 nationalist Sinn Féin chapters active throughout the country, with about 250,000 members organized in the largest political mass movement since Parnell's time. Holding a convention in October, they planned to elect members of Parliament who would boycott Westminster and form a Dáil Éireann in Dublin, with Eamon de Valera to preside as president.

The British prime minister, Lloyd George (1863–1945), called an Irish Convention on Home Rule, a conference that met between July 1917 and April 1918.

Fiction

Joyce wrote the first chapter of *Ulysses,* "Telemachus," depicting the interaction of Stephen Dedalus, Buck Mulligan, and the Englishman Haines in and about the Martello Tower near the south Dublin town known today as Dún Laoghaire.

The Threshold of Quiet captured the lives of "quiet desperation" in Cork observed by Daniel Corkery. Corkery's solution is not the "silence, exile, and cunning" advocated by Joyce in *A Portrait of the Artist as a Young Man,* but rather acceptance, resignation, and Catholic piety. At the end of this novel, Lily Bresnan, Corkery's heroine, enters a convent.

Poetry

Francis Ledwidge (1887–1917), a promising young nature poet from county Meath whose first published work appeared the year before, was killed in World War I in Belgium. Austin Clarke's (1896–1974) "The Vengeance of Fionn," one of his first poems, was a long narrative in epic style drawn from the legend of Diarmuid and Grainne.

Yeats married Georgie Hyde-Lees, whose automatic writing ("shorthand from the gods," or parapsychological free writing tapping into the unconscious) immediately began to influence his poetry and played a crucial role in *A Vision* (1924).

1918

Irish abandonment of involvement in or cooperation with the English Parliament was encouraged by the death in March of John Redmond, the leader of the Irish Parliamentary party, who had earlier lost credibility by encouraging Irish participation in the British war effort.

After months of resentment over British prime minister Lloyd George's attempts to enact military conscription of Irishmen and withhold Irish Home Rule, Sinn Féin won a landslide victory in the December election, winning seventy-three Irish seats and moving toward formation of the Dáil Éireann.

One of the surviving leaders of the 1916 Easter Rising, Eamon de Valera, was establishing himself as a leading force in the nationalist movement. He declared in an interview in the *Christian Science Monitor* in this year, "Irishmen will never fight as slaves. . . . England is guilty in Ireland of all the crimes she alleges against Germany. There is not a single crime ever committed by a strong nation against a weak that cannot be illustrated and paralleled from the catalogue of England's crimes in Ireland" (*Eamon de Valera States His Case*, 1918, 1).

Partly in recognition of women's efforts in World War I auxiliary organizations, and partly as the result of years of struggle, the Representation of the People Act granted the vote in national elections to women over the age of thirty.

Architecture

R. M. Butler designed University College in central Dublin (de Breffny 1983, 30).

Drama

Written four years earlier, Joyce's only play, *Exiles,* was published —and produced in the following year in Munich (and only rarely since then). In what Joyce called "three cat-and-mouse acts," Richard Rowan and Robert Hand vie for the love of Bertha, Richard's wife. Richard was a version of Joyce, and Bertha of Nora Joyce, while Robert was an amalgamation of Joyce's friends Oliver St. John Gogarty, Vincent Cograve, Thomas Kettle, and Roberto Prezioso (Ellmann 1982, 356). The basic premise of the play had its source in Joyce's visit to Dublin in 1909. As linked to *Ulysses* and Joyce's letters to Nora, a major theme of the play is Richard's simultaneous passion for Bertha yet fascination with the possibility of her infidelity.

Lennox Robinson's play at the Abbey, *The Lost Leader,* rested on the premise that Parnell had in fact survived and was living in the west of Ireland under the name of Lucious Lenihan.

Fiction

The Valley of the Squinting Windows, the first novel of Brinsley MacNamara (John Weldon, 1890–1963), became a cause célèbre; it was "publicly burned in the best medieval fashion in Delvin" (Hogan 1980, 418), his hometown in county Westmeath, immortalizing the virulent reaction of many in the town. It recounts the townspeople's disdain for the characters' love affairs; more memorable than the story itself was MacNamara's unforgettable image of the Free State as captured in his stodgy, nosy, bourgeois townspeople, personified in their "squinting" windows.

In *A Story Teller's Holiday,* a collection of short stories and novellas, George Moore—in contrast to his earlier collection *The*

Untilled Field (1903)—adopted more of the style of a *seanchaí* or oral storyteller.
Installments of Joyce's *Ulysses* began to appear in the *Little Review.*

Irish Language and Literature

Pádraic Ó Conaire's *Seacht mBuaidh an Eirghe-Amach* (Seven battles of rebellion) was a collection of stories focused on 1916.

Periodicals

An tÓglach (The volunteer) succeeded the *Irish Volunteer* as the newspaper of the Irish Volunteers and was published until the end of the Civil War four years later (Hickey and Doherty 1987, 435).

Poetry

James Stephens's *Reincarnations,* a volume of poems inspired by (and in some respects translations of) Gaelic poems of earlier periods, showed the influence of Douglas Hyde's earlier *Love Songs of Connacht* (1893).

1919

In January the Dáil Éireann met in the Mansion House in Dublin and elected Eamon de Valera (still in prison after his arrest for subversive activities in previous years) as president and Cathal Brugha (1874–1922) as acting president; in the following month de Valera escaped from prison and spent the second half of the year in the United States. A raid by Republican opponents of British rule on Royal Irish Constabulary quarters began the Anglo-Irish War, and the assassination of Lord French, the lord lieutenant of Ireland, was unsuccessfully attempted in December.

Drama

Lennox Robinson returned to the Abbey, serving as its main director of plays until 1935.

Also in this year Robinson, Yeats, and James Stephens
founded the Dublin Drama League in an attempt to import to the
Irish theater international trends in drama, such as expressionism
(Maxwell 1984, 72, 91–92).

Yeats's Cúchulain play *The Only Jealousy of Emer* (published
in this year though not staged until 1922 in Amsterdam and 1929
at the Abbey) contained daring new experimentation with masks
and ritual action inspired by Japanese Noh drama. The play is a
morality play of sorts involving Cúchulain's struggle of conscience
caused by conflicting love and loyalty to his wife, Emer, and his
mistress, Eithne Inguba.

Fiction

Part roman à clef, part bildungsroman, part political novel, and
part romance, Eimar O'Duffy's (1893–1935) *The Wasted Island*
presented a critical view of the Easter Rising. Like O'Duffy
himself, who served with the Irish Volunteers, his protagonist,
Bernard Lascelles, joins Eoin MacNeill in opposing the Rising and
trying to stop it.

Seumas O'Kelly's (1875–1918) *The Weaver's Grave* was a
remarkable novella set in a graveyard in which an atmosphere of
pervasive mortality is established, made all the more poignant by
the fact that O'Kelly had died the year before. The graveyard is so
fully described that it becomes as important as any of the
characters who visit it in search of the correct site in which to bury
the weaver. O'Kelly's tale may have influenced Máirtín Ó Cadhain
in his later great novel in Irish, *Cré na Cille* (Churchyard clay,
1949).

Irish Language and Literature

Pádraic Ó Conaire's collection of stories *An Crann Géagach* (The
branching tree) appeared.

Periodicals

The *Irish Statesman,* later edited by Æ (beginning in 1923),

became a major Irish literary and critical forum through the
1920s, publishing Liam O'Flaherty and many other important
Irish writers.
Darrell Figgis (1892–1925) edited the *Republic* from June to
September.
Dáil Éireann's *Irish Bulletin* was edited by Frank Gallagher,
Desmond Fitzgerald (1888–1947), and Erskine Childers (1870–
1922) up until 1921 (Kain 1962, 196).

Poetry

Yeats's *The Wild Swans at Coole* contained some of his most
celebrated poems, including "Easter 1916."
The Complete Poems of Francis Ledwidge appeared.
Ledwidge, a native of county Meath, had died on the Belgian front
two years earlier at the age of twenty-six (Hickey and Doherty
1987, 303). He wrote some fine short lyrics, including an elegy to
his friend Thomas MacDonagh, executed after the 1916 Easter
Rising ("He shall not hear the bittern cry . . .").

Prose Nonfiction

A little-known Irish laborer and activist named Seán O'Casey
published *The Story of the Irish Citizen Army,* a short history of
this army—which had been begun by the labor movement to
protect union members from attacks by management thugs during
the 1913 lockout (when O'Casey served as its secretary) and then
joined forces, under James Connolly, with the Irish Volunteers in
the 1916 Easter Rising. O'Casey was highly critical, however, of
this latter involvement, seeing it as part of the cooptation of
socialism by the forces of nationalism during the World War I era.
He declared in his preface: "It appears certain that Nationalism
has gained a great deal and lost a little by its union with Labour in
the Insurrection of Easter Week, and that Labour has lost much
and achieved nothing by its avowal of the National aspirations of
the Irish Nation" (vi). The fifteen pounds that O'Casey was paid
by his publisher was the first sum of money that he had ever
earned with his pen, but "most of it went to pay for his mother's
funeral" (Kain 1962, 118–19).

1920

In January the first "Black and Tans"—auxiliary British troops nicknamed after the colors of their uniforms—were recruited in response to Irish resistance to British rule, and a brutal guerrilla war (the Anglo-Irish War) with the underground Irish Republican Army (IRA) in the countryside accelerated. The Republican mayor of Cork, Terence MacSwiney (b. 1879), went on a seventy-four-day hunger strike in Brixton Jail in London and died in October, becoming a national hero and provoking the outrage even of James Joyce (who wrote angry letters about it from Trieste, Italy). In November the IRA killed eleven unarmed British officers in Dublin; later that same day, Black and Tans fired into a Dublin football crowd and killed twelve people. Michael Collins (1890–1922) directed anti-British espionage. In December, Black and Tan soldiers set fires in Cork City and caused three million pounds of damage (Kain 1962, 196).

At the end of the year the Government of Ireland Act provided for two Irish parliaments, one in Dublin governing twenty-six counties and one in Belfast for the six most Protestant northern counties.

Fiction

Daniel Corkery's *The Hounds of Banba* contained stories portraying the Anglo-Irish War from a nationalist point of view. Corkery was much influenced by Turgenev, further encouraging the reverberations of Russian fiction among Irish writers (particularly Corkery's students Frank O'Connor and Seán O'Faoláin).

In sharp counterpoint to Corkery's positive view of the struggle for Irish independence, Brinsley MacNamara's *The Clanking of Chains* depicted a Sinn Féin idealist trapped in the town of Ballycullen with its stultifying, small-town social hiearchies.

James Joyce moved to Paris.

Irish Language and Literature

The first novel of Séamus Ó Grianna (1891–1969)—often known

as "Máire" after the name of the fictional female narrator of most of his books—*Mo Dhá Róisín* (My two Roseens), was a romantic tale of the Easter Rising in Dublin.

1921

A truce was agreed to in July, and a treaty conference met in London in October. On 6 December an Anglo-Irish Treaty was signed, providing for dominion status and virtual domestic independence for the twenty-six southern counties and the full maintenance within the Union of the six most Protestant northern counties. However, this treaty would not settle these issues, but rather perpetuate strife and controversy over the coming months and decades. A columnist in the *Irish Review* spoke for many when writing in the following year, "As a vague threat partition was universally unpopular in Ireland—as an accomplished fact it will bring consequences that will be calamitous to both north and south" (1, no. 2 [11 November]: 15).

The Communist party of Ireland was founded with Roderic Connolly (1901–), James Connolly's son, as its first president. This organization remained small but included such members as Liam O'Flaherty, Peadar O'Donnell (1893–1986), and others (Hickey and Doherty 1987, 85).

Fiction

Gerald O'Donovan's novel *Vocations* described a new Irish social order according to which the Catholic church interacted with farmers, grocers, and publicans in a powerful alliance promoting public conservatism and private advancement. Benedict Kiely (1919–) later remarked that the "terrible beauty" of Easter 1916 had resulted merely in "a grocers' republic."

Edith Somerville's novel *An Enthusiast* suggested that its author felt it was impossible for a former Ascendancy landlord to survive in this brave new Irish world: at the end Dan Palliser rushes to the scene of an Irish rebel attack on the home of the woman he loves, intending to save her, and is shot dead by her husband, who fires from his window at the rebels.

Periodicals

Evidence that the Irish Republican Army continued to gear up for further struggle was reflected in the December issue of *Oglāigh na hÉireann* (Volunteers of Ireland), the officers' staff journal, which contained such contributions as Major Kelly's "Notes on the Tactical Employment of the Thompson Submachine in Guerilla Warfare" (1, no. 2: 12–16).

Poetry

Yeats's *Michael Robartes and the Dancer* was marked by his theory of opposites and included such visionary poems as "The Second Coming" and "A Prayer for My Daughter." Concerning Ireland and the wider world in the 1920s and 1930s, "The Second Coming" would seem prophetic: "What rough beast, its hour come round at last, / Slouches towards Bethlehem to be born?"

The poet and Gaelic scholar Austin Clarke, who had succeeded Thomas MacDonagh in his professorship at University College, Dublin, following MacDonagh's execution in 1916, was fired from the job when the administration learned he had been married in a registry office rather than a Catholic church. His volume of poems *The Sword of the West* was published in this year.

1922

The Anglo-Irish Treaty was approved by Dáil Éireann by a small majority (sixty-four to fifty-seven) in January, but opponents led by Eamon de Valera—bitterly upset not only by the political partition of Ireland but by the required oath of allegiance to England—withdrew and the stage was set for the guerrilla Civil War of 1922–23 between supporters of the treaty ("Free Staters") and their opponents ("Irregulars"). Treaty supporter Kevin O'Higgins (1892–1927) defined the opposition to the new government as 20 percent idealism, 20 percent crime, and 60 percent "sheer futility." In contrast, de Valera famously claimed (despite electoral majorities repudiating the claim) that he could "examine my own heart and it told me straight off what the Irish people wanted" (quoted in Foster 1988, 508–9).

In January Liam O'Flaherty and a small army of unemployed men seized the Rotunda government building in Dublin and raised a red flag in protest over the unemployment of 30,000 Irish citizens. Driven out after four days, O'Flaherty fled first to Cork and then to London. Later he wrote in *Shame the Devil* (1934): "Ever since then, I have remained, in the eyes of the vast majority of Irish men and women, a public menace to faith, morals and property, a Communist, an atheist, a scoundrel of the worst type. . . . Crave forgiveness? Clip the wings of my fancies, in order to win the favour of the mob? To have property and be esteemed? Better to be devoured by the darkness than to be haunted by dolts into an inferior light" (21–22, 23). O'Flaherty then briefly joined Rory O'Connor and the IRA in the government courts on the Liffey River, the Four Courts, in their equally futile attempt to overthrow the new Free State forces. Soon thereafter, O'Flaherty abandoned his activism and turned to writing.

At this point the twenty-six counties had four different "governments" (not to mention the separate Ulster government): the already existing Dáil with Arthur Griffith as president, the newly formed provisional Free State government under Michael Collins, the disaffected Republicans under Eamon de Valera, and the Irish Republican Army under Rory O'Connor. In April O'Connor and the IRA occupied the Four Courts in Dublin and refused to recognize the new government; the Free State army subsequently stormed the building and recaptured it. In a last-ditch, futile attempt to avoid armed conflict, Collins and de Valera agreed in May to mount a coalition slate in the upcoming election, but Collins's government renounced the deal in June and fifty-eight Free Staters and thirty-four supporters of de Valera (who would boycott the new parliament) were elected. In August Arthur Griffith died and Michael Collins was killed (in a secret Republican ambush that even today stirs strong passions throughout the country); thereafter W. T. Cosgrave took over as head of the Free State government until 1932. In September 1922 the Dáil gave Free State leaders emergency powers permitting the execution of leading opponents. The Free State was officially established on 6 December.

In the 1922 elections, seventeen of the eighteen Labour party candidates were elected and Labour won 21.4 percent of the overall national vote—more than the antitreaty supporters of de

Valera (Foster 1988, 514). This was the best the Labour party would ever do, however: to this day it has remained a small minority party whose influence is increased only by the fact that the two dominant parties (Fianna Fáil and Fine Gael) often need to form a coalition with Labour in order to have the votes necessary to form a government.

W. B. Yeats became one of the first members of the new Irish Senate. He would serve in more than a titular role, often advocating unpopular positions such as the legalization of divorce.

The Garda Siochana (Guardians of the peace) were established as an unarmed peacekeeping force in the Free State, under the original title of Civic Guards, while the Royal Ulster Constabulary (RUC) were formed as the equivalent police force in Northern Ireland (Hickey and Doherty 1987, 187, 512). The fact that the Garda were unarmed while the RUC were armed says something about the contrasting levels of popular support for the governments in place in the South and the North.

Fiction

Sylvia Beach made possible the book publication on 2 February, Joyce's fortieth birthday, of *Ulysses,* parts of which had earlier appeared periodically in the *Little Review.* In addition to encyclopedic coverage of dozens—indeed, hundreds—of minor Dublin characters, Joyce's masterly, radically innovative novel includes three early chapters focusing on the now aimless Stephen Dedalus, the protagonist of *A Portrait of the Artist as a Young Man,* and fifteen more attending mainly to Leopold and Molly Bloom, a thirty-eight-year-old Jewish newspaper canvasser and his wife, a singer. In the course of a single day Leopold cooks breakfast for Molly, visits the public baths, attends a funeral, goes about his work at the newspaper, eats lunch and dinner, visits a couple of pubs, continues a titillating correspondence with another woman, is sexually excited by a young woman at the beach, endures some anti-Semitism, worries about the affair Molly is having, meets the drunken Stephen at a party in a hospital, and finally rescues him from a whorehouse and a scrape in the street with an English soldier, taking him home to sober him up before he goes on his way. Before encountering Leopold, Stephen leaves the Martello tower where he has been staying with his eccentric friend Buck Mulligan, teaches his morning class at a school in Dalkey, walks along Sandymount Strand, delivers his schoolmaster's letter to the editor of Leopold's newspaper, and then drinks and carouses the rest of the day. Molly stays home all day, makes love in the late afternoon to the manager of her singing tour, and eventually lies in bed thinking after Leopold comes home. The delicious Homeric parallels and parodies have been copiously traced: Leopold as Ulysses, Stephen as his unwittingly faithful "son," Telemachus; Molly as his certainly not conventionally faithful wife, Penelope (as well as Calypso); Nestor transformed into Stephen's bigoted schoolmaster; Proteus into language beside the Irish Sea; the Cyclops into a bad drunk; Nausicaa into a young woman who has read too many romances; Circe into a whorehouse madam; and so on. Joyce had explained to a friend in Paris five years earlier, "The most beautiful, all-embracing theme is that of the Odyssey. It is greater, more human, than that of *Hamlet, Don Quixote,* Dante, *Faust.* . . . The most beautiful, most human traits are contained in the Odyssey. I was twelve years old when we took up the Trojan War at school; only the Odyssey stuck in my memory. I want to be frank: at twelve I liked the supernaturalism in Ulysses. When I was writing *Dubliners,* I intended at first to choose the title *Ulysses in Dublin,* but gave up the idea. In Rome, when I had finished about half the *Portrait,* I realized that the Odyssey had to be the sequel, and I began to write *Ulysses*" (quoted in Ellmann 1982, 416). After *Ulysses* Irish and world literature would never be the same again.

Irish Language and Literature

The Irish National Schools began following a new curriculum requiring the teaching of the Irish language, at the expense of elementary science, nature study, hygiene, home economics, and drawing (each of which was eliminated in order to free time for the new emphasis on Irish). "Public notice no. 4" mandated that "the Irish language shall be taught or used as a medium of instruction for not less than one full hour each day in all national schools where there is a teacher competent to teach it." The most extreme (and unrealistic) recommendation was that "in the two grades of the infant class the work be conducted entirely in the Irish language" (quoted in Akenson 1975, 42, 44). Thus began many years of required Irish in schools, which was resented by many speakers of English much as required English had been resented by Irish speakers a century earlier in government schools during British rule. As Osborn Bergin (1873–1950), professor of Early Irish at Trinity College, Dublin, later noted about the attempt to revive Irish, "Today the people leave the problem to the Government, the Government leaves it to the Department of Education, the Department of Education to the teachers and the teachers to the school-children" (quoted in T. Brown 1985, 53).

Periodicals

Erskine Childers edited *Poblacht na hÉireann* (Republic of Ireland) from January to June. *War News* appeared until the following March (Kain 1962, 197, 198). Childers was executed by the Free State in November, for possession of a revolver, as was IRA leader Rory O'Connor (b. 1883) in December, in reprisal for the assassination of Free State politician Seán Hales.

Dublin Opinion, a satirical monthly that ran until 1972, was begun by Arthur Collins.

P. S. O'Hegarty edited the nationalist newspaper the *Separatist* for six months.

Cathal O'Shannon began the *Voice of Labour*—later the *Irishman* (1927–30) and then the *Watchword of Labour* (1930–32)—as an organ of the Labour party and the trade union movement (Hickey and Doherty 1987, 138, 527, 593).

Poetry

Chronicles and Poems of Percy French (1854–1920) included such popular songs as the still well-known "The Mountains of Mourne" (Deane et al. 1991, 2: 104).

1923

De Valera ordered a suspension of the Irregulars' campaign in April.

Free State leader W. T. Cosgrave founded the Cumann na nGaedheal (Society of the Gaels) party, which he led until its reorganization as Fine Gael ten years later.

James Larkin founded the Irish Workers' League, which replaced the Communist party of Ireland as the Irish section of the Communist Comintern, and was later absorbed by Larkin's Workers' Union of Ireland (Hickey and Doherty 1987, 268).

Writing on "The Lessons of Revolution" in *Studies*, Æ argued that "the champions of physical force have, I am sure, without intent, poisoned the soul of Ireland. All that was exquisite and lovable is dying. They have squandered a spirit created by poets, scholars and patriots of a different order, spending the treasure lavishly as militarists in all lands do, thinking little of what they squander save that it gives a transitory gilding to their propaganda" (12 [March]: 4).

Drama

Seán O'Casey made an auspicious debut at the Abbey with the first of his three great Dublin plays, *The Shadow of a Gunman,* the story of two foolish roommates, Seumas Shields and Donal Davoren, in working-class Dublin during the Anglo-Irish War. Davoren is a would-be poet who eventually is left lamenting his own egotism that allowed him to let people think that he was a gunman on the run, and his cowardice for hiding in his room while Minnie Powell sacrifices herself to protect him when British soldiers arrive. Intermixed in this play were comedy, tragedy, and Irish-English dialogue in a new blend unique to O'Casey and preceded only by Synge's *The Playboy of the Western World* (1907). Joseph Holloway felt that "what it lacked in dramatic construction, it certainly pulled up in telling dialogue of the most topical and biting kind, and the audience revelled in the telling talk" (Hogan and O'Neill 1967, 215).

Film

Foreshadowing the more notorious Censorship of Publications Act six years later, the lesser known Censorship of Films Act established a film censor with "power to cut or refuse a licence to

films which, in his opinion, were 'subversive of public morality' "
(Whyte 1971, 36).

Periodicals

Seamus O'Sullivan founded and persistently edited the *Dublin Magazine,* which provided for more than thirty years (ceasing only with O'Sullivan's death in 1958) an important forum and means of publication for Irish writers, comparable in the 1920s to Seán O'Faoláin's *Bell* in the 1940s. It published such writers as James Stephens, Liam O'Flaherty, Brinsley MacNamara, Pádraic Fallon, and Austin Clarke. The first volume alone, without any editorial pronouncement or self-congratulation, offered works by such excellent writers as Patraic Colum, Stephens, O'Flaherty, Lennox Robinson, John Eglinton, Æ, and Clarke.

Meanwhile, at Horace Plunkett's request, Æ took over as editor of the *Irish Statesman,* rejuvenating it and turning it into the other Dublin literary journal of quality and conscience during the 1920s. Æ argued that Irish writers and thinkers should adopt an international view, advocated a merged Anglo-Irish and Gaelic cultural melting-pot version of Ireland, and tirelessly opposed Irish xenophobia and the close-minded side of "Irish Ireland," much as O'Faoláin would also do later. Describing his own point of view (in the third person) in his first issue of 15 September, Æ noted in "A Confession of Faith" that he would be "even more interested in the future than in the past, and he hopes that this journal may help to create alluring images of the future society and the moulds into which it will be cast, and for this purpose he has enlisted the cooperation of many of the best writers and thinkers in this country."

Poetry

With sixteen years of great poems still ahead of him, Yeats was awarded the Nobel Prize for Literature.

Oliver St. John Gogarty's volume *An Offering of Swans* appeared.

1924

The Irish Transport and General Workers' Union expelled James Larkin, lately returned from the United States, from the union he had created in 1908 because of his socialism; other ITGWU leaders had moved to the right of Larkin during his years away from Ireland. His brother Peter formed the Workers' Union of Ireland, and two-thirds of the ITGWU membership, in a measure of Larkin's support, transferred to the new union (Ellis 1973, 268). The Irish labor movement was marked by increasing factionalism and began to decline.

Prohibition never came to Ireland. An Irish version was the Intoxicating Liquor Act, which reduced the hours that pubs could be open (Whyte 1971, 36).

Drama

Matching the mood of the time, T. C. Murray's *Autumn Fire* was a despairing play comparable to Eugene O'Neill's *Desire under the Elms* in its focus on the love of a father and son for the same woman.

Set in the midst of the Irish Civil War, O'Casey's *Juno and the Paycock* powerfully exposed Irish male bravado in the form of pathetic "Captain" Jack Boyle and his sidekick, Joxer Daly, and countered it with the feminist actions and vision of Boyle's wife, Juno. Juno leaves home at the end of the play, after their son Johnny has been killed in the war, to care for their daughter Mary, whom even her old socialist boyfriend, Jerry Devine, rejects when he learns that she has become pregnant out of wedlock by Charles Bentham, the English opportunist who has abandoned her. Wrote Joseph Holloway in his journal, "The last act is intensely tragic and heart-rendingly real to those who passed through the terrible period of 1922. . . . The tremendous tragedy of Act III swept all before it, and made the doings on the stage real and thrilling in their intensity. The acting all round was of the highest quality, not one in the long cast being misplaced or for a moment out of the picture" (Hogan and O'Neill 1967, 226). Added a reviewer in *Studies,* "Since *The Playboy* was produced at the Abbey almost twenty years ago, it may safely be said that no play staged there has aroused as much interest as *Juno and the Paycock"* (493). Shaw's play *St. Joan* achieved a huge success in London.

Fiction

Liam O'Flaherty's first volume of stories, *Spring Sowing,* appeared. In such stories as "The Cow's Death," written under the advice of the London editor Edward Garnett, O'Flaherty wrote some of the best animal stories and best naturalistic stories of the century (see Cahalan 1991).

The Loughsiders was Shan Bullock's belated sequel to *The Squireen* (1903). In this novel an arranged marriage is refused; Richard Jebb gets his revenge on Rachel Nixon for refusing to marry him, however, by eventually marrying her widowed mother, thereby obtaining her family farm after all.

Irish Language and Literature

Séamus Ó Grianna's novel *Caisleáin Óir* (Castles of gold) focused on a Donegal man who, after he returns home after many years in America to look for the woman he loved, finds her, but they fail to recognize each other. Learning her identity, Séimi realizes that he can't go home again to depopulated rural Gaelic Ireland, and so he leaves town on foot, passing an old man who mutters, "Tá sé fuar" (It is cold). Séimi can only agree, and face his permanent exile.

There were now only 139 local branches of the Gaelic League whereas two years earlier there had been 819 (T. Brown 1985, 54).

Writing in the *Catholic Bulletin* in April, priest and professor Timothy Corcoran (who could not himself speak Irish) typified the type of culturally conservative Free State mentality later lampooned by Myles na Gopaleen: "The Irish nation is the Gaelic nation; its language and literature of the Gaelic language; its history is the history of the Gael. All other elements have no place in Irish national life, literature and tradition, save as far as they are assimilated into the very substance of Gaelic speech, life and thought" (quoted in T. Brown 1985, 63).

Literary Criticism

James Joyce's friend Herbert Gorman published a pioneering critical study entitled *James Joyce: The First Forty Years.*

Periodicals

Liam O'Flaherty played a part in starting *Tomorrow,* a periodical edited by Francis Stuart and Cecil Salkeld, which lasted for just two issues before encountering a controversy surrounding its publication of Lennox Robinson's story "The Madonna of Slieve Dun," about a country girl who thinks that she is about to give birth to a new messiah (Denman 1987, 128). *Tomorrow* published pieces by Yeats (including his sexually bold poem "Leda and the Swan"), Joseph Campbell, and Margaret Barrington (1896–1982).

Poetry

F. R. Higgins's (1896–1941) first volume, *Salt Air,* was published. Higgins remained a gifted poet who—like several other writers of the time—was strongly influenced and overshadowed by Yeats.

Prose Nonfiction

Daniel Corkery's *The Hidden Ireland: A Study of Gaelic Ireland in the Eighteenth Century* championed past Gaelic literature and civilization, lamented its erosion in the face of the rise of the Anglo-Irish Ascendancy, and encouraged a return to Gaelic culture.

Yeats's *A Vision,* filled with prose and diagrams, was the culmination and expression of his mystical system.

1925

The Irish Republican Army split from Sinn Féin, whose leader, Eamon de Valera, formed (in the following year) a new party, so that he could enter the Irish parliament. The true radicals dedicated to a thirty-two-county Irish republic thus parted company with de Valera, who became increasingly conservative.

Yeats delivered a much noted speech in the Senate defending the right to divorce, "but he seems chiefly to have aroused disgust among those not already of his way of thinking." Political leaders ensured the opposite of what Yeats advocated: "Mr Cosgrave refused to legalise divorce; Mr de Valera made it unconstitutional" (Whyte 1971, 59–60).

Architecture

The Royal Dublin Society buildings in Ballsbridge were designed by the firm of O'Callaghan, Webb, and Giron (de Breffny 1983, 30).

Drama

Following Yeats two years earlier, Shaw became the second Irish winner of the Nobel Prize for Literature.

The Abbey Theatre accepted a subsidy from the Free State (850 pounds in the first year, increased to 1,000 pounds in the following year), becoming the first state-supported theater in the English-speaking world and belying its increasing conservatism. The subsidy was largely due to the influence of Ernest Blythe (1889–1975), a northern Protestant, Irish-language advocate, Abbey enthusiast, and member of the new Free State Executive Council (Maxwell 1984, 93). Blythe was to join the Abbey board in the 1930s and remain a very influential figure at the Abbey during its midcentury, most conservative phase.

Fiction

Much influenced by Maria Edgeworth's *Castle Rackrent* (1800) and by the gothic tradition, Edith Somerville's *The Big House of Inver* was a Big House chronicle novel delving far back into the Prendeville family history in order to learn how the protagonist was reduced to the status of "Shibby Pindy," a dispossessed peasant aristocrat, a "strange mixture of distinction and commonness" (quoted in Flanagan 1966, 75). This novel was the Ascendancy's death knell, though effective Big House novels would continue to be written. *The Informer* was Liam O'Flaherty's best-known novel. Its protagonist, Gypo Nolan, is a poor lumbering, animalistic man who informs on a rebel for a 20-pound reward and is ultimately and inevitably destroyed. This novel draws on O'Flaherty's knowledge of the Irish political scene just after the Civil War, borrows from the "thriller" formula of suspense fiction, and was subsequently immortalized on the Hollywood screen by John Ford in a very popular 1935 film.

Storm was Peadar O'Donnell's first novel, an apprentice work with a protagonist suspiciously resembling himself—a schoolteacher who eventually leaves his island off the western coast to join the nationalist struggle.

Periodicals

The IRA began *An Phoblacht* (The republic), a newspaper edited by Peadar O'Donnell. Contributors included Frank Gallagher (1898–1962) and Frank Ryan (1902–44), who was later an editor.

1926

Accommodating himself to the political processes of the Free State, Eamon de Valera founded a new political party, Fianna Fáil (Soldiers of destiny), with plans to enter the Dáil.

Census data showed that in the Free State over 800,000 people were living in overcrowded conditions (with more than two people per room)—many of them in North Dublin City, where the average mortality rate was 25.6 per 1,000 for children between the ages of one and five (T. Brown 1985, 16).

Drama

The biggest public outcry in Dublin over a play since Synge's *Playboy* in 1907 was provoked by O'Casey's *The Plough and the Stars,* which portrayed the 1916 Easter Rising with uncompromis-

ing realism from the point of view of the working classes, who in
April 1916 viewed the Rising not as a great nationalist apocalypse
but as an opportunity to loot the shops. In 1916 the Irish people in
general had been equally apathetic, but by 1926, by virtue of pious
hindsight, they had come to revere the event and would brook no
such uncomplimentary picture of it; even O'Casey's fellow socialist and realist Liam O'Flaherty, along with the poets Austin Clarke
and F. R. Higgins, attacked the play in letters to the *Irish
Statesman,* with Yeats defiantly defending O'Casey and the play
much as he had nineteen years earlier defended Synge and the
Playboy. On 11 February Joseph Holloway wrote in his journal,
"alas, tonight's protest has made a second *Playboy* of *The Plough
and the Stars,* and Yeats was in his element at last" (Hogan and
O'Neill 1967, 254). O'Casey's most celebrated drama, the *Plough*
includes such memorable characters as the self-parodic socialist
"Young Covey," the Falstaffian Fluther Good, the Irish volunteer
Jack Clitheroe and his wife, Nora (who is driven mad by his
death), and Bessie Burgess, a hardheaded Protestant neighbor who
is shot dead trying to protect Catholic Nora from British gunfire
and after speaking some of the strongest lines of the play in sharp
indictment of the violence of the Rising. Lady Gregory described
one of the play's first performances in her journal: "When the
disturbance began and [Lennox Robinson] wanted to call for the
police he found . . . the telephone had been closed up. But at last
the Civic Guards came and carried the woman [protestor] off the
stage and the play went on without interruption to the end. At the
end of the second act, a good many people had thought it was not
to be resumed and had gone, and the disturbers had seized their
places and kept up the noise from there while some climbed on to
the stage breaking two lamps and tearing a piece out of the curtain
and attacked the actresses. . . . I thought the play very fine indeed" (Kilroy 1975, 27–28).

Lennox Robinson's Abbey play *The Big House* focused on the
opposite end of Irish society from the Dublin proletariat in
O'Casey's *Plough:* the increasingly alienated Anglo-Irish Ascendancy. Kate Alcock, the play's heroine, is depressed about the
cultural divide separating Anglo-Irish people such as herself from
the Catholic population of the country, but is convinced that she
is as Irish as anyone and remains determined to rebuild her
family's decaying Big House. The play was well received by its

audiences, though some Catholic Free Staters attacked it—and were met by a spirited defense by Æ in his *Irish Statesman:* "We do not want uniformity in our culture or our ideals, but the balancing of our diversities in a wide tolerance. . . . Many who saw *The Big House* felt a liberating thrill at the last outburst of Kate Alcock" (quoted in T. Brown 1985, 120).

Fiction

Liam O'Flaherty's second volume of stories, *The Tent,* included such biting studies of peasant life as "The Outcast," the account of a young woman who has had a baby out of wedlock, visits the parish priest looking for help, is scorned by him, and commits suicide. His novel *Mr. Gilhooley* depicted a man who tries to care for, reform, and live with a young prostitute, but ends up strangling her after she cannot return his feelings for her.

Like its sequels in the "Cuanduine trilogy," *The Spacious Adventures of the Man in the Street* (1928) and *Asses in Clover* (1933), Eimar O'Duffy's *King Goshawk and the Birds* was a marvelous, unfairly neglected novel in which he combined Swiftian satire on contemporary Ireland with entertaining fantasy. In *Goshawk* the ancient hero Cúchulainn appears in modern Dublin to do battle with evil King Goshawk (who charges people money to hear birds sing), play tennis at the Bon Ton Suburban Tennis Club, and observe the battles of Dublin's two mirror-image political parties, the Yallogreens and Greenyallows (send-ups of the Cumann na nGaedheal, which would become Fine Gael, and the Fianna Fáil parties). In *The Spacious Adventures,* Aloysius O'Kennedy (whose body had been borrowed by Cúchulainn in *Goshawk*) is transported to the planet of Rathé (an anagram of "Earth"), where the natives freely share sex with everyone but are "monophagous," eating just one fruit all their lives and viewing fruit consumption as an intensely private, often sinful activity. In *Asses in Clover* O'Duffy returns to Dublin in order to deliver scathing satires of military, economic, and other matters.

Irish Language and Literature

An Gúm (The plan) was founded by the Free State government as a publisher of books in Irish. However, An Gúm proved to be very conservative, publishing many more translations and imitations of the classics—seemingly aimed at "children or nuns," in the acerbic view of the fiction writer Máirtín Ó Cadhain (1971, 147)—than new writings of any quality.

The government-funded Radio Éireann began broadcasting from Dublin (and in the following year from Cork); Radio Éireann reinforced—especially after 1933 when a high-powered station opened in Athlone—the dominance of spoken English throughout the country (T. Brown 1985, 153). This was partially offset only many years later, in 1972, by the establishment of an Irish-language radio station.

Periodicals

The *Irish Hammer and Plough* was the weekly of the Workers' Union of Ireland, begun in this year by Roderic Connolly and other survivors of the now-defunct Communist party of Ireland (Hickey and Doherty 1987, 609).

The closing of the Maunsel publishing company—which had earlier published Yeats, Æ, and many of the Anglo-Irish writers of the Literary Revival (yet refused to print Joyce's *Dubliners*)—reflected the slippage of Anglo-Irish hegemony in Irish writing and publishing.

Poetry

James Stephens's *Collected Poems* appeared.

1927

Fianna Fáil won forty-four seats in the Dáil to the forty-seven of the government party (subsequently restructured in 1933 as Fine Gael), and their representatives entered the Dáil, taking the required oath—earlier so vehemently opposed by de Valera—with the rationalization that it was a meaningless ritual.

Kevin O'Higgins, a noted Free State minister (and hero of Yeats), was assassinated by members of the IRA in July.

A second Intoxicating Liquor Act made provisions for reducing the massive number of licensed premises in Ireland (Whyte 1971, 36). It met with little success.

Drama

The small, experimental Peacock Theatre was created by renovations within the Abbey premises. Yeats's play *The Resurrection* focused on the bizarre struggle of a Greek, a Hebrew, and a Syrian over Christ following his Crucifixion. The Hebrew believes Christ to have been only a man; the Greek, a phantom. Yet both doubting Thomases must confront the bizarre image of the beating heart of the image of Christ at the end of the play.

Brinsley MacNamara's comedy *Look at the Heffernans!* enjoyed a successful debut at the Abbey.

Folklore

An Cumann le Béaloideas Éireann (The society for Irish folklore) began its work collecting folklore throughout the countryside, which would grow into the largest single national folklore collection in the world.

Irish Language and Literature

A revised edition of Father Patrick Dineen's celebrated Irish-English dictionary, *Foclóir Gaedhilge agus Béarla* (1904), was published.

When the Irish enthusiast Una MacClintok Dix complained in the *Irish Statesman* that Liam O'Flaherty did not write in Irish—thereby repeating earlier (and inaccurate) complaints made elsewhere by Padraic Colum and Walter Chambers—O'Flaherty's reply, a letter entitled "Writing in Gaelic," was the most bitter piece of writing he ever published. In no uncertain terms, he explained that he had written a Gaelic play (*Dorchadas* [Darkness], 1925) and won a schoolboy prize for an essay in Irish, that native-English-speaking zealots such as Dix and Colum had no business criticizing him, and that "all the best Irish patriots live in America" (quoted in Cahalan 1991, 16–17, 120–22).

Poetry

James Joyce's *Pomes Penyeach* appeared.

1928

Drama

The Abbey Theatre betrayed its newfound conservatism by reject-
ing two remarkable (and since, much-celebrated) plays, Seán
O'Casey's experimental World War I play, *The Silver Tassie,* and
Denis Johnston's (1901–84) *The Old Lady Says "No!"* (a phantas-
magoric farce swirling around the figure of the Irish rebel Robert
Emmet). Yeats felt that O'Casey had better stick to Dublin;
O'Casey responded by breaking with the Abbey and remaining in
England, where he had been staying since 1926—he made his
home in Devon for the rest of his life. Johnston's play was staged
by the Gate Theatre in the following year (see 1929 entry).

Determined to bring to Dublin the continental classics that
the Abbey had been avoiding for years, the new Gate Theatre
(founded by the English actor-director Hilton Edwards [1903–82]
and the Irish actor and artist Micheál MacLiammóir) staged
Ibsen's *Peer Gynt* as their first production. Edwards and
MacLiammóir established themselves, and long endured, as the
Irish theatrical Gilbert and Sullivan or Rodgers and Hammerstein
of their day, even though the bubbly Gael and the brilliant
Anglo-Irishman made a strange pair. MacLiammóir was one of
the most talented actors and artists, not to mention director-
producers, of his time. As for Edwards, MacLiammóir recalled in
his memoir *All for Hecuba* that "his mind galloped away from a
brain that could not always take the reins and his speech from a
tongue that with all its astonishing nimbleness could not keep pace
with his thought. His energy, both physical and mental, was
apparently without limit; so, it must be said, was his patience,
especially in stage matters" (1946, 29).

Fiction

James Joyce composed "Anna Livia Plurabelle," part of what was
to become *Finnegans Wake.*

Samuel Beckett met Joyce in Paris and became his steadfast friend and follower. The connection remained close enough that subsequently Beckett was invited to court Joyce's daughter, Lucia, whose schizophrenia deepened after he could not return her infatuation—and he remained a friend of the family, serving as best man at the wedding of Joyce's grandson, Stephen, in 1955.

In his novel *Islanders* Peadar O'Donnell concentrated on the ethnography of his native county Donegal island people and their attempts to resist the tide of emigration to the Lagan Valley in county Down, to Scotland, and to America, but he imposed on his material a romantic plot of only passing interest.

James Stephens's second collection of stories, *Etched in Moonlight,* was more fabulist than his earlier, more realist *Here Are Ladies* (1913).

Irish Language and Literature

The government granted an annual subsidy (as it had to the Abbey three years earlier) to An Taibhdhearc (The theater), the new Irish-language theater in Galway founded by the ever-energetic Micheál MacLiammóir.

Music

The Reverend Richard Henebry's *A Handbook of Irish Music* appeared (Kain 1962, 199).

Poetry

Considered by many to be his greatest volume, Yeats's *The Tower* included such poems as "Sailing to Byzantium," "Leda and the Swan," and "Among School Children." "The Tower" and the great sequence "Meditations in Time of Civil War" focus on the unifying emblem of Thoor Ballylee, the tower near Lady Gregory's estate in county Galway that Yeats restored and lived in, as a literal and symbolic site of violent conflict yet also great beauty. The high point of the volume is "The Stare's Nest by My Window," where the poet beautifully synthesizes his reactions to nature and to the public, violent world. He laments that he and other Irish romantics and revolutionaries had "fed" their hearts "on fantasies," and had now "grown brutal from the fare," with "more substance" in their "enmities" than in their love. In a beautiful image, and in the midst of violence, he invites the "honey-bees" he sees near an abandoned bird's nest to "Come build in the empty house of the stare."

Wild Apples was a collection by Oliver St. John Gogarty.

Prose Nonfiction

Shaw's *The Intelligent Woman's Guide to Socialism and Capitalism* was published.

Tim Healy's *Letters and Leaders of My Day* was a characteristically partial memoir by this former deputy of Parnell who turned against Parnell and later became a Free State minister. In the previous year Liam O'Flaherty had published his sardonic *Life of Tim Healy,* noting that "When His Excellency the Governor-General heard that I was about to write his life, he humorously threatened to write my life in revenge" (quoted in Cahalan 1991, 115).

1929

The Censorship of Publications Act was passed in July. It enforced a reactionary, puritanical code on publications, banning many of the best Irish writers as well as any literature advocating birth control. It established a five-person board, chaired by a priest, with power to prohibit the sale and distribution of any book that it considered "in its general tendency indecent or obscene." J. J. Horgan (1881–1967) noted in the following year, "To attempt a censorship of modern literature . . . is not unlike trying to drink a river" (quoted in T. Brown 1985, 76). Later Merwyn Wall (1908–   ), in *The Return of Fursey* (1948), depicted a censor with two separately aimed eyes—one just for the "dirty" words and the other for everything else.

Due largely to continued high emigration rates caused by poverty, at this stage the Irish average age of marriage was the latest in the world: 34.9 for men and 29.1 for women (Foster 1988, 539).

Drama

The Abbey passed on Denis Johnston's rejected play *The Old Lady Says "No!"* along with a small subsidy to the Gate Theatre, where it was brilliantly produced in the Peacock Theatre by Hilton Edwards with Micheál MacLiammóir in the lead. Johnston claimed that his title constituted the words written on his manuscript (reputedly reporting Lady Gregory's reaction) when it came back to him from the Abbey, though it appears that the real basis of the decision was Lennox Robinson's feeling that the play would be too difficult to direct and produce. The first part of *The Old Lady Says "No!"* is a pseudohistorical pastiche about Robert Emmet and his abortive 1803 rebellion, dominated by a collage of parodies and pastiches from earlier Irish literature, including the ballads of Thomas Moore. During the remainder of the play Johnston's unfortunate hero—now lost in the 1920s, though he also has bizarre conversations with statues of public figures from earlier periods—tries to make his way to the Dublin suburb of Rathfarnham in search of Sarah Curran, his lover. Instead he encounters a series of satiric contemporary personages including "O'Cooney" (Seán O'Casey) and "O'Rooney" (Liam O'Flaherty). In the process Johnston sharply satirizes many aspects of the puritanical Free State. This play entertainingly explodes the cultural world of the time, utilizing humorously innovative, expressionist techniques to do so.

Fiction

The Mountain Tavern and Other Stories, Liam O'Flaherty's third collection, contained more stories of animal and peasant life, often set on the Aran Islands. His satiric *A Tourist's Guide to Ireland* attacked and cautioned against priests, politicians, and publicans as the dominant groups in Ireland (adding a fourth, much more sympathetic chapter on peasants as the group oppressed by the other three).

Peadar O'Donnell's *Adrigoole* was a compelling novel based on a real incident concerning a mother and her children who were found dead of starvation after the mother was shunned by her Free State neighbors following the imprisonment of her Republican husband during the Civil War. Hughie Dalach, who returns home at the end of this novel to find most of his surviving family victimized by such a fate, goes mad.

Elizabeth Bowen's (1900–73) most celebrated Irish novel, *The Last September,* focused on the effects of Irish guerrilla war on the opposite end of the social spectrum—within the county Cork Ascendancy. During the Anglo-Irish War (1919–20), young Lois Naylor promises to marry an English soldier, but she is unable to love him and he is not accepted by her domineering mother. Finally he is shot dead in an ambush, and the Naylors' Big House is burned to the ground (in a fictional projection of Bowen's feelings about her own family estate).

Daniel Corkery's *The Stormy Hills* included such stories as "Rock-of-the-Mass," which takes as its central symbol the Mass Rock of penal times where priests said Mass as fugitives (but which has now been dynamited to build a road).

Within an experimental fictional mode, Brinsley MacNamara's protagonist in *The Various Lives of Marcus Igoe* lives what most of us only fantasize about occasionally: What if our lives had taken a different course? For example, Marcus marries and has children with Nancy the bookkeeper instead of Mary Margaret Caherlane—yet soon thereafter we learn that Mary Margaret "had never gone away only remaining to become the plump and somewhat strong-tempered woman he had married."

Irish Language and Literature

Tomás Ó Criomhthain's (1856–1937) *An tOileánach (The Islandman)* was a vivid memoir of life on the Great Blasket Island off the Kerry coast, the first of three such books along with Muirís Ó Súilleabháin's (1904–50) *Fiche Bliain ag Fás (Twenty Years A-Growing,* 1933) and Peig Sayers's (1873–1958) *Peig* (1936).

Literary Criticism

Our Exagmination round His Factification for Incamination of Work in Progress, a book of essays on what was to become *Finnegans Wake,* championed the book a full ten years before its actual publication in book form. Organized by James Joyce himself, it included essays by Samuel Beckett, William Carlos Williams, Joyce (briefly and cryptically under the pen name of "Vladimir Dixon"), and other notables.

Periodicals

An Phoblacht (The republic), edited by Frank Ryan and Peadar O'Donnell, now became the newspaper of Comhairle na Poblachta (Council of the republic), a new Republican and socialist political party founded by Maud Gonne, Seán MacBride (1904–   ) (son of Maud Gonne and John MacBride), Frank Ryan, and others (Hickey and Doherty 1987, 83).

Poetry

Austin Clarke (1896–1974) recorded his reaction to censorship in a brief, defiant and satiric lyric in his volume *Pilgrimage:* "Burn Ovid with the rest. Lovers will find / A hedge-school for themselves, and learn by heart / All that the clergy banish from the mind / When hands are joined and heads bow in the dark." In this collection Clarke employed Gaelic techniques of assonance (internal vowel rhymes) in his English verses. Clarke explained, "Assonance . . . takes the clapper from the bell of rhyme. . . . The natural lack of double rhymes in English leads to an avoidance of words of more than one syllable at the end of the lyric line. . . . But by cross-rhymes or vowel-rhyming, separately, one or more of the syllables of longer words . . . lovely and neglected words are advanced to the tonic place and divide their echoes" (quoted in Garratt 1986, 110).

The *Poems of Eva Gore Booth* appeared (Lapisardi 1991, 216).

Prose Nonfiction

P. L. Dickinson's book *The Dublin of Yesterday* was representative of Anglo-Irish nostalgia for the glory days of the Ascendancy (also found in Yeats's poetry during this period) and sense of alienation from the conservative, Catholic-dominated, Gaelic-obsessed Free State. Dickinson, a Dublin architect, wrote, "I love Ireland; few people know it better. There is hardly a mile of its coastline or hills I have not walked. There is not a thought in me that does not want well-being for the land of my birth; yet there is no room today in their own land for thousands of Irishmen of similar views" (quoted in T. Brown 1985, 117).

1930

Drama

At the Abbey, Yeats's *The Words upon the Window-Pane* was written in a highly realistic manner unusual for him yet explored with delicious ambiguity the seeming reappearance of Jonathan Swift at a Dublin séance, allowing Yeats to exploit simultaneously his interests in occult phenomena and in Swift as an important personal prototype. As Andrew Malone (1888–1939) noted in the *Dublin Magazine,* "Yeats managed to evoke the spirit of Dublin's Gloomy Dean without the necessity for his bodily presence on the stage" (1931, 6).

The Gate Theatre moved into the Rotunda building at the head of O'Connell Street, where it has remained ever since. Pointing to the opening of this new venue, and complaining about the decrease in the number of new productions at the Abbey, Andrew Malone wrote that "probably for the first time in the recent history of the drama and the theatre in Ireland it is necessary to look elsewhere than to the Abbey Theatre for the outstanding events of the year in the theatre in Ireland" (1931, 1).

Fiction

Peadar O'Donnell's novel *The Knife* was set in the Lagan Valley in county Down, and focused on the difficulties encountered by the Godfrey Dhus, a Catholic family who bought a farm in a Protestant region, and the role played by their sympathetic Protestant neighbors, the Rowans.

Folklore

The Irish Folklore Institute, which later became the Irish Folklore Commission, was constituted as a result of a government grant to a committee appointed by An Cumann le Béaloideas Éireann (The society for Irish folklore) and the Royal Irish Academy (T. Brown 1985, 148).

Literary Criticism

Stuart Gilbert's pioneering critical study (aided and abetted by Joyce himself), *James Joyce's "Ulysses,"* was published.

Poetry

Poems contained the first published verses of both Brian Coffey (1905–　) and Denis Devlin (1908–59), marked by European, particularly French, influences.

Prose Nonfiction

Two Years was Liam O'Flaherty's memoir about his wanderings in America and elsewhere as a young man.

1931

Peadar O'Donnell had continued his political activities, serving as editor of the IRA newspaper *An Phoblacht* (The republic) since 1925. He was also involved in Saor Éire (Free Ireland), a movement formed in 1931 as an offshoot from the IRA to create "an independent revolutionary leadership for the working class and working farmers towards the overthrow in Ireland of British imperialism and its ally, Irish capitalism" (quoted in Ellis 1973, 279). Saor Éire was condemned by the Catholic Church and eschewed by the established political parties.

In county Tipperary Father John Hayes founded Muintir na Tire (People of the land), which developed from a farmers' "marketing organisation to being a movement for the social uplift of the Irish countryside" (Whyte 1971, 68–69).

The extent of conservative Catholicism in the Free State was evidenced when the county Mayo Library Committee refused to approve the appointment of Letitia Dunbar-Harrison, a Protestant and graduate of Trinity College, Dublin, as county librarian. In response, the national government dissolved the Mayo County Council and appointed Dunbar-Harrison, but when a resulting boycott of the library was organized (and publicly supported by de Valera), the government was forced to back down over the next couple of years, transferring Dunbar-Harrison to another position and restoring the county council (Whyte 1971, 44–46).

Drama

Denis Johnston's *The Moon in the Yellow River* was a realistic problem play centered on Irish rebels' schemes to blow up a power plant.

Fiction

Ironically, in the same year when Daniel Corkery was arguing that Irish literature in English could not fully succeed (see below), his protégé and fellow Corkman, Frank O'Connor, published his first volume of stories, *Guests of the Nation*—the brilliant title story and several others serving to refute Corkery's thesis. "Guests of the Nation" was an unforgettable story narrated by an Irish Republican soldier who has to help carry out the execution of two British soldiers whom he and his fellow Irishmen have befriended. Several of the other stories in O'Connor's first collection were similarly drawn from his earlier experiences in the Irish Republican Army. The *Dublin Magazine* reviewer declared about these stories, "To Irish readers who have lived through the eventful period with which they deal, they come with the shock of surprise of something amazingly good and real. The first story, which gives the book its title, is profoundly moving. And so powerful is the impression produced that its influence lasts right through the reading of the others. This creates a definite atmosphere that binds these sketches together and gives them a feeling of continuity that is rare in books of short stories" (1932, 71).

O'Flaherty's novel *The Puritan* was a full-fledged assault on the Free State puritanism that led to censorship, stretched by O'Flaherty into what he saw as its logical conclusion: murder.

Francis Ferriter kills a supposed prostitute as a result of his fanatical puritanism as expressed in his manuscript "The Sacrifice of Blood." O'Flaherty turned naturally to a rural rodent, the incorrigible ferret, to capture the Dublin Free State mentality. In this same year, his tale (or novella) *The Ecstasy of Angus* borrowed from and transformed Irish mythology (a rare strategy for O'Flaherty) in order to tell the story of how the god of love, Angus, conceived Genius in the goddess Fand and died, having lost his youth and immortality.

Kate O'Brien's (1897–1974) first novel, *Without My Cloak*, appeared and subsequently won the Hawthornden and James Tait Black prizes. In this family chronicle set in O'Brien's characteristic upper-middle-class Catholic world of "Mellick" (Limerick), even the best-meaning characters, Denis and Caroline Considine, are unable to transcend the boundaries of their social world in order to make new lives with lovers from beyond that world.

Along with its companion novels *The Retreat* (1936) and *Young Tom* (1944), Forrest Reid's (1875–1947) *Uncle Stephen* explored the alternately realistic and fantasy worlds of Tom Barber, a youthful autobiographical protagonist in the north of Ireland.

Literary Criticism

Daniel Corkery's *Synge and Anglo-Irish Literature* rejected the Literary Revival notion of Yeats and others that Irish literature in English could be established as the national literature.

The first book of Samuel Beckett—who was a university lecturer in Belfast, Dublin, and Paris between 1928 and 1931 and passed up a promising academic career in order to devote himself to writing—was his insightful and self-revelatory critical study, *Proust*.

Periodicals

The *Irish Press* began and soon established itself as one of the major Dublin dailies alongside the *Irish Times* and the *Irish Independent* (the major threesome today). The *Press* was initially perceived as a strong nationalist, polemical paper; de Valera was involved in it, and Pádraic Pearse's mother was present at the launching. It eventually developed into much more, however, and later literary editor David Marcus would create within its pages the most important organ for new Irish fiction since the *Dublin University Magazine* and the *Irish Homestead* (and rivaling the *Bell* in the 1940s).

Prose Nonfiction

In the tradition of Swiftian satire, O'Flaherty's pamphlet *A Cure for Unemployment* suggested that the unemployed masses be adopted by the wealthy few as house pets.

1932

In February the Fianna Fáil party won the general election and Eamon de Valera, earlier the instransigent opponent of the Irish Free State, became its prime minister. De Valera and Fianna Fáil monopolized Irish political life for the next decade and a half. The previously revolutionary de Valera now did all in his power to enforce a socially, economically, and religiously conservative, Catholic, Gaelic, rural cultural code on the country.

Architecture

Sir Arnold Thornley designed the northern Irish parliament building at Stormont, outside Belfast (de Breffny 1983, 30).

Cultural Institutions

Yeats, Æ, and George Bernard Shaw founded the Irish Academy of Letters in order to combat (in the words of their letter inviting writers to join the academy) "an official censorship possessing, and actively exercising, powers of suppression which may at any moment confine an Irish author to the British and American market, and therefore make it impossible for him to live by distinctive Irish literature" (quoted in T. Brown 1985, 132). Yeats spoke in praise of O'Flaherty's novel *The Puritan,* a heated satiric

attack on censorship. While maintaining an exclusive membership, the academy awarded the Harmsworth Prize for fiction
annually from 1934 to 1938, the Casement Award for poetry or
drama from 1934 to 1939, and an annual prize during the same
years for writing in Irish. The awarding of similar prizes then
resumed only when funding was obtained from the Arts Council
in 1969 and subsequently from the Allied Irish Banks (de Breffny
1983, 115).

Drama

T. C. Murray's *Michaelmas Eve* and Paul Vincent Carroll's
(1900–68) *Things That Are Caesar's* were produced at the Abbey.

Fiction

Skerrett was (along with *Famine* [1937]) one of Liam O'Flaherty's
two best novels. David Skerrett was O'Flaherty's idea of a
hero—a defiant schoolteacher, based on his own childhood
teacher. He comes to the island of "Nara" (Inis Mór or "Aran"
thinly disguised) as an outsider, becomes a champion of its
traditional culture and language in spite of his initial aversion to
them, but is destroyed by the island's priest because his ideas and
practices are too revolutionary.

Midsummer Night's Madness, the first collection of stories by
Seán O'Faoláin, appeared; like Frank O'Connor's *Guests of the
Nation,* published in the previous year, O'Faoláin's stories registered the disillusionment of a former idealistic Irish rebel about
the tragedies of guerrilla war and the quotidian realities of the
conservative Irish Free State.

O'Connor's first novel, *The Saint and Mary Kate,* centered on
a young woman who has to endure a cast of Irish comic grotesques
surrounding her—particularly "the saint," a young man whose
religious mania prevents him from loving or understanding her.

Sex was equally difficult and risky in Austin Clarke's prose
romance *The Bright Temptation*—and in its sequels, *The Singing-
Men at Cashel* (1936) and *The Sun Dances at Easter* (1952).
Clarke veiled his critique of the sexually repressive Free State in
the guise of medieval romance, as he had earlier done in verse (see

1929 entry on *Pilgrimage*)—but the Free State banned these prose volumes anyway.

Prose Nonfiction

Dorothy MacArdle's (1889–1958) *The Irish Republic* appeared and soon established itself as the standard history of the events leading up to the establishment of the Irish Free State in 1922. *The Gates Flew Open* was Peadar O'Donnell's memoir of his revolutionary prison days at the hands of the Free State in the early 1920s.

1933

The Cumann na nGaedheal (Society of Gaels) party joined forces with the followers of General Eoin O'Duffy (1892–1944)—the former commissioner of police (dismissed by de Valera) who sympathized with Mussolini and led the closest thing to an Irish fascist movement, the "Blueshirts"—and formed the Fine Gael (Race of Gaels) party. Fine Gael cast off O'Duffy two years later and has continued until today as the major opposition party to Fianna Fáil.

Drama

Teresa Deevy's (1903–63) *Temporal Powers* (1932) shared an Abbey Theatre prize with Paul Vincent Carroll's *The Things That Are Caesar's.* Lennox Robinson's *Drama at Inish,* a comedy, was put on at the Abbey. It focuses on the effects on a small Irish town of a touring theater's bleak plays; in response, the impressionable townspeople begin planning affairs and suicides. Reviewing "The Irish Theatre in 1933" in the *Dublin Magazine,* Andrew Malone felt that "the year 1933 was merely a good average year . . . with a dozen new plays. . . . With such notable writers as Liam O'Flaherty, Brinsley MacNamara, Francis Stuart, Frank O'Connor, Peadar O'Donnell and Seán O'Faoláin devoting themselves almost entirely to the writing of novels it will be plain that for the present, at least, the drama has lost the overwhelming appeal it once had for Irish writers" (9 [July–September 1934]: 45).

Denis Johnston's *A Bride for the Unicorn* was staged at the Gate Theatre.

Fiction

When George Moore (b. 1852) died in London, James Joyce asked Harriet Shaw Weaver to send a wreath to his funeral carrying the inscription "To George Moore from James Joyce," and "then filled his letters of the next two months with bitter references to the failure of the newspapers to mention his gift. It was as if in the end he felt the need to acknowledge publicly a debt that he had long owed, but could only then admit" (McCarthy 1983, 114). In 1912 the young, ambitious Joyce had dismissed his rival modernist novelist in his broadside "Gas from a Burner" as "Moore, a genuine gent / That lives on his property's ten per cent," but now—his own acclaim having eclipsed the declining Moore's—he could afford to be more gracious, however belatedly.

Seán O'Faoláin's first novel, *A Nest of Simple Folk,* concentrated on Leo Donnel, a vagabond nineteenth-century Fenian who passes on his rebelliousness to young Denis Hussey (shades of O'Faoláin himself) in the early twentieth century.

The Ante-Room was Kate O'Brien's second novel and her own favorite. Agnes Mulqueen is plagued by a secret love for her sister's husband that he encourages, but she refuses to get more involved because her loyalty to her sister runs deeper.

Lord Dunsany's (1878–1957) novel *The Curse of the Wise Woman* combined a nostalgia for old Ireland and its folkways with an anti-industrial, environmentalist critique. Dunsany's old wise woman, believing that Tir-na-nOg (the Land of Youth) is buried in the bog bordering her house, delivers her curse upon the Peat Development Syndicate that would destroy it, and is obliged by the arrival of storms that wreck the project.

Film

Denis Johnston directed and edited a silent feature film adapted from Frank O'Connor's short story "Guests of the Nation," with an Irish cast and photographed by John Manning and Jim Douglas (de Breffny 1983, 64).

Poetry

Yeats's *The Winding Stair* included "In Memory of Eva Gore-Booth and Con Markiewicz," "A Dialogue of Self and Soul," and the "Crazy Jane" poems of *Words for Music Perhaps* (with the two volumes published together). The "Crazy Jane" poems injected a newly vigorous, demotic voice into Yeats's characteristically passionate themes, as the persona of a peasant woman is adopted—in, for example, "Crazy Jane Grown Old Looks at the Dancers," in which his female speaker repeatedly declares that love *"is like the lion's tooth."* In this poem and others, Crazy Jane speaks in Irish-English idiomatic phrases such as "I cared not a thraneen" and "God be with the times." In general, Yeats's Crazy Jane could not sound more different from his early romantic speakers of the 1890s or the more abstracted, intellectual persona of his middle period.

1934

Along with Frank Ryan and George Gilmore (1898–1985), Peadar O'Donnell formed the Republican Congress as a socialist and republican movement after a split in the IRA along socialist versus more narrowly nationalist lines. The Republican Congress remained active until 1936, when de Valera banned its weekly newspaper (Ellis 1973, 283–84).

Fiction

Originally published in Paris, Joyce's *Ulysses* was printed for the first time in the English-speaking world, by Random House in New York, after a court battle to ban it there was ended by Judge John Woolsey's sensible verdict in favor of the book.

In Samuel Beckett's story collection *More Pricks than Kicks,* his protagonist Belacqua Shuah confronts an inconsequential Dublin that shows the influence of Joyce. Belacqua is the first of Beckett's inert fictional antiheroes.

Another antihero was the protagonist of Joseph O'Neill's (1878–1952) *Wind from the North,* a historical fantasy that reflected its author's unease and boredom with his career as a civil servant in the Irish Department of Secondary Education, which he headed from 1923 to 1944. Here an unnamed clerk, after being hit by a Dublin tram in Dame Street, finds himself in the body of one Olaf Ulfson during the days just before Brian Boru defeated but was himself killed by the Norsemen at the Battle of Clontarf in 1014.

Peadar O'Donnell demonstrated his sense of humor in *On the Edge of the Stream,* a novel about the comic consequences of the "communist" red-baiting of a rural cooperative.

Like its sequels *Candle for the Proud* (1936) and *Men Withering* (1939), Francis MacManus's (1909–65) historical novel *Stand and Give Challenge* concentrated on the eighteenth-century Gaelic poet and schoolmaster Donnacha Ruadh MacConmara, portrayed as struggling through the Penal Age and surviving to witness the 1798 rising in Wexford.

Like her other novels, Molly Keane's (1905–   ) *Devoted Ladies* (published under the pen name M. J. Farrell) explored the sexual conflicts of Ascendancy women with a boldness not found anywhere else. A woman wants to marry a generous if dull Anglo-Irishman, but is blackmailed and prevented from doing so by her cruel lesbian ex-lover.

Periodicals

The socialist-republican threesome of O'Donnell, Ryan, and Gilmore (see above) brought out a newspaper as a sounding board for their views, entitled *Republican Congress.*

Prose Nonfiction

O'Flaherty's *Shame the Devil,* concerning his early life on Aran and his struggle to overcome writer's block, was written in order, he asserted, to steal the thunder of any later would-be biographer who might want to attempt his life.

1935

An act prohibited the importation of contraceptives into the Free State by married as well as unmarried couples. Nearly forty years would pass before the Supreme Court would find that this act "violated a married couple's right to privacy" (Beale 1987, 13). Contraceptives could not be legally bought or sold by anyone within the Republic of Ireland until 1979.

Yet another attempt to enforce conservative Catholic moral standards by legislation was the Public Dance Halls Act, which specified that a license from the local district court was necessary for all public dances and stipulated criteria for its granting. It backfired, though: ironically, "one writer has complained that it stamped out informal dances in private houses, where the young people danced under the eyes of their elders, and diverted them to commercial dance halls where there was less supervision" (Whyte 1971, 50).

Drama

Yeats sponsored Frank O'Connor as a new director of the board of the Abbey Theatre, Hugh Hunt took over from Lennox Robinson as the main director of plays, and Ernest Blythe joined the board. In the late 1930s O'Connor spent much time trying to get the Abbey to live up to its high Yeatsian ideals, during years of continued decline in the theater. This decline was evident in Andrew Malone's review of "The Irish Theatre in 1935" in the *Dublin Magazine,* which was bleaker than any of his previous ones: "The year 1935 revealed in a most remarkable manner the poverty of the Irish theatre, the number of new plays presented having been the lowest for thirty years" (1936, 48).

Film

By this date film had become a major popular form of entertainment; "the estimated number of cinema admissions [in Ireland] was 18.25 million" (Kennedy 1990, 115).

Folklore

The Irish Folklore Commission was established in place of the Irish Folklore Institute. Patrick Sheeran notes that "it is generally agreed . . . among folklorists that the seaboard of Galway had more unrecorded folktales in 1935 (when the Irish Folklore Commission replaced the more amateur Irish Folklore Institute) than had all the rest of Western Europe" (1976, 140). The hard work of the commission's many collectors—working their way through the countryside, astride bicycles and armed only with pen, paper, and ediphone (an early tape recorder)—eventually resulted in the world's largest single national folklore archive, housed today at University College, Dublin.

Literary Criticism

Literary Revival essayist John Eglinton's *Irish Literary Portraits* appeared.

Poetry

After a highly distinguished and immensely varied career as poet, editor, activist, artist, mystic, and mentor to many others, Æ (George Russell) (b. 1867) died.

Sounding (in the *Dublin Magazine*) a note very close to Andrew Malone's bleak assessment of Irish drama (see above), Austin Clarke began an essay on "Irish Poetry Today" with the assertion, "Irish poetry seems to be rapidly approaching a state of destitution but there is, of course, always the shabby genteel consolation that it has seen better days" (1935, 26). He concluded that "Irish poetry has lost the ready ear and the comforts of recognition. But we must go on. We must be true to our own minds" (32).

1936

Dublin's population, which would rise throughout the century as people moved there from the countryside, was now 472,935. By 1951 it would be 575,988 and by 1961, 595,288 (T. Brown 1985, 211).

After several brutal murders were attributed to the Irish Republican Army, in June the government proclaimed the IRA to be an illegal organization (Whyte 1971, 91)—a status that it has maintained ever since.

Irish fascist and "Blueshirt" leader Eoin O'Duffy organized an Irish Brigade to fight with Franco in Spain, "and that was his last political activity" (Whyte 1971, 81).

Aer Lingus was incorporated as the government-owned airline of Ireland (Hickey and Doherty 1987, 3).

Drama

The Gate Theatre was divided into Gate Theatre Productions (Hilton Edwards and Micheál MacLiammóir) and Longford Productions (Lord Longford) [Maxwell 1984, xii]. Longford Productions was to handle all nontheatrical endeavors, such as MacLiammóir's subsequent films.

Fiction

Bones of Contention, Frank O'Connor's second collection, contained such masterful realistic studies of life in the provinces as "In the Train" and "The Majesty of the Law."

Seán O'Faoláin's second novel, *Bird Alone,* focused on Corney Crone, a young man resembling Dennis Hussey in *A Nest of Simple Folk* (1933) who models himself on a grandfather much like Dennis's and experiences the loss of all that he loves.

Irish Language and Literature

Peig, the autobiography of the celebrated Kerry storyteller Peig Sayers, was published.

Periodicals

The journal *Ireland Today* was a forum for progressive, European interests. It supported the Republicans in Spain against Franco, flying in the face of popular Irish opinion and leading to its demise two years later (T. Brown 1985, 169–70).

Poetry

The first volume of the best Irish poet in the generation after Yeats, Patrick Kavanagh (1904–67), *Ploughman and Other Poems,*

contained reflective lyrics of rural life in his native county of
Monaghan. In his review in *Ireland Today,* Donagh MacDonagh
(1912–68) was unable to recognize in these poems the work of a
major Irish poet, the first who would be able to move significantly
beyond Yeats's influence. MacDonagh dismissively concluded
that "there is little thought and little beauty in these verses," and
ironically advised, "Mr. Kavanagh would do well to read the later
Yeats and leave his archaic musings" (1936, 86).

1937

De Valera's new Irish constitution was approved in June. It
provided for a powerful taoiseach, or prime minister, a popularly
elected president (Douglas Hyde served as the first one) whose role
was often ceremonial but who could refuse to sign a bill if
convinced that popular opinion should be determined by referendum, a more powerful senate, a "special position" for the Catholic
church, the prohibition of divorce and the denunciation of
working mothers, and continued hopes for the restoration of
the Irish language and the achievement of a united Ireland. This
last hope was ironic in light of some of the aforementioned
stipulations, which Protestant Ulster inevitably found abhor-
rent. Maurice Harmon notes that this constitution "mirrored
the bourgeois mind" and "was characterized not by bold affirma-
tions of individual liberties, but by cautious qualifications
of and restrictions upon just about every freedom it granted"
(1986, 34).

Architecture

City Hall in Cork was built by the firm of Jones and Kelly (de
Breffny 1983, 30).

Drama

At the Abbey, *Shadow and Substance* by Paul Vincent Carroll
focused on an intellectual priest and his simple housekeeper,

whose visions force the priest to reexamine his own abstract ideas and achieve some measure of humility. This was Carroll's best play; he never quite lived up to its promise.

When *She Had to Do Something* was staged at the Abbey, Seán O'Faoláin remarked about the response to his play (in a wry comment on the fate of writers during this close-minded period), "I am very pleased to say, it was soundly booed. One likes to be in the tradition" (quoted in Doyle 1968, 38).

Fiction

O'Flaherty's novel *Famine,* published in the same year as his anthology *The Short Stories of Liam O'Flaherty,* was his best novel, a historical novel about the Great Hunger based in part on the author's own knowledge of famine experiences at the turn of the century on his native island of Inis Mór. Its heroes are an old man and his young daughter-in-law, Brian and Mary Kilmartin, who come to gain each other's admiration (despite early antipathy) in the midst of crisis. *Famine* is far superior to its two historical sequels, *Land* (1946) and *Insurrection* (1950). *The Short Stories of Liam O'Flaherty* was the first anthologized selection from his collections published up until that time, including many of his most celebrated stories: "Spring Sowing," "The Cow's Death," "The Landing," "Going into Exile," "Milking Time," "The Conger Eel," "The Wounded Cormorant," "Poor People," "The Fairy Goose," "Red Barbara," and other vivid accounts of the rural existence of people and animals.

Seán O'Faoláin's collection *A Purse of Coppers* contained such stories as "A Broken World"—closely comparable to Frank O'Connor's "In the Train" in its exploration of the loneliness and spiritual desolation of the era through close attention to a few characters traveling on a train.

Francis MacManus's novel *This House Was Mine* centered on a young man who is prevented by his prideful father, who approaches marriage like he does the purchase of land, from marrying their servant, and witnesses the eventual loss of the family home, which is regarded as divine retribution for the family hubris.

Molly Keane's *The Rising Tide* focused on an assertive

Ascendancy woman who survives marriage, widowhood, and two affairs—finally feeling herself to be outdated, and emerging as an image of the decaying Ascendancy.

Irish Language and Literature

Leon Ó Broin's biography in Irish, *Parnell,* appeared; it was the first of a series of significant historical works by this author, and demonstrated that Irish could be an effective scholarly (not only literary or folk) language.

Periodicals

The *Irish Democrat* was a socialist newspaper begun by Peadar O'Donnell as a successor to his *Republican Congress.* It lasted only a year (Hickey and Doherty 1987, 244).

Hibernia magazine began as a monthly and subsequently continued as a fortnightly from 1968 and as a weekly from 1977 until it ceased in 1980. *Hibernia* was a significant forum for political and literary opinion in Dublin.

Prose Nonfiction

As I Was Going Down Sackville Street by Oliver St. John Gogarty was a riotous memoir of Dublin in the days of revolution and literary revival. A libel suit ensued, during which Samuel Beckett (among others) was cross-examined and derided as a Parisian degenerate. Thereafter Beckett returned to Paris, subsequently explaining after World War II (when he was a fugitive working in the French underground) that "I preferred France in war to Ireland in peace."

1938

Clann na Talmhan (Family of the land) was founded by Michael Donnellan as a political party looking out for the interests of small western farmers. This party would become a minor part of the coalition government formed in 1948 and would last until the 1960s (Hickey and Doherty 1987, 76).

Cultural Institutions

Austin Clarke and Robert Farren (1909–   ) founded the Dublin Verse-Speaking Society, which brought together many poets and fostered radio plays—and also new plays at the Abbey produced by the Lyric Theatre Company, which the society sponsored.

Drama

Yeats's play *The Herne's Egg,* published in this year though not produced at the Abbey until 1950, was a strangely sexual yet abstract play concerning the mythical mating of God (the Great Herne) and humanity (the priestess Attracta), recalling "Leda and the Swan" thematically and the "Crazy Jane" poems stylistically. Yeats's play *Purgatory* was performed at the Abbey in this year, with a curtain call at what proved to be Yeats's final public appearance. It was a spare, effective drama concerning an old man and his son talking beside the ruins of a Big House. Feeling cursed by the demise of his Big House as well as by the degeneration of the noble blood of his mother (who mated with a mere groom to produce him), the Old Man has killed his father and now kills his son. He begs that his mother be released from her purgatory but is doomed to constantly relive her mistake and the consequences of his own act.

F. R. Higgins, a writer much influenced by Yeats, was appointed managing director of the Abbey Theatre.

Fiction

Samuel Beckett's first novel, *Murphy,* was really an antinovel. Like the narrator of Flann O'Brien's *At Swim-Two-Birds* (1939), Murphy appears to be in part a ludicrous parody of Joyce's Stephen Dedalus, another intellectual who cherishes his privacy. The putative plot of *Murphy* involves an absurd comedy of manners in which Murphy is sought out in London by a whole crew of people. Beckett relentlessly derides traditional romantic conventions of love stories and nature writing, and interrupts his prose with charts listing characters' attributes and long digressions on the philosophy of dualism. In a clear slap at the Literary Revival, Murphy's will dictates that his ashes be flushed down the Abbey

Theatre's toilet in Dublin, but instead they are tossed aside in a London pub after he dies.

Patrick Kavanagh's autobiographical book *The Green Fool* explored his repressed upbringing in county Monaghan. As Frank O'Connor remarked, "It is O'Faoláin's second novel [*Bird Alone*]; my own second novel [*Dutch Interior*]; it is Gerald O'Donovan's *Father Ralph;* it is *A Portrait of the Artist as a Young Man;* it is the novel every Irish writer who isn't a rogue or an imbecile is doomed to write when the emptiness and horror of Irish life begins to dawn on him" (quoted in Lubbers 1980, 70).

Periodicals

The journal *Irish Historical Studies* began publishing, facilitating the professional, intensive work of historians.

Begun in 1928, the *Standard* was taken over by a new team of directors and editor Peadar O'Curry, serving "united public opinion in the cause of Catholic reconstruction." By 1939 this weekly enjoyed a circulation of 50,000, one of the largest in the country (Whyte 1971, 70–71).

Poetry

Though Yeats had passed him over for inclusion when he edited the *Oxford Book of Modern Verse* (1935), Austin Clarke published *Night and Morning,* after several other excellent volumes and with many more to come. From the time of "The Vengeance of Fionn" (1917), Clarke had sought to outdo Yeats in drawing from Gaelic tradition and legend, but in *Night and Morning* and throughout the rest of his career, he moved sharply away from Yeats's style and material.

Prose Nonfiction

Seán O'Faoláin's *King of the Beggars* was a biography of Daniel O'Connell, one of several historical and cultural studies— including *De Valera* (1939), *The Great O'Neill* (1942), and *The Irish* (1947)—in which O'Faolain extended his range beyond the fiction that made his name and sought to define an Irish identity. As Terence Brown notes, "his fundamental thesis was that Gaelic

Ireland had died in the eighteenth century and that there was little point in trying to resurrect it. . . . The modern Ireland that the twentieth century had inherited was not the outcome of many centuries of Gaelic and Catholic civilization but the fruit of the democratic victories won by Daniel O'Connell in the nineteenth century" (1985, 156).

Among many other recollections, Maud Gonne's autobiography, *A Servant of the Queen,* presented a hardheaded and realistic if sympathetic enough view of her friend "sillie Willie Yeats," in sharp contrast to the poet's highly romanticized portrait of her in his own autobiographical volumes (and, of course, in his poetry).

1939

The United Kingdom officially entered World War II in September, and de Valera declared Ireland's intent to remain neutral—an official position that he maintained throughout the war while following a de facto practice of quiet support for Britain. As he stated to the Dáil Éireann parliamentary session on 2 September, announcing Ireland's neutrality, "I know that in this country there are sympathies, very strong sympathies, in regard to the present issues, but I do not think that anybody, no matter what his feelings might be, would suggest that the Government policy, the official policy of the state, should be other than what the Government suggests" (1946, 9). Meanwhile, the Irish Republican Army maintained a campaign in Britain throughout the war.

Drama

Seán O'Casey's play *The Star Turns Red* conveyed his theme of "a communist following in the footsteps of Christ" through a series of pageantlike confrontations between the reactionary Red Priest and Red Jim, the labor leader.

The Ulster Group Theatre was founded in Belfast (Maxwell 1984, xii).

Fiction

After seventeen years of work with periodical publication as "Work in Progress," *Finnegans Wake* was released in book form.

Joyce wrote to a friend: "I have at last finished finishing my book. For three lustra I have been combing and recombing the locks of Anna Livia. It is now time that she tread the boards" (quoted in Ellmann 1982, 714). Joyce noted that he expected his "ideal reader suffering from an ideal insomnia" (*Finnegans Wake*, p. 120, l. 14) to spend at least as long studying the book as he had spent writing it. This multilingual, continually punning, cyclical work in four books without a definite beginning or end— structured to reflect both the Renaissance Italian philosopher Vico's model of the four eternally recurring ages of humankind (as well as the circuitous course of the Vico Road in Dalkey) and his countryman Bruno's binary model of opposites—has eluded easy comprehension yet provoked endless scholarship in the decades since then. Having organized his own critical *Exagmination Round His Factification for Incamination of Work in Progress* (1929) a full decade *before* the publication of *Finnegans Wake,* Joyce succeeded grandly in his stated intent of "keeping the professors busy." In December he left Paris (then occupied by the Nazis) for southern France.

Another highly celebrated experimental novel, Flann O'Brien's *At Swim-Two-Birds,* appeared in the same year, though it did not attract anything like the attention that Joyce's did until its republication in the 1960s. Coincidentally, O'Brien (whose real name was Brian O'Nolan) used Finn MacCool as one of his touchstones just as Joyce did. And like Joyce, O'Brien "deconstructed" his own fiction. This novel contains novels-within-novels-within-the-novel, and O'Brien provides several quick synopses in lieu of full narration of action. Among other narrative strands in this amazing and hilarious book—which opens with three separate, alternate beginnings— the unnamed student narrator, who suspiciously resembles Joyce's Stephen Dedalus, is writing a novel about a pubkeeper whose son writes one in which his father is tortured, and the son is so taken by one of his own characters that he makes love to her.

Daniel Corkery's final collection of stories, *Earth out of Earth,* was not up to the level of his previous ones.

Michael McLaverty's (1907–92) first and perhaps best novel, *Call My Brother Back,* was divided into two books, "The Island" and "The City." The MacNeill family is forced to leave Rathlin

Island for the Falls Road area of Belfast, and in the process young Colm MacNeill loses his link to the land, his education, and his older brother Alec (an IRA member).

Oliver St. John Gogarty's novel *Tumbling in the Hay* contained a series of loose, rambling, lighthearted experiences of a set of young Trinity College vagabonds. Gogarty poked fun at James Joyce in the character of "Kinch."

Irish Language and Literature

The most important author of innovative modern fiction in Irish, Máirtín Ó Cadhain (1907–70), published his first collection of stories, *Idir Shúgradh agus Dáiríre* (Half in jest, half in earnest).

Poetry

Yeats's *Last Poems* and his play *The Death of Cuchulain* were his final, summary statements; he died in France, where he had moved a year earlier, in 1939. "The Circus Animals' Desertion" and "Under Ben Bulben" provided great, defiant, but also slightly bemused epitaphs, while such poems as "Lapis Lazuli" and "The Man and the Echo" reflect a deep maturity. The old man who stumbles onto the stage to rant and rave at the beginning of *The Death of Cuchulain* (completed just before Yeats's own death in this year)—who is ostensibly the play's producer and clearly the author himself with his mask removed—shows Yeats in a rare humorous mode. Following an interruption by drum and pipe, the old man explains, "That's from the musicians; I asked them to do that if I was getting excited." This play was not staged until 1945 (by Austin Clarke's Lyric Theatre Company in Dublin [Maxwell 1984, 134]).

Prose Nonfiction

I Knock at the Door, the first volume of O'Casey's six volumes of autobiography, appeared in this year; the series would eventually include *Pictures in the Hallway* (1942), *Drums under the Windows* (1945), *Inishfallen, Fare Thee Well* (1949), *Rose and Crown* (1952), and *Sunset and Evening Star* (1954). On the one hand, O'Casey's autobiographies (like the autobiographies of many writers and public figures) as much mythologize the author and his world as provide reliable sourcebooks of biographical and historical fact; on the other hand, some believe that these volumes are literary achievements surpassing all but his very best plays.

Under the pen name "Myles na Gopaleen" (a Gaelic rogue in Dion Boucicault's play *The Shaughraun* [1874], whose name means "Myles of the little horses"), Brian O'Nolan/Flann O'Brien began publishing his famous "Cruiskeen Lawn" (little full jug) column in the *Irish Times*. This column (since collected in such anthologies as *The Best of Myles*) continued until his death in 1966 and contained some of the most hilarious satires of Irish matters since Jonathan Swift.

1940

John Charles McQuaid (1895–1973) was appointed archbishop of Dublin and was to become "the most-talked-about Irish prelate," very active in the area of social welfare (Whyte 1971, 75).

Cultural Institutions

The government founded the Dublin Institute for Advanced Studies, with research specialties in physics and Celtic studies (Hickey and Doherty 1987, 137).

Drama

Quite unlike any of his earlier plays, O'Casey's *Purple Dust* was a "wayward comedy" about the attempt of two English people to create an Anglo-Irish Big House.

At the Abbey, George Shiels's (1886–1949) *The Rugged Path* enjoyed the longest run of any play during the period; Shiels was an immensely popular though inferior playwright.

Fiction

O'Faoláin's novel *Come Back to Erin* centered on Frankie

Hannafey, an older man who slowly comes to realize that his rebel stance has become outdated in the Ireland of the 1930s.

Frank O'Connor's second and last novel, *Dutch Interior,* examined Stevie Dalton and, through his eyes, the lives of people with potential and people who failed. O'Connor made a kind of *Winesburg, Ohio* out of the working-class world of Cork from which he emerged.

Irish Language and Literature

In his autobiography *Mo Bhealach Féin* (My own way), Seosamh MacGrianna (1901–90) captured a sense of sharp division between a traditional life-style in Donegal and the harsher world of Dublin.

Periodicals

The *Bell* was founded by Seán O'Faoláin, who edited the journal until 1946. The *Bell* became the most important cultural and literary journal at midcentury, with O'Faoláin—the most influential figure in Irish literature since Yeats—courageously speaking out against censorship and the close-mindedness of the Free State in general and arguing for a liberal, bilingual, inclusive brand of Irishness that recalled Æ's editorials in the *Irish Statesman* twenty years earlier. O'Faoláin declared in his opening editorial, "This Ireland is young and earnest. She knows that somewhere, among the briars and the brambles, there stands the reality which the generations died to reach—not, you notice, the Ideal; our generation is too sober to talk much about Ideals. . . . we are lively experimentally" (1940, 8). The list of contributors to the first issue reads like a hall of fame of Irish literature at midcentury: Frank O'Connor, Flann O'Brien, Patrick Kavanagh, Elizabeth Bowen, Peadar O'Donnell, Brinsley MacNamara, O'Faoláin himself, and several other notables. Liam O'Flaherty, Austin Clarke, and various other important writers also published their work in the *Bell,* and several more recent writers such as James Plunkett (1920–   ) got their start in its pages. Conor Cruise O'Brien (writing as Donat O'Donnell) and Vivian Mercier began their long careers as influential critics by writing for the *Bell.* Also notable is the fact that its poetry editor, Geoffrey Taylor, encouraged the inclusion of the work of northern Protestant poets such as Louis MacNeice (1907–63), John Hewitt (1907–87), and W. R. Rodgers (1909–69).

Poetry

W. R. Rodgers's volume *Awake! and Other Poems* was influenced by the modernist mode of Auden and MacNeice.

1941

Architecture

Desmond Fitzgerald designed the terminal building at the new Dublin Airport, using a markedly modern style that helped usher in the arrival of air transportation to Ireland (de Breffny 1983, 30).

Drama

F. R. Higgins (b. 1896) died and was succeeded as managing director of the Abbey Theatre by Ernest Blythe, who led the theater into its most conservative phase.

Fiction

Two years after the publication of *Finnegans Wake* and one year after moving to Switzerland, James Joyce (b. 1882) died in Zurich, where he is buried.

One of the most astonishing acts of Irish censorship was the banning (in the following year) of Kate O'Brien's superb novel *The Land of Spices* due to a single, stylistically veiled sentence referring to a homosexual act committed years earlier by a young musician and the heroine's father. This is the story of Helen Archer, whose isolation as the English superior of an Irish convent is overcome by her generous, platonic love for a young student, Anna Murphy, whose educational and personal development she nurtures.

Michael McLaverty's novel *Lost Fields* depicted the conflict between rural and urban life in the north of Ireland. The surviving members of the Griffin family finally choose rural over urban poverty by moving into their dead grandmother's empty house.

Irish Language and Literature

The Irish National Teachers' Organisation issued a *Report of the Committee of Inquiry into the Use of Irish as a Teaching Medium,* indicating that a majority of teachers were "opposed to using Irish as the sole medium of instruction when English is the home language." This report, however, fell on deaf ears in the Department of Education, which was controlled by Irish Irelanders (T. Brown 1985, 190).

The most biting and hilarious satire ever of the whole Irish Ireland movement, and many other Irish matters, appeared in the form of *An Béal Bocht* (*The Poor Mouth*), a novel by Myles na gCopaleen (Brian O'Nolan/Flann O'Brien). Ostensibly a parody of Tomás Ó Criomhthain's 1929 autobiography, *An tOileánach* (*The Islandman*), this short, Swiftian novel narrates the disastrous experiences of its unfortunate narrator—who has no name of his own, only the name imposed by the cruel English-speaking schoolmaster on every boy in school: "Jams O'Donnell." Like Ó Criomhthain, this narrator nostalgically assures us that "Ní bheidh ár léitheidí arís ann" ("Our likes will not be there again"), but ridiculously repeats it ad nauseam: Ambrose the Pig's likes will not be there again, nor will the likes of the fireplace's bad smell be there again, and so on. This novel mercilessly lampoons folklorists who believe that the purest Irish is that grunted by a pig, Gaelic fanatics whose every other word is "Gaelic," and many of the other obsessions and stereotypes of Irish Ireland.

Music

The Dublin Grand Opera Society was founded by John F. Larchet (1884–1967) (its president until 1967), William T. O'Kelly (its chairman until 1979), musical director James Doyle, and others (de Breffny 1983, 175).

Poetry

Veterans was a volume by Donagh MacDonagh, the son of the Irish rebel, poet, professor, and 1916 martyr Thomas MacDonagh.

1942

The most ludicrous chapter of the story of Irish censorship focused on *The Tailor and Ansty,* a delightful, harmless memoir published in this year by Eric Cross (1903–80) about West Cork storyteller Tim Buckley, "The Tailor," and his wife. Along with Kate O'Brien's novel *The Land of Spices* (1941), *The Tailor and Ansty* (1942) was banned because of its supposedly "Rabelaisian qualities"— provoking a Senate debate that resulted in the defeat (thirty-four to two) of Sir John Keane's motion criticizing the Censorship Board, by Board Chairman William Magennis and his followers. Frank O'Connor remarked that reading the published account of the debate was "like taking a long, slow swim through a sewage bed" (quoted in Cahalan 1979, 116).

Architecture

J. R. Boyd Barrett designed the new government buildings in Kildare Street in Dublin, adjacent to the National Library and the National Gallery (de Breffny 1983, 30).

Art

Corkman Séamus Murphy (1907–75) completed *The Virgin of the Twilight,* a fine limestone sculpture in his early style that stands in Fitzgerald Park in Cork. A student of Daniel Corkery (as were Frank O'Connor and Seán O'Faoláin), Murphy was one of modern Ireland's finest sculptors.

Drama

The novelist Michael Farrell (1899–1962) wrote in the *Bell* that "dramatic activity in the country is abundant and enthusiastic.

... It is not necessary to list among the difficulties of the Country Theatre a lack of talent. Possibly at no time has there been so much of it; or so much talk of drama and plans for drama" (quoted in T. Brown 1985, 154, 178).

O'Casey's *Red Roses for Me* effectively evoked the world of the 1913 Dublin lockout, but in a much more reflective, detached, experimental mode than his earlier and better-known Dublin plays.

Fiction

Tales from Bective Bridge by Mary Lavin (1912–   ) appeared, examining the quiet subtleties of middle-class, small-town Irish life which came to be Lavin's characteristic theme.

Maura Laverty's (1907–66) *Never No More* was the story of young Delia Scully, who grows up surrounded by the warm love of her grandmother.

Francis MacManus's novel *Watergate* portrayed a woman who returns from America to find her family home inhabited by her sister and husband but controlled by a grasping peasant, the tinker woman whom she eventually supplants—but only at the expense of her own freedom and dignity.

Irish Language and Literature

The literary and cultural journal *Comhar* (Cooperation) emerged. It was to publish such important writers in Irish as Máirtín Ó Cadhain, Máirtín Ó Direáin (1910–88), Seán Ó Riordáin (1916–77), Máire Mhac an tSaoi (1922–   ), Eoghan Ó Tuairisc (Eugene Watters, 1919–82), and Micheál Mac Liammóir (1899–1978).

Coinnle Geala (Bright candle), the first volume by Máirtín Ó Direáin (who was originally from the Aran Islands), has been assessed as bringing modernism into poetry in Irish.

Literary Criticism

In an article in *Horizon* entitled "The Future of Irish Literature," Frank O'Connor lamented that "after the success of the

Revolution . . . Irish society began to revert to type. . . . Every year that has passed, particularly since de Valera's rise to power, has strengthened the grip of the gombeen man, of the religious secret societies like the Knights of Columbanus, of the illiterate censorships."

Poetry

Patrick Kavanagh's long poem "The Great Hunger," which first appeared in Cyril Connolly's journal *New Horizons*, was the most important statement by a new poetic voice at midcentury (even though Kavanagh himself, later and in a more optimistic phase, tended to discount the poem). Paddy Maguire, its protagonist, is a county Monaghan farmer who embodies all that is despairing in the rural Ireland of the time, with late (or no) marriage, sexual repression, maternal dominance, and close-mindedness creating a new rural Irish "famine"—sexual and spiritual more than physical. This work is also marked by Kavanagh's characteristically direct, natural style: "No hope. No lust. / The hungry fiend / Screams the apocalypse of clay / In every corner of this land."

1943

In a famous St. Patrick's Day speech, head of government Eamon de Valera advanced a romantic, antiquated, clichéd, unrealistic, yet very influential vision—insisting that the Ireland he dreamed of was "a land whose countryside would be bright with cosy homesteads, whose fields and villages would be joyous with the sounds of industry, with the romping of sturdy children, the contests of athletic youths, the laughter of comely maidens, whose firesides would be the forums for the wisdom of serene old age" (quoted in Beale 1987, 20).

During this year and the next, the Labour party and the labor movement in general were wracked by factionalism. The president of the Irish Transport and General Workers' Union, William O'Brien, a long-standing enemy of James Larkin (who had just been elected to the Dáil), accused Larkin of being a Communist.

The result was that bad press about supposed Communist infiltration into the Labour party and the labor movement, especially in the pages of the widely circulated Catholic *Standard,* badly damaged both the party and the movement (Whyte 1971, 85–86).

Art

The establishment of the Irish Exhibition of Living Art "provided a plurality of exhibiting groups in Dublin" (de Breffny 1983, 186).

Drama

At the Abbey, *Old Road* by M. J. Molloy (1917–   ) dramatized the problems of emigration in a mode influenced by Chekhov.

Flann O'Brien's play *Faustus Kelly* focused on a government official who sells his soul to the devil in exchange for a seat in parliament.

Like his other verse-plays *The Son of Learning* (1932) and *The Moment Next to Nothing* (1958), Austin Clarke's *The Plot Is Ready* was based on a medieval Irish tale recurrent in Irish folklore and focused on human passions, in this case a king who refuses to abandon his mistress.

Fiction

Like Thomas Kilroy's (1934–   ) later novel *The Big Chapel* (1971), Francis MacManus's *The Greatest of These* was based on ecclesiastical conflicts in Callan, county Kilkenny, during the 1870s. Here the Bishop of Dunmore befriends an ex-priest who was banished by the former bishop, with both of them rediscovering kindness and friendship in old age.

Irish Language and Literature

Comhdháil Náisiúnta na Gaeilge (The national Gaelic congress) was formed, eventually leading to the establishment ten years later of Gael-Linn (Irish with us) (T. Brown 1985, 194).

Inniu (Today), a newspaper in Irish, commenced publishing and continued until 1984.

1944

For the next six years two political parties divided by factionalism, Labour and National Labour, sat separately in the Dáil, "and all hope that Labour might overtake Fine Gael as the main opposition party [to de Valera's dominant Fianna Fáil party] disappeared" (Whyte 1971, 86).

Drama

The Lyric Theatre Company was founded by Austin Clarke.

George Shiels's *The Old Broom* was produced by the Group Theatre in Belfast (Maxwell 1984, xii).

Fiction

Frank O'Connor's excellent story collection *Crab Apple Jelly* was published.

Mary Lavin's *The Long Ago* contained such stories as "The Will," characteristically focused on a young woman left out of her mother's will because she is seen as having married below the family's middle-class position in small-town Ireland.

1945

Drama

Hubert and Dorothy Wilmot founded the Arts Theatre Studio in Belfast.

Fiction

Michael McLaverty's novel *In This Thy Day* showed how rural old people can oppress the young, preventing marriage by refusing to let go of their land.

In her novel *The House in Clewe Street* Mary Lavin depicted an eventually futile relationship between a young middle-class, small-town man and a peasant woman, in the process characteristically indicting narrow-minded, middle-class, small-town life.

Irish Language and Literature

Seán Ó hÉigeartaigh (1917–67) founded the Irish-language publishing house Sáirséal agus Dill, which published among others the novelist Máirtín Ó Cadhain and the poet Seán Ó Ríordáin. David Marcus wrote the following year, "During the last ten years or so Gaelic writing in Ireland has moved into a new era. There has been an eager and widening awareness among the reading public and an atmosphere of excitement in the writing itself—two factors which, in supplementing each other, have generated continuous growth; and among the new writers which this activity has produced are many whose freshness and modernity might be said to have given Irish literature in Gaelic something it never had at any previous stage of its long development—an *avant garde* movement" (quoted in T. Brown 1985, 231).

1946

By this date, only one Irish farmhouse in five had *any* form of toilet, and only one in twenty had one indoors. Only the major towns had any electricity, most rural roads were still dirt, turf remained the main fuel, and women cooked over the open fire (Beale 1987, 21). Halfway through the twentieth century, Ireland had not yet achieved modernity.

Clann na Poblachta (The Republican family) was founded in July by Seán MacBride, Noel Hartnett, Jack McQuillan, and Michael Kelly (general secretary) as the political party furthest to the left. This party began with IRA connections and developed into a force for reform, managing to become part of the coalition government formed two years later. The most controversial government minister of the period, Dr. Noel Browne (1915–   ) (see 1951 entry), was a member of Clann na Poblachta (Hickey and Doherty 1987, 75).

Bord na Móna (The turf board) was established to look over the country's natural turf or peat resources.

Education

In March the Irish National Teachers' Organisation (INTO) staged an ingenious strike: Dublin primary teachers struck while teachers in the rest of the country stayed on the job but supported their Dublin colleagues with contributions from their own salaries. Even though backed by Dublin archbishop John McQuaid, however, INTO was up against governmental intransigence; at the end of October teachers conceded defeat and returned unconditionally to work (Whyte 1971, 120–21).

Fiction

The title story of Mary Lavin's *The Becker Wives and Other Stories* focuses on characters lost in fantasy or trapped in middle-class reality, in either case doomed to failure.

Mervyn Wall's hilarious satire *The Unfortunate Fursey* and its sequel, *The Return of Fursey* (1948), centered on a pseudomedieval monk and slyly avoided censorship by avoiding any overt mention of sex. *The Return of Fursey* depicted a Censor with two independently moving eyes—one to focus exclusively on the "dirty" words in books and one to read everything else—who finds the Old Testament to be "in general tendency indecent."

Like *In a Harbour Green* (1949), Benedict Kiely's early novel *Land without Stars* was set in a northern town in the days leading up to World War II, telling the story of a bookish man who wins a woman after his rival falls prey to violence (a policeman's bullet in *Land without Stars,* and the war in *In a Harbour Green*). As Kiely himself had done, the protagonist of *Land without Stars* leaves a Catholic seminary in the North and sets off for a worldly life in Dublin.

Irish Language and Literature

Liam O'Flaherty returned from America, where he had spent much of the 1930s and early 1940s, to take up more or less permanent residence in Dublin, lasting until his death in 1984. In the 1920s he had bitterly attacked the futility of writing in Irish (see 1927 entry); now more mellow and nostalgic (and financially

more secure) after years in exile, he insisted in an interview in the
Irish Press that Irish publishers should publish only writing in
Irish and that the speaking of English should be banned altogether
for ten years (see Cahalan 1991, 17, 123–25).

Periodicals

Suspicious of Clann na Poblachta (see above) and the involvement
of republicans in official politics, *Resurgence* was a short-lived
newspaper published by a different splinter group of the IRA
(Hickey and Doherty 1987, 506).

Seán O'Faoláin turned over the editorship of the *Bell* to
Peadar O'Donnell. The *Bell* continued until 1954 with O'Donnell
as editor.

Poetry

Denis Devlin's *Lough Derg and Other Poems* were marked by his
choice of characteristically quiet, meditative subjects and wide-
ranging European stylistic influences.

1947

Education

In Northern Ireland, an education act established compulsory and
free secondary education (Darby 1976, xii). This and other
measures, such as the following year's national assistance and
health services programs, improved social services in the North,
keeping them at a level superior to the Republic (and thus
deepening motives to maintain partition).

Fiction

Seán O'Faoláin's *Teresa and Other Stories* incorporated such
stories as "The Silence of the Valley," in which the death of an old
storyteller registers the loss of a traditional way of life, "Lady
Lucifer," and other ironic critiques of Irish society.

Frank O'Connor's collection of stories *The Common Chord*

contained such humorous and ironic glimpses of Irish society as "News for the Church" and "Judas."

Irish Language and Literature

By this time the Irish school system had redoubled its attempts to enforce the government mandates dating from 1922 that sought to require the teaching of Irish in the schools, which had never been effectively carried out to the extent originally envisioned. In this year it was estimated that "the average Irish primary school (excluding infant classes) spent half its total teaching time on the language" (Akenson 1975, 49). The percentage of the population actively speaking Irish outside of school, however, continued to decline.

The Irish-language periodical *Feasta* (Henceforth) was begun by Conradh na Gaeilge (the Gaelic League).

Periodicals

Irish Writing was a quarterly based in Cork and edited by David Marcus and Terence Smith until 1954 (and then by Seán White until 1957). Contributions by O'Flaherty, O'Faoláin, Stephens, O'Connor, MacNeice, and Kavanagh all appeared in its first issue (Denman 1987, 135). *Irish Writing* also published writing from the Continent—Sartre and Beckett, among others—and essays by such non-Irish critics of Irish literature as Donald Davie and Hugh Kenner (T. Brown 1985, 227).

Poetry

In an assessment of "Trends in Irish Poetry" in the *Irish Bookman,* Robert Greacen (1920–) recognized the distinct achievements of northerners such as John Hewitt, Louis Mac-Neice, and Roy McFadden (1921–), and "south of the border" praised Patrick Kavanagh, F. R. Higgins, and Austin Clarke, among others. Greacen concluded, "In the big sense it is still true that the poets are the legislators of the new Ireland, unacknowledged and certainly without much influence in either of our two parliaments" (1947, 63).

Prose Nonfiction

Irish Miles was Frank O'Connor's highly readable account of his bicycle journeys around Ireland, with much attention paid to the monastic sites whose preservation he championed.

O'Faoláin's book *The Irish* classified the country (rather in the fashion of Liam O'Flaherty's *A Tourist's Guide to Ireland* [1929]) into five basic types: rebels, peasants, the Anglo-Irish, priests, and writers.

1948

Eamon de Valera was defeated and Fine Gael leader John A. Costello (1891–1976) became taoiseach until 1951.

Cultural Institutions

An Taisce (The trust) was founded and has since served as the most important independent environmental organization in Ireland. With headquarters in Dublin, An Taisce is concerned with environmental planning and the natural heritage of Ireland in general (de Breffny 1983, 233–34).

Drama

M. J. Molloy's *The King of Friday's Men* was staged at the Abbey; it was set in 1787 in the west of Ireland and dealt with "the feudal mentality." This play was excellent, but the theater and its company were in a period of decline during this period.

Fiction

In a banner year for short fiction, Seán O'Faoláin's collection of stories *The Man Who Invented Sin* and his critical study *The Short Story,* Liam O'Flaherty's *Two Lovely Beasts and Other Stories,* and Máirtín Ó Cadhain's second volume of stories in Irish, *An Braon Broghach* (The dirty drop), all appeared.

The Lion-Tamer and Other Stories was Bryan MacMahon's

(1909–) first collection. A translator of the Kerry storyteller Peig Sayer's Gaelic autobiography, MacMahon is a writer in English quite indebted to the Irish storytelling tradition, and his stories show the influence of folktales.

Patrick Kavanagh's *Tarry Flynn* was a bildungsroman or *Künstlerroman* (artist-novel) about the thirtyish Tarry/Kavanagh's decision to leave his native Monaghan farm and village for Dublin. Tarry has to leave because his inner artistic vision is too much at odds with the grotesque social world of a place where "hating one's next-door neighbour was an essential part of a small farmer's religion."

Irish Language and Literature

An Club Leabhar (The book club) was begun, making literature in Irish available to a surprisingly large readership—with a new book guaranteed a sale of 3,000 copies (T. Brown 1985, 194).

Periodicals

Poetry Ireland, a companion publication to *Irish Writing,* was published until 1956, featuring the work of such poets as Denis Devlin. David Marcus served as its editor between 1948 and 1952; Liam Miller (1924–1987), between 1952 and 1956.

In the North, *Rann: An Ulster Quarterly of Poetry* was edited by Barbara Hunter and Roy McFadden and ran until 1953 (Denman 1987, 135).

1949

In April the Republic of Ireland was officially declared under the recently new coalition government of John Costello. In June the Ireland Act, passed at Westminster, declared that Northern Ireland would remain within the United Kingdom unless its representatives decided otherwise.

The government sponsored the Industrial Development Authority (IDA), which remains today as an agency furthering business growth and encouraging foreign investment in Ireland (Hickey and Doherty 1987, 236).

Drama

Like his earlier play *Purple Dust* (1940) and his later ones *The Bishop's Bonfire* (1954) and *The Drums of Father Ned* (1958), O'Casey's *Cock-a-Doodle Dandy* was a satirical fantasy quite different from his earlier, more celebrated, realistic Dublin plays of the 1920s.

By this date, the Abbey Theatre had produced since its founding a total of 449 plays, of which 384 had been written specifically for the Abbey (Hickey and Doherty 1987, 1).

Fiction

Mary Lavin's novel *Mary O'Grady* focuses on a heroic woman who endures many trials and travails. At the end Mary O'Grady is left consoling her surviving daughter in a scene recalling the conclusion of O'Casey's *Juno and the Paycock* (1924).

Irish Language and Literature

The *Ulysses* of writing in Irish, Máirtín Ó Cadhain's brilliant novel *Cré na Cille* (Churchyard clay), was published. As Caoilfhionn Nic Pháidín noted, "Rinne Ó Cadhain an rud céanna don Ghaeilge is a rinne Joyce don Bhéarla" (Ó Cadhain did the same thing for Irish that Joyce did for English; 1987, 48). A series of voices speak from a graveyard. The first and most central is that of Caitríona Pháidín, an old woman obsessed by a lifelong resentment against her sister Neil, who married the man she loved; Caitríona views her placement in a mere fifteen-shilling grave as Neil's latest assault upon her dignity. The other dominant character is An Máistir Mór (The Big Master), a linguistically learned though nonnative schoolteacher, who, when he discovers that his young widow has remarried to the postman, delivers a series of curses upon him that would have made a Middle Irish satirist proud. *Cré na Cille* is marked by Ó Cadhain's imaginative use of the Irish language and his uncanny, often comic insights into rural Gaelic society.

Periodicals

Much as Fianna Fáil founder Eamon de Valera had helped begin the *Irish Press* in 1931 before he became taoiseach, future Fianna Fáil taoiseach Seán Lemass launched the *Sunday Press* as a rival to the *Sunday Independent*. Lemass demonstrated his characteristic craftiness by enlisting parish priests to help distribute the paper after Sunday masses (Oram 1983, 238–39).

The monthly *Envoy: A Review of Literature and Art* was edited by John Ryan (1925–) and Valetin Iremonger (1918–) until 1951, publishing among others Patrick Kavanagh, Flann O'Brien, Samuel Beckett, Francis Stuart, and Mary Lavin (Denman 1987, 137–38). It also published such relative newcomers as Pearse Hutchinson (1927–), Patrick Galvin (1927–), Thomas Kinsella (1928–), Benedict Kiely, James Plunkett, and John Montague (1929–) (T. Brown 1985, 226).

1950

Cultural Institutions

Thomas McGreevy (1893–1967) became director of the National Gallery of Ireland and served in this position for the next fourteen years (Hickey and Doherty 1987, 339). A scholar and poet, McGreevy was a close friend of James Joyce, Samuel Beckett, and Jack B. Yeats.

Drama

George Bernard Shaw (b. 1856) died in London after a remarkably long and distinguished career.

Fiction

Molloy, the first volume of Samuel Beckett's masterly fictional trilogy written originally in French, was released. In *Molloy* the protagonist sets out looking for his mother, Moran later looks for Molloy, and neither one attains his objective. In *Malone Meurt* (*Malone Dies,* 1951), Malone, who often recalls Molloy as well as Murphy and Watt, sits and writes, preparing to die. *L'Innomable* (*The Unnamable,* 1952) removes any pretence of protagonist or plot: the narrator (who now appears to be the author himself) disparages his own life and writings, deciding in his final words that "I don't know, I'll never know, in the silence you don't know, you must go on, I can't go on, I'll go on."

Walter Macken's (1916–67) novel *Rain on the Wind,* like his subsequent *The Bogman* (1952), concerned the struggles of a young Galwayman to establish an identity and find love despite the worst machinations of his relatives and surrounding society. Macken described the arranged marriages still common in rural Ireland at this time; the protagonist of *The Bogman* thinks to himself, "She could cook, couldn't she, and she had 250 pounds in the bank as Barney stated and you could buy a new mowing-machine for that and a new plough and maybe another cow and they would be living on the fat of the land. Where was all the love business you read about in books long ago? He never saw any of it around Caherlo. They got married this way."

1951

Minister for Health Noel Browne's "Mother and Child Scheme" was an attempt to provide government-funded health care to mothers before and after childbirth and to newborns. In the face of opposition by the Catholic hierarchy, the coalition government did not back the socialist Browne (who resigned afterward), and withdrew the plan.

Soon thereafter John A. Costello was defeated as taoiseach and Eamon de Valera took over again, until 1954. Subsequently de Valera would serve a final term as taoiseach from 1957 to 1959 and then as president from 1959 to 1973.

Later to be the most popular (for the extreme Unionist) or infamous (for the nationalist), working-class, Protestant leader in Northern Ireland, the Reverend Ian Paisley (1926–   ) began his Free Presbyterian church of Ulster, a splinter denomination of the mainstream Presbyterian church.

Cultural Institutions

An Chomhairle Ealaíon (The Arts Council) was established by the Republic to support and fund work in literature, theater, dance, visual arts, film, and music. It disburses annual grants to creative artists.

Drama

The Abbey Theatre building was destroyed by an accidental fire; coming during a low phase in the history of the theater, its temporary demise seemed symbolic.

The Lyric Players were founded in Belfast by Mary and Pearse O'Malley, and ever since (particularly since the opening of the Lyric Players' Theatre in 1968) have provided a crucial, respected center for drama in the North.

Fiction

Francis MacManus examined sexual repression in his novel *The Fire in the Dust,* in which the frenzy of an unmarried woman leads to the death of another character.

Mary Lavin's collection of stories *A Single Lady* was released.

Frank O'Connor published *Traveller's Samples,* a collection of stories.

Michael McLaverty's novel *Truth in the Night* characteristically focused on the tension between city life and country life in the North. Martin Gallagher moves back to Rathlin Island from Belfast only to encounter mounting tragedy: he falls in love with a widow from the mainland who feels rejected by her dead husband's island family, but after he marries her both she and her daughter die and Martin is left to eke out an existence all by himself.

Sam Hanna Bell's (1909–   ) novel *December Bride* was the story of a ménage-à-trois between Hamilton and Frank Echlin, farmers and brothers, and Sarah Gomartin, originally their servant.

Film

The feature film *Return to Glenascaul*, written by Micheál MacLiammóir, was produced and directed by Hilton Edwards with a Gate Theatre cast. In the following year MacLiammóir-Edwards Productions made a documentary about a production of *Hamlet*, and in 1953 a second short feature, *From Time to Time* (de Breffny 1983, 64).

Literary Criticism

Austin Clarke's *Poetry in Modern Ireland* sought to explain the special qualities of Irish writing that distinguished it from literature in England.

Music

Comhaltas Ceoltóirí Éireann (The association of musicians of Ireland, originally called Cumann Ceoltóirí na hÉireann) was founded to foster the appreciation and sustenance of traditional Irish music, greatly contributing over the years to the subsequent revival and rejuvenation of musical interest and activity in recent decades.

The Pipers' Club of Dublin held the first National Fleadh (festival) in Mullingar in this year, with traditional musicians from around the country competing on various instruments. By the following year this annual event was given the name Fleadh Cheoil na hÉireann (Music festival of Ireland), and has been sponsored annually since then by Comhaltas Ceoltóirí Éireann. It has grown steadily to the point where it typically attracts 100,000 or so people to whatever town hosts it each August, serving as a significant gathering point for the upsurge of interest in Irish traditional music since the 1950s.

Poetry

Liam Miller founded the Dolmen Press, which would adopt a very high standard of design and production in its many publications of poets and other Irish writers over the years.

1952

Fiction

Mervyn Wall's novel *Leaves for the Burning* captured his own real, confined world living in a small town and working for the Irish Civil Service.

Stories, a mostly retrospective collection by Frank O'Connor, served as recognition of his growing and major reputation as an author of short stories. It did contain some new stories, including perhaps his most celebrated comic work, the much anthologized "My Oedipus Complex."

Irish Language and Literature

Seán Ó Ríordáin's volume *Eireaball Spideoige* (A robin's tail) introduced a rich vocabulary and texture into contemporary poetry in Irish. Born in an Irish-speaking area in western county Cork, Ó Ríordáin managed to turn personal difficulties—his mother's death, his own tuberculosis—into the stuff of excellent poetry throughout his career, which lasted until his death in 1977.

1953

With the establishment of the Divis transmitter in Northern Ireland, BBC television began to be picked up in Ireland much more widely (Maxwell 1984, 159).

Architecture

Michael Scott designed the most notable modern building in central Dublin, the Bus Éireann building at Store Street near (and in direct conflict with) Gandon's classical Custom House on the River Liffey (de Breffny 1983, 30).

Drama

Beckett's *Waiting for Godot* made its historic debut in Paris. This absurdist work of genius was the most influential play of the contemporary period in world literature, entertaining and confusing audiences in its first performances in London and Miami as well as Paris, and provoking a number of plays by others and much talk about the "theater of the absurd." In it Vladimir and Estragon wait for Godot, who never arrives. It was said that this two-act work was a "play in which nothing happens, twice." The two engage in much existential repartee, interrupted only by a traveler, his slave, and a boy (Godot's messenger).

In Dublin Alan Simpson (1920–80), a young director, and Carolyn Simpson founded the Pike Theatre, a tiny, experimental venture, which staged Brendan Behan's (1923–64) *The Quare Fellow* in 1954 and Beckett's *Godot* in its Irish premiere (and only its second production in English) in 1956.

Fiction

Beckett's novel *Watt* also appeared, though he had written it before World War II. *Watt* is set in Beckett's own boyhood, south-suburban area of Dublin and is his most direct fictional response to the tradition of the Irish novel. Watt journeys by train from central Dublin to Leopardstown (described though never named) to work in the home of Mr. Knott; he mysteriously sojourns in a mental institution where he tells his story to "Sam," a fellow inmate; and he finally leaves Knott's house, returns to the nearby train station, and waits for another train, taking him in we know not which direction. If Watt ("what?") is the question, then Knott ("naught" or "not") is Beckett's answer.

Benedict Kiely's novel *The Cards of the Gambler* was a new departure—a tour de force making very deliberate use of a folktale. Brief "interludes" recounting segments of the gambler's story in its original fireside form alternated with chapters transforming the story into a novel.

Irish Language and Literature

Dúil (Desire) was Liam O'Flaherty's only volume in Irish, and in the view of many the best collection of modern short stories in that language. It included versions of eighteen stories of animal and peasant life that also appeared in O'Flaherty's English collections, as well as three stories never published in English ("An tAonach" [The fair], "An Charraig Dhubh" [The black rock], and "An Fiach" [The hunt]). Máirtín Ó Cadhain's story collection *Cois Caoláire* (Beside the inlet) also appeared. Particularly impressive was its long story, almost a novella, "An Strainséara" (The stranger). Gael-Linn (Irish with us) was formed, becoming—especially as distributor of films such as *Saoirse?* (Freedom?) and *Mise Éire* (I am Ireland), as well as tapes and records—a major disseminator of Irish-language materials over the next four decades.

Poetry

Louis MacNeice's *Autumn Journal,* a long poem in terza rima, was an attempt to unify his views about life and poetry. MacNeice was often cited as a British poet, but he recognized his roots in Ireland.

1954

Fine Gael leader John Costello once again formed a coalition government replacing that of his rival, Eamon de Valera, as had occurred also in 1948.

Drama

The Quare Fellow by the celebrated playwright, rebel, and character Brendan Behan made its debut at Alan Simpson's Pike Theatre in Dublin. This controversial prison drama had earlier been rejected by both the Abbey and Gate theaters (reflecting the fact that theatrical innovation had been pushed elsewhere). After its Pike premiere, the play was a great success in its six-month run in London, arriving there in timely fashion at the height of the campaign against capital punishment. It is notable for its gallows humor and realistic, gritty dialogue—recalling O'Casey and based on Behan's own experiences in Dublin's Montjoy Prison—and the fact that the play's central character, the "quare" (or isolated, odd) man who is hung at the end of the play, never appears onstage.

1955

Bord Fáilte, the Irish Tourist Board, was established (Hickey and Doherty 1987, 40).

Drama

The actor-director Cyril Cusack (1910–   ) managed to stage O'Casey's *The Bishop's Bonfire* at the Gaiety Theatre for five weeks over the objections of the archbishop of Dublin, John Charles McQuaid (T. Brown 1985, 229).

In an essay on "The Future of the Irish Theatre" in *Studies,* Gabriel Fallon (1898–1980) argued that "a people gets the theatre it deserves, and . . . the present condition of the Irish theatre reflects the condition of the Irish people. The nationalist impulses which led to the foundation of the Abbey Theatre are no longer with us and seemingly we have nothing to take their place. . . . The Irish Theatre lacks vision because we, its audiences, lack vision" (1955, 99).

Fiction

Encountering strong censorship in Ireland (where it was banned again as late as 1969), Irish-American J. P. Donleavy's (1926–   ) first novel, *The Ginger Man,* created quite a stir in Dublin. It is the racy story of a student at Trinity College and his comrades in youthful debauchery.

Brian Moore's (1921–   ) *The Lonely Passion of Judith Hearne* was immediately and widely hailed as an impressive first novel and remains Moore's most consistently praised work. Focused on her desperate consciousness, it tells the story of how a middle-aged Belfast piano teacher fails in her attempt to match herself with a returned Yank (the blowhard brother of her land-lady), is discovered to be an alcoholic, dismissed by her landlady and dropped by her clients, treated with indifference by the local priest, and finally committed to a nursing home, having been virtually destroyed by societal forces.

In *The Big Windows* Peadar O'Donnell showed that he was not opposed to change in rural Donegal, as he also proved many times in his long life of political and social activism. In this novel Brigid Manus insists to her husband that their home will have big windows, not the traditional claustrophobic panes, and she also wins out in her insistence on having a doctor attend to the birth of their first child, to the secret relief of women who lost children in childbirth under the traditional taboo against the presence of a doctor.

James Plunkett, who had begun by publishing stories in the *Bell* under Seán O'Faoláin's mentorship, made his debut in book form with his excellent collection of stories *The Trusting and the Maimed*. The title story and others such as "The Eagles and the Trumpets" were penetrating glimpses of lower-middle-class life in Dublin at midcentury. This was the best volume of Dublin stories of this kind since Joyce's *Dubliners*. In this same year Plunkett visited the Soviet Union as part of a delegation of Irish writers and artists, including Anthony Cronin (1925–   ) and others, at the invitation of the Soviet secretary of arts. As a result he was attacked by the conservative *Catholic Standard,* which called for his resignation as secretary of Jim Larkin's Workers' Union. Plunkett was strongly backed by his union, and left this position later in the year quite voluntarily in order to take a new job as drama assistant for Radio Éireann.

Poetry

Austin Clarke's volume *Ancient Lights* marked the beginning of the last, best, most prolific phase of his career, which continued until his death in 1974. Here his poems became significantly more conversational and anecdotal in tone and style than those of previous volumes.

1956

The census revealed that almost 200,000 people had left Ireland during the previous five years. A government Commission on

Emigration reported that "emigration has been due to two fundamental causes—the absence of opportunities for making an
adequate livelihood, and a growing desire for higher standards of
living on the part of the community, particularly the rural
community. . . . Nowadays, fewer people are satisfied with a
subsistence standard of living and they find an easy alternative in
emigration" (quoted in Beale 1987, 39).

Fiction

The Stories of Liam O'Flaherty included not only some of his best
earlier works but also such later, masterly stories as "Two Lovely
Beasts," "The Touch," "The New Suit," "Galway Bay," "The
Blow," "Desire," and "The Post Office." This collection did more
than any other to solidify O'Flaherty's international reputation,
but he virtually ceased publication after this date though he lived
another three decades.

Irish Language and Literature

Máire Mhac an tSaoi's *Margadh na Saoire* (Market of freedom)
contained poems praised for their craft, their command of Munster Irish, and their erudition. Born in Dublin but spending much
of her childhood on the Irish-speaking Dingle peninsula in county
Kerry, Mhac an tSaoi (the daughter of a Free State minister and
the wife of Conor Cruise O'Brien, the outspoken author and
government official) has worked as a scholar and foreign service
officer as well as a poet (Murphy and MacKillop 1987, 362).

1957

Eamon de Valera formed his third separate Fianna Fail government, serving in his final term as taoiseach until 1959. On New
Year's Day two young Catholic IRA men, Seán South and Fergal
O'Hanlon, were killed during an IRA attack on Brookeborough
police barracks in Northern Ireland. Seán South's funeral in
Limerick was the occasion of nationalist mourning and renewed
support for the IRA (Whyte 1971, 321–22).

    In response to a petition circulated in the previous year by the

Irish Association of Civil Liberties for an inquiry into the workings of the Censorship Board–which had banned more books than ever during the years 1950–55, including works by André Gide, Jean-Paul Sartre, Ernest Hemingway, John Steinbeck, Tennessee Williams, and Graham Greene—liberals were appointed to the board, conservatives resigned, and the board from this date onward banned mostly only clearly pornographic works (Whyte 1971, 315–16).

Drama

The Dublin Theatre Festival was begun—bringing together many playwrights (including international ones) and involving numerous theaters ranging from the Abbey to much smaller, newer venues. Plays produced included O'Casey's *Juno and the Paycock,* Synge's *The Playboy of the Western World,* Wilde's *The Importance of Being Earnest,* Denis Johnston's *The Old Lady Says "No!,"* seven of Yeats's plays, Tennessee Williams's *The Rose Tattoo,* and Swedish playwright Stig Dagerman's *The Shadow of Mart.* Concluded Gabriel Fallon in a review of the festival in *Threshold,* "If something which leads to an examination of conscience, to a reassessment of values, may be termed a success, then Dublin's first International Theatre Festival may, I think, be described as successful" (1957, 75). This festival has continued in virtually every year since, with the notable exception of 1958 (see below). It typically entails thirty to forty different productions over a three-week period in September.

Meanwhile, Alan Simpson was arrested for "presenting for gain an indecent and profane performance"—Tennessee Williams's *The Rose Tatoo.* Even though the entire cast was subsequently threatened with arrest, the play went on and Simpson was eventually cleared in Dublin District Court. Terence Brown calls this "a turning point in Irish theatrical life" (1985, 229–30).

Beckett's *Fin de Partie* (*Endgame*) was performed for the first time at the Royal Court Theatre in London. A play that *begins* with the words "Almost finished . . . ," *Endgame* is considered by many to be Beckett's masterpiece. In a single focused act, the blind Hamm and his attendant and companion Clov remain in a stark room, accompanied only by Hamm's father and mother, Nagg and

Nell, who live in trash cans. Often performed together with *Endgame* is Beckett's short mime *Acte sans parole* (*Act without Words*), in which the Chaplinesque sole character pursues a series of futile attempts to grasp a container of water that is always withdrawn beyond his grasp.

Also in this same year, Beckett's *All That Fall* was broadcast by the BBC. Written (in Beckett's words) for "voices coming out of the dark," this radio play focuses on elderly Mr. and Mrs. Rooney, who struggle to meet at a train station and then (after the arrival of the train, which has been delayed after a child has fallen out and been crushed beneath its wheels) trudge homeward. Like Hamm in *Endgame,* Mr. Rooney is blind, but unlike *Endgame* and all of Beckett's other plays, this one has a realistic Irish setting— Leopardstown and Foxrock, near Beckett's boyhood home.

Fiction

Frank O'Connor's story collection *Domestic Relations* furthered his art of presenting childhood experiences through deliciously naive narrative exteriors, as in "The Genius."

Periodicals

Threshold began as a quarterly journal, edited by Mary O'Malley, of the Lyric Players Theatre, with John Hewitt as poetry editor. Later it employed guest editors including Brian Friel (1929–   ), Roger MacHugh, Seamus Heaney (1939–   ), John Montague (1929–   ) and Seamus Deane (1940–   ) (Denman 1987, 136).

Prose Nonfiction

In a book review in the Dublin Jesuit scholarly journal *Studies,* a young (and later immensely influential) historian at Trinity College, F.S.L. Lyons (1923–83), introduced the notion of "historical revision," arguing that modern Irish history needed to be reexamined with a new critical objectivity (T. Brown 1985, 227–28). From then until the present day, Irish historical "revisionism" has been a dominant trend, with historians such as Lyons, R. Dudley

Edwards (1944–   ), and numerous others determined to examine Irish history in an unsentimental, detached manner.

1958

Finance Secretary T. K. Whitaker (1916) published an influential plan for economic development that stressed attracting foreign investors to Ireland and generally internationalizing and modernizing the country's economy. The true "modernization" of Ireland is dated from around this time—and during the prime ministership (1959–66) of Seán Lemass—by many historians and remembered by many Irish people in general. Terence Brown asserted in 1985 that "Irishmen and women believe now, as they believed then, that those five years [between 1958 and 1963] represented a major turning point in Irish fortunes" (241).

Drama

This was the year of Brendan Behan's most famous play, *The Hostage,* which (with Joan Littlewood's encouragement and collaboration) he rewrote from its lyric Gaelic original version, *An Giall* (commissioned by Gael-Linn), into a tragicomic drama full of macabre songs and humor. It focused on an Englishman taken hostage by the IRA who falls in love with a young Irishwoman.

In what would have been its second year, the Dublin Theatre Festival was canceled after ecclesiastical disapproval of the inclusion of work by James Joyce and O'Casey's *The Drums of Father Ned.*

Lennox Robinson (b. 1886) died.

Samuel Beckett's *Krapp's Last Tape* was produced at the Royal Court Theatre in London (Maxwell 1984, xiii).

Fiction

The Feast of Lupercal was Brian Moore's second Belfast novel, portraying (like *The Lonely Passion of Judith Hearne* [1955]) a protagonist defeated by a narrow-minded Catholic society. A thirty-seven-year-old schoolteacher nicknamed "Dev" (like the

puritan southern head of state, de Valera), Diarmuid Devine takes
up an interest in Una Clarke, a nineteen-year-old Protestant from
Dublin, but he has to endure both his failure to consummate any
affair with her and the public humiliation of having her uncle, his
superior, cane him like a schoolboy after he hears of Una's
overnight stay in Diarmuid's flat.

The Stories of Seán O'Faoláin was a retrospective anthology
that also contained some new work, such as "Lovers of the Lake."

Irish Language and Literature

Richard Power (1928–70) published a novel in Irish set in Galway
and the Aran Islands, *Úll i mBárr an Ghéagáin* (*Apple on the
Treetop*).

Poetry

Another September, Dubliner Thomas Kinsella's first collection,
launched his distinguished career.

Prose Nonfiction

Borstal Boy was Brendan Behan's alternately grim and hilarious
memoir, focused on his days as an IRA prisoner in England.

1959

Fianna Fáil leader Seán Lemass became taoiseach, serving until
1966. Eamon de Valera moved to the more ceremonial position of
president, until 1975. As head of state Lemass is credited with
enacting many aspects of T. K. Whitaker's economic plan—in
general taking steps toward modernizing and internationalizing
Ireland's economy (see 1958 entry). A persuasive case could be
made that Lemass as taoiseach was Ireland's Franklin Delano
Roosevelt; he would be remembered as such a turning-point figure
by the Irish people. Lemass concluded a talk on "The Role of the
State-Sponsored Bodies in the Economy," published in this year,
with the characteristic thesis that "state boards and companies

267

... can by leadership and example, set standards of performance which can inspire private enterprise to greater achievements and help to build up confidence in the country's future" (14).

The Irish Congress of Trade Unions (ICTU) was formed out of the previous organizations the Irish Trades Union Congress and the Congress of Irish Unions. Its ninety-three affiliated unions had a combined membership of 438,000; by 1977 this figure would increase to 564,000 (Hickey and Doherty 1987, 243).

Drama

Sive by county Kerry author John B. Keane (1928–   ) won several awards at the National Amateur Drama Festival and became one of the most frequently performed plays of the period. It concerned a young woman forced into marriage by her father in Keane's characteristically vivid county Kerry. Keane's home base was Cork's Southern Theatre Group.

Fiction

Walter Macken's historical novel *Seek the Fair Land,* and its sequels *The Silent People* (1962) and *The Scorching Wind* (1964), focused respectively on the adventures of romantic heroes during the seventeenth-century Cromwellian reign of terror, the nineteenth-century Great Hunger, and the twentieth-century Civil War.

Film

The very popular historical film *Mise Éire* (I am Ireland)— compiled, edited, and directed by George Morrison with a musical score by Seán Ó Riada (1931–71), was sponsored by Gael-Linn.

Irish Language and Literature

A reflection of the extent of the failure to revive Irish by requiring it in the schools—and one source for the resentment of non-Irish speakers—was the fact that of the 1,068 students who failed the leaving certificate examination (at the end of secondary schooling) in this year, "373 would have passed but for their failure in Irish" (Akenson 1975, 53).

Tomás de Bhaldraithe's major *English-Irish Dictionary* was published by the government.

Máire Mhac an tSaoi's *A Heart Full of Thought,* poems translated from the Irish, appeared.

Literary Criticism

Richard Ellmann's *James Joyce* was the most significant Irish literary biography, and many believe the best biography in world literature, of any writer in the twentieth century. This noted American scholar earlier published books on Yeats, and subsequently spent years completing another large biography of Oscar Wilde.

Echoing Patrick Kavanagh's poem "Who Killed James Joyce?," Myles na gCopaleen (Brian O'Nolan/Flann O'Brien) complained in the *Irish Times,* "Witness the shower of gawms who erupt from the prairie universities to do a 'thesis' on James Joyce" (quoted in Powell, 60).

Music

Seoirse Bodley's (1933–) Symphony No. 1 enjoyed its first performance; since then Bodley has remained the Irish composer most devoted to avant-garde techniques (de Breffny 1983, 44).

1960

The 1960s would be the decade of Irish prominence in the United Nations, the advent of Irish television, the second Vatican Council, the sharp increase of tourism to Ireland, and the growth of the economy in general and modest liberalization of social mores and widening of horizons.

The Economic and Social Research Institute was founded by the government, reflecting Taoiseach Lemass's determination to base social and economic decisions on hard data (T. Brown 1985, 257).

Irish television began under the terms of an act passed in this year, though it was not until 1962 (after its first public transmission on 31 December 1961) that it began to broadcast regularly. This act directed Radio Telefís Éireann (as it was called) to bear constantly in mind the needs of the Irish language, but over the years television—with many shows imported from England and America—has instead served to maximize the influence of the English language and its culture throughout the country. Given its major role in the increasing "Americanization" of Ireland, it seems appropriate that RTE's first broadcast was "The Cisco Kid" (Maxwell 1984, 159).

Cultural Institutions

The Yeats Summer School commenced its annual gatherings in Sligo, providing a meeting place and inspiration for an international bevy of scholars and Yeats enthusiasts.

Fiction

Edna O'Brien's (1932–   ) first novel, *The Country Girls,* and its sequels, *The Lonely Girl* (1962) and *Girls in Their Married Bliss* (1964), created quite a stir. The subject of these novels was located in previously uncharted fictional territory: the struggles, sexual and otherwise, of two young girls from county Clare, the earnest Kate and the racy Baba, who make their way together from a rural Catholic boarding school to jobs and flats in Dublin, and then, as young women, into unsuccessful marriages in London.

Benedict Kiely's novel *The Captain with the Whiskers* was dedicated "to the memory of my father, Tom Kiely, who talked with the wizard Doran on the Cornavara Mountain in the County Tyrone"—with the wizard lurking as one of several emblematic figures haunting the boyhood of Kiely's protagonist.

Felo de Se, a collection of stories, was Aidan Higgins's (1927–   ) first book.

Literary Criticism

In an article in *Catholic World,* Stephen P. Ryan asked, "What has become of the Emerald Isle's once promising literary revival?"

The emergence of a new generation of diverse literary talents, however, belied his query.

Periodicals

The *Kilkenny Magazine: An All-Ireland Literary Review* appeared quarterly until 1970 under the editorship of James Delehanty. Established writers such as Frank O'Connor, Pádraic Colum, and Austin Clarke appeared in its pages, as did such new writers as Seamus Heaney, John Banville (1946–   ), and Thomas MacIntyre (Denman 1987, 138–39).

1961

The population of the Republic was down to 2.8 million, more than 400,000 having emigrated (many to Britain) during the preceding decade (Foster 1988, 578).

Ireland applied for membership in the European Economic Community (granted eleven years later).

In this year there were in Ireland 7.3 psychiatric beds per 1,000 citizens, compared to 4.6 in England and Wales and 4.3 in Scotland—reflecting the fact that "southern Ireland has the highest proportion of persons in psychiatric hospitals of any nation in the world" (Akenson 1975, 142).

Drama

The ramifications of Irish emigration to Britain were powerfully examined in *A Whistle in the Dark* by Thomas Murphy (1936–   ), a tragedy focused on the intense lives of Irish laborers in Coventry. It had a very successful run in London's West End.

Fiction

O'Faoláin's story collection *I Remember! I Remember!* was published.

Beckett's *Comment c'est* (*How It Is*) was a long narrative that departed from conventional punctuation and syntax. Subsequently he abandoned the novel form altogether, writing progressively shorter and shorter fictions and drama.

Encouraged by the successful new edition of *At Swim-Two-Birds* (1939) in the previous year, Flann O'Brien broke a long silence as a fiction writer and published *The Hard Life,* an amusing but lesser Dublin novel.

Irish Language and Literature

Gaelic poet Máirtín Ó Direáin's *Feamainn Bhealtaine* (May seaweed), recounted his boyhood on the Aran Islands.

Music

Seán Ó Riada founded Ceoltóirí Cualann, an innovative traditional music ensemble whose members included the talented piper Paddy Moloney and several other future members of the Chieftains, the world-famous Irish musical group.

Periodicals

The *Dubliner* was a poetry magazine that ran until 1972, under the editorship of Donald Carroll and then Bruce Arnold, publishing early poems by poets connected to Trinity College, Dublin, such as Derek Mahon, Michael Longley, Brendan Kennelly (1936–   ), and Eavan Boland (1945–   ), as well as John Montague, Austin Clarke, and Seamus Heaney (Denman 1987, 139).

Poetry

Poisoned Lands was the first collection by John Montague, who was born in Brooklyn in 1929 but raised in county Tyrone.

Prose Nonfiction

Frank O'Connor published *An Only Child,* a memoir of his difficult but delicious youth.

1962

Art

Originally founded as the Belfast Municipal Museum and Art Gallery in 1892, the Ulster Museum opened in greatly enlarged quarters in Belfast (de Breffny 1983, 245).

Cultural Institutions

Michael J. O'Kelly and his team of archeologists began their excavations of an impressive ancient passage grave at Newgrange, county Meath, known since 1699 and open to the public today (with a reconstructed exterior). One of the most impressive discoveries was that the entryway to the grave had been constructed so that sunlight perfectly illuminated the interior at winter solstice.

Drama

Brian Friel's *The Enemy Within* premiered at the Abbey. Friel was to become the most celebrated current Irish playwright.

Samuel Beckett's *Happy Days* was staged at the Royal Court Theatre in London (Maxwell 1984, xiii).

Irish Language and Literature

Eogan Ó Tuairisc's *L'Attaque,* a historical novel in Irish, examined the impact upon the Irish peasantry brought to bear by the French soldiers and Anglo-Irish republicans who joined them in the 1798 rising in county Mayo.

As in his earlier *Saol Saighdiura* (A soldier's life, 1960), Donal MacAmhlaigh (1926–   ) in his autobiographical *Dialann Deorai* (Journal of an Irish navvy) focused on the difficult experiences of an Irish speaker in England.

Literary Criticism

Frank O'Connor's *The Lonely Voice* was a provocative and influential study of the short story as a form.

Music

The Cork composer and musician Seán Ó Riada delivered a series of talks on Irish radio about "Our Musical Heritage." Ó Riada was arguably the father of the contemporary Irish folk music revival that grew up during the 1960s and 1970s. He died in 1971.

Periodicals

Poetry Ireland, reviving the name of David Marcus's earlier journal, was edited by John Jordan (1930–   ) until 1968, carrying the work of young poets such as Longley, Mahon, Heaney, and Paul Durcan (1944–   ) (Denman 1987, 140).

Poetry

Downstream was a collection of poems by Thomas Kinsella.

1963

The moderate Terence O'Neill (1914–   ) succeeded Lord Brookborough (1888–1974) as prime minister of Northern Ireland.

The American journalist Donald Corkery wrote that "returning to Ireland in early 1963 it was impossible not to feel the atmosphere change or notice the many signs of modernization. There was an unaccustomed briskness about the way Dubliners moved and a freshness of complexion which I had not seen before" (quoted in T. Brown 1985, 244).

Fiction

John McGahern (1934–   ) made an impressive debut with his novel *The Barracks,* focused on a policeman's wife who is dying of cancer. Here illness and death, existentially confronted, are revealed as humanizing forces.

Michael Farrell's *Thy Tears Might Cease* was a bildungsroman and roman à clef examining the growth from boyhood to manhood of Martin Matthew Reilly during the placid, then turbulent 1910–20 decade, with particular attention to the Easter Rising as a turning point.

Northerner Anthony C. West's (1910–88) novel *The Ferret Fancier* focused on a boy's dual, overlapping pastimes: his husbanding of ferrets that are used to kill rabbits for sport and profit, and his fantasies about sex.

Benedict Kiely's first collection of stories, *A Journey to the Seven Streams,* appeared.

Periodicals

Arena was edited until 1965 by James Liddy (1934–   ) and Liam O'Connor, featuring poetry by Patrick Kavanagh, Derek Mahon, Paul Durcan, and Michael Hartnett (1941–   ) (Denman 1987, 140).

Poetry

Sailing to an Island was the first collection by Richard Murphy (1927–   ), who had settled on the island of Inishbofin off the west coast of Ireland after graduating from Oxford. This volume was informed by the knowledge of fishing that Murphy gained on Inishbofin.

1964

Architecture

Desmond Rae O'Kelly designed the Connolly Building, headquarters for the Irish Transport and General Workers Union and also Dublin's tallest building (de Breffny 1983, 31).

Drama

Seán O'Casey (b. 1880) died at the age of eighty-four.

Brian Friel, the greatest living Irish playwright, came to wide recognition with his remarkable fourth play, *Philadelphia, Here I Come,* a probing study of the tension between a father and his about-to-be exiled son and between the son's inner and outer personalities—"Gar O'Donnell (Public)" and "(Private)"—as separately represented on the stage. Friel's play and Eugene McCabe's (1930–   ) *King of the Castle* were both produced at the Dublin Theatre Festival. Friel had written many more short stories than plays at this point, noting in an interview in *Acorn* (a magazine of Magee University in Derry), "I don't concentrate on the theatre at all. I live on short stories" (no. 8 [Spring 1965]: 4). His continued success in the theater would change that.

Fiction

Janet McNeill's (1907–   ) novel *The Maiden Dinosaur* dealt with the theme of sexual frustration from the perspective of a woman who was sexually abused by her father and whose later interactions with men are marked by that experience.

Anthony Cronin's novel *The Life of Riley* was a picaresque, rather comic account of Patrick Riley's downward progression from itinerant jobs in Dublin to total lethargy in England.

According to the typically confusing publication history of this man with the many names, Flann O'Brien's *The Dalkey Archive* was a highly entertaining though inferior revision of a novel that he had written many years earlier, but which was published in its original form only after his death: *The Third Policeman* (see 1967 entry).

Frank O'Connor's *Collection Two* helped solidify his reputation as a master of short fiction.

Poetry

Denis Devlin's *Collected Poems* brought belated recognition to this writer, who died in 1959.

The *Collected Poems* of Patrick Kavanagh (appearing three years before his death) facilitated a retrospective view of his work.

Prose Nonfiction

Seán O'Faoláin's memoir *Vive Moi!* explored the formative influences on the imagination of this writer who in turn influenced more younger Irish writers than anyone since Yeats.

1965

Northern Ireland prime minister Terence O'Neill and Republic of Ireland taoiseach Seán Lemass held talks in an unsuccessful attempt to improve North–South border relations.

Drama

John B. Keane's play *The Field,* like the even more popular 1990 film version starring Richard Harris, was a tragedy focused on the Lear-like paterfamilias Bull McCabe, who destroys both his sons and himself in the process of trying to hold onto a patch of land that he had rented and nurtured for years, after he is outbid for it at a public auction by an American.

Fiction

Brian Moore published his third Belfast novel, *The Emperor of Ice-Cream,* after he had already published two novels set in North America, where he had been living since 1948. It recounted a variety of episodes united under the theme of Gavin Burke's maturation during World War II. Included are Moore's glimpses of 1930s socialists in Belfast, Gavin's unresolved relationship with his girlfriend, his rebellion against his narrow-minded Catholic father, and his adventures with an army air-raid unit, culminating in his heroic and cathartic work among the victims of the German bombing of Belfast.

An even more impressive autobiographical novel was John McGahern's *The Dark,* focused on a boy who grows up in conflict with his father yet nonetheless comes to accept him. This novel's graphic descriptions of the boy's masturbatory fantasies provoked its banning even though the Censorship Board was by then considerably less rigid than it had been in the 1930s.

The protagonist of John Broderick's (1927–) novel *The Waking of Willie Ryan,* having had a homosexual love affair and having been committed to an institution by his sister-in-law and the parish priest, returns to vanquish his foes quietly in his own way.

Iris Murdoch's (1920–) *The Red and the Green* was a

historical novel dealing with conflicts within an Anglo-Irish family at the time of the 1916 Easter Rising.

Film

Samuel Beckett's *Film* premiered at the Venice Film Festival (Maxwell 1984, xiv).

Irish Language and Literature

Seanchas ón Thiar (Folklore from the west) was a book of stories by the great Blasket Island storyteller Tomás Ó Criomhtháin, dictated the year before his death in 1937, to Robin Flower.

The government's White Paper on the Irish Language recognized that "competent knowledge of English will be needed even in a predominantly Irish-speaking Ireland" since English provides access to "the large body of Irish literature written in English and to the prose, poetry, songs and speeches in which Irish national aspiration have to a large extent been expressed" (quoted in T. Brown 1985, 315).

Music

The Irish National Opera was founded and has since given hundreds of performances throughout the country (de Breffny 1983, 175).

1966

Fianna Fáil leader Jack Lynch (1917–   ) replaced Seán Lemass as taoiseach, remaining in power until 1973, with Eamon de Valera continuing until the same year in the ceremonial role of president.

In the North, the Protestant extremist Ulster Volunteer Force (UVF) declared war on "the IRA and its splinter groups" (quoted in Darby 1976, xii).

During observances of the fiftieth anniversary of the Easter Rising, a group of radical revivalists named Misneach (Courage)

278

Modern Irish Literature and Culture

mounted a week-long hunger strike in Belfast and Dublin to remind Irishmen and women of past idealism; this group's founders included Máirtín Ó Cadhain and two of his best contemporary successors as novelists in Irish, Eoghan Ó Tuairisc and Diarmaid Ó Súilleabháin (1932–85) (T. Brown 1985, 270).

Drama

The Abbey and Peacock Theatres moved to their present location in Lower Abbey Street, in a building designed by Michael Scott and Ronald Tallon. Hugh Hunt has described its "fan-shaped auditorium" with "a seating capacity of 628 of which ninety-seven are located in a shallow balcony. . . . The open stage, with its forestage mounted on two lifts that descend to form an orchestra pit, can extend forward to a total of fourteen feet from the curtain line, and provides a sense of intimacy between players and audience" (quoted in Maxwell 1984, 160). Tomas MacAnna was appointed artistic adviser of the Abbey. Liam Miller wrote in an article in *Studies,* "it is on the National Theatre that our hopes for the future of theatre in Ireland must be based. Despite the depressions and disappointments, we have in the Abbey a company with a long-standing tradition, with the necessary technical equipment and with the facilities for training the next generation of players. The Government have provided an excellent permanent home for the company and now it is the duty of the public to indicate what it wants from its national theatre and to see that its wishes are carried out. A National Theatre of international quality and reputation would be a most valuable addition to the image we try to project abroad of the Ireland of today" (1966, 235).

Education

Investment in Education, the report of a special government commission, took an unsentimental look at the Irish educational system and advocated many important reforms. This allowed Irish schools to begin to move gradually away from the narrow-minded reinforcement of "Irish Ireland" ideals toward the fulfillment of the modern needs of students, with significant reorganization and reorientation at both primary and secondary levels.

Nollaig Ó Gadhra remarked in the journal of the Irish-American Cultural Institute, *Éire-Ireland,* that "many who still proclaim allegiance to the ideals of the 1916 leaders played down the vital importance which almost all of these men attached to the task of reviving the native language. The economic gospel seemed to have ousted the social and cultural ideals" (T. Brown 1985, 249–51, 269–70).

Fiction

Aidan Higgin's novel *Langrishe, Go Down* was a penetrating, brilliantly written examination of the inhabitants of a decayed Anglo-Irish estate in north Kildare during the 1930s—the sisters Imogen and Helen Langrishe—and their intellectual and cynically ruthless visitor, the German student Otto Beck.

Séamus Ó Grianna's novel *Bean Ruadh de Dhálach* (A red-haired O'Donnell woman) focused on a heroine who helps lead her whole village out of poverty in Donegal to Scotland and then to America.

Seán O'Faoláin's story collection *The Heat of the Sun* appeared.

Frank O'Connor (b. 1903) and Flann O'Brien (b. 1911) both died in this year.

Irish Language and Literature

Eoghan Ó Tuairisc's novel in Irish *Dé Luain* (Monday) employed several interwoven streams of consciousness, in his own words "designed to commemorate the 50th anniversary of 1916," dealing "with the opening hours of the Revolution in Dublin, minute by minute, from midnight Easter Sunday to noon on Monday" (1981 letter to author).

Periodicals

The *Protestant Telegraph,* a newspaper controlled by Ian Paisley, began publication—centered on attacks on Catholics and any attempt to include them in Northern Ireland governments.

Poetry

Seamus Heaney, the most celebrated contemporary Irish poet, published his first volume, *Death of a Naturalist,* which introduced several of his recurrent and well-known, powerful settings and symbols, especially the Ulster bogs, farms, and images of digging.

Excellent poetry was also to be found in Austin Clarke's *Mnemosyne Lay in Dust,* written in the confessional mode of Americans such as Robert Lowell and W. D. Snodgrass.

Louis MacNeice's *Collected Poems* underscored the range of his achievement.

Eiléan Ní Chuilleanáin (1942–   )—daughter of the novelist Eilís Dillon (1920–   ) and University College, Cork, professor of Irish Cormac Ó Cúilleanáin—won the *Irish Times* poetry award (Murphy and MacKillop 1987, 396). Her poetry is precise in diction and informed by an imaginative sense of history.

1967

The mostly Catholic Northern Ireland Civil Rights Association (NICRA) was founded in January, with its members soon thereafter identifying themselves with nonviolent activists in France and the United States and leading to the People's Democracy movement in the following year.

Further relaxation of censorship (already evident since 1956–57) came in the form of a bill introduced by Brian Lenihan, the minister for justice, that provided for the removal of bans on books after twelve years. This act released over 5,000 titles, including many of those banned by conservative earlier Censorship Boards (Whyte 1971, 344).

Architecture

St. Aengus church at Burt, county Donegal, was designed by Derry architect Liam McCormick in a boldly modernist style (de Breffny 1983, 31).

Drama

Brian Friel's *Lovers* was produced at the Gate Theatre, and his *The Loves of Cass Maguire* was staged at the Abbey, with the great Irish actress Siobhan McKenna (1923–86) in her first role there in eighteen years.

After an absence of twenty years from its stage, the great Irish actor Cyril Cusack returned to the Abbey Theatre to play Con the Shaughraun in Dion Boucicault's classic play *The Shaughraun* (O'Donnell 1986, 8).

Education

University College, Dublin, was authorized to begin building its new suburban Belfield campus, and the university colleges of Dublin, Cork, and Galway became fully independent universities. The New University of Ulster (now Coleraine University) opened in county Derry, becoming Ireland's first entirely new university in more than fifty years (O'Donnell 1986, 14).

Fiction

Though written many years earlier and already published in a different (and lesser) form as *The Dalkey Archive* (1964), Flann O'Brien's hilarious novel *The Third Policeman* was finally published in this, the year following the death of O'Brien (Brian O'Nolan). Its unnamed narrator hatches a scheme with one John Divney to kill old Phillip Mathers for his money, in order to finance his research on the crackpot scientist and philosopher de Selby (whose theories are explained in interchapters and footnotes running through the book). The narrator kills Mathers but— unbeknownst to himself (and until the end of the book, the reader)—is in turn killed by Divney. He then experiences a bizarre series of events and characters in a kind of twilight zone: his arrest by Sergeant Pluck and Policeman MacCruiskeen, for whom everything is "about a bicycle" and who assure him that he can be happily hanged since he has no name and therefore is nobody; his own soul, Joe, who constantly advises him; and, of course, de Selby. *The Third Policeman* remained so popular that in

1976, for example, a series of people published tongue-in-cheek letters to the editor in the *Irish Times* under the name of de Selby.

Film

In November a government-sponsored Film Industry Committee, chaired by American film director John Huston, began meeting to examine the feasibility of fostering a revivified Irish film industry (O'Donnell 1986, 11).

Irish Language and Literature

Máirtín Ó Cadhain's *An tSraith ar Lár* (The swath laid low) collected some of his best later stories.

Diarmaid Ó Súilleabháin's second novel, *Caoin Tú Féin* (Keen for yourself), portrayed a hung over schoolteacher who wonders why his wife has just left him and what his whole life means.

Poetry

New Territory was Eavan Boland's first collection of poems. Born in 1944, Boland was educated at Trinity College, Dublin, has won several prizes including one from the Irish-American Cultural Institute, and has developed an increasingly strong feminist attitude in her work.

Thomas Kinsella's *Nightwalker and Other Poems* appeared. The title poem recaptures the speaker's long walk at night through the streets of a Dublin suburb, as he imaginatively refashions what he sees.

1968

Inspired partly by the civil rights movement in the United States and determined to win full civil rights for Catholics in Northern Ireland, a thousand students demonstrated at Queen's University, Belfast, and formed the People's Democracy movement. Its leadership included Bernadette Devlin (later McAliskey)

(1947–   ), Eamonn McCann (1943–   ), Michael Farrell, and others. In Derry a Citizen's Action Committee was formed by a thirty-one-year-old businessman, John Hume (1937–   ), who later led the Social Democratic and Labor party. Both groups organized civil rights meetings, rallies, and marches. The first civil rights march occurred on 24 August, from Coalisland to Dungannon. In November moderate Northern Ireland prime minister Terence O'Neill announced a reform program including "a points system of housing allocation, . . . franchise reform," and "a review of the Special Powers Act" (Darby 1976, xiii).

The Council for the Status of Women was founded as a liaison between the Republic's government and women's organizations. As a result it was to represent 250,000 women from thirty organizations (Hickey and Doherty 1987, 99).

Cultural Institutions

The Merriman Summer School, an annual series of symposia on contemporary cultural concerns, met for the first time, in Ennis, county Clare (O'Donnell 1986, 14).

Drama

Thomas Murphy's *Famine* was staged at the Peacock Theatre.

Thomas Kilroy's *The Death and Resurrection of Mr. Roche* was presented as part of the Dublin Theatre Festival.

Brian Friel's *Crystal and Fox* was produced at the Gaiety Theatre.

Probably the first production of the entire cycle of Yeats's Cúchulain plays occurred at the Lyric Theatre in Belfast (Maxwell 1984, xiv).

Fiction

Benedict Kiely's novel *Dogs Enjoy the Morning* was set in the imaginary town of Cosmona, a strange place located somewhere in Ireland not too far from Dublin and populated by medieval pagans as well as by twentieth-century characters.

We Might See Sights was a collection of stories introducing the work of Julia O'Faoláin (1932–   ), Seán O'Faoláin's daughter.

Irish Language and Literature

Diarmaid Ó Súilleabháin's novel *An Uain Bheo* (The moment of decision) focused on a Jew who experiences the isolation of a Leopold Bloom and loses the woman he loves in a car accident.

Periodicals

The *Honest Ulsterman* began with James Simmons (1933–   ) as editor, succeeded at the end of the following year by Michael Foley and Frank Ormsby (1947–   ), who published the journal throughout the 1970s in Belfast as a collection of poetry, prose, and commentary (Denman 1987, 142).

David Marcus began a lengthy term as literary editor of the *Irish Press*. He fostered the careers of many young writers, but also published established writers.

The new *Economic and Social Review* was a forum for scientific analyses of Irish society by sociologists (T. Brown 1985, 257).

Poetry

Collected Poems 1932–67 by John Hewitt spanned the long career of this Ulsterman, a liberal Protestant who in 1957 was denied promotion as an art director in Belfast because of his broadminded, socialist beliefs. He thereafter exiled himself to Coventry for a number of years but finally returned to Belfast, where he served as a model for many younger poets—for the courage of his views as well as for his direct, earthy style and imagery.

Night-Crossing was the first volume of Derek Mahon (1941–   ), a young Trinity College graduate from Northern Ireland.

Richard Murphy's *The Battle of Aughrim* took the 1691 downfall of England's King James II and the solidification of Protestant hegemony in Ireland as the touchstone for a sequence of poems also exploring the poet's own heritage.

Prose Nonfiction

Two years following his death, Frank O'Connor's second autobiographical volume, *My Father's Son,* was released.

1969

On 1 January the People's Democracy movement, led among others by Bernadette Devlin, set off from Belfast City Hall and marched across Northern Ireland westward toward Derry. Three days later as they approached Derry, they were attacked by Protestant extremists and many were beaten while the Protestant-controlled police stood by and did nothing.

In April Northern Ireland's prime minister, Terence O'Neill, resigned and was replaced on 1 May by James Chichester-Clark (1923–   ).

Elected in this year as the youngest female member of the British Parliament ever, Bernadette Devlin was instrumental in leading a demonstration of working-class Derry Catholics in August—dubbed the "battle of the Bogside"—and as a result was sentenced in December to six months in prison allegedly for inciting riots (O'Donnell 1986, 17, 21).

After months of violence, largely involving Protestant and police attacks on Catholic communities where social activists lived, in August British troops were reluctantly sent to Northern Ireland, and the soldiers—though later viewed as the agents of British oppression and harrassment—were at first welcomed by many Catholics as defenders against their attackers.

Minister for Finance Charles Haughey (1925–   ) was responsible for legislation that permitted writers and artists to avoid paying income tax on their royalties. A country already by and large appreciative of its writers and artists therefore became even more of a haven for them.

Drama

Thomas Murphy's *A Crucial Week in the Life of a Grocer's Assistant* was produced at the Abbey, where Hugh Hunt was now artistic director.

Samuel Beckett was awarded the Nobel Prize for Literature. He accepted the award but declined to travel to Stockholm to accept it, and was reported to have been "distressed" by the announcement (O'Donnell 1986, 21).

Fiction

Three years after his death, Frank O'Connor's *Collection Three* (in its American edition, *A Set of Variations)* included his final works of short fiction, such as "A Story by Maupassant."

James Plunkett's *Strumpet City* was an impressive, panoramic historical novel drawing on the experiences of the author's father and other relatives and friends during the big Dublin transport labor lockout of 1913, on his own later acquaintance with Jim Larkin (the union leader), and on his own earlier radio and stage plays about Larkin and the lockout. *Strumpet City* was an immediate best-seller in Ireland and received further fame through its 1980 Irish television adaptation starring Peter O'Toole as Larkin, Peter Ustinov as King Edward VII, and Cyril Cusack as Father Giffley.

Richard Power's novel *The Hungry Grass* began by describing the death of Father Tom Conroy, who by all public accounts has led an uneventful, mediocre life; it then illustrated via extended flashbacks that his life was difficult but anything but mediocre.

Cork native but Devon resident William Trevor's (1928–) novel *Mrs. Eckdorf in O'Neill's Hotel* centered on an unfortunate British woman who married a German and whose misguided attempt to beautify a Dublin flophouse ultimately lands her in an insane asylum.

Irish Language and Literature

Thomas Kinsella's remarkable modern translation of the *Táin Bó Cuailnge* (The cattle raid of Cooley), the ancient epic from the Ulster cycle—and the rough Irish equivalent, in subject matter and reputation, to the *Iliad*—was published, accompanied by Louis le Brocquy's striking inkblot-style brush drawings. This edition of the *Táin* was important not only in scholarly circles, but also for its impact on Irish writers and readers, in reasserting the power of Old Irish subjects and themes in contemporary writing and consciousness.

Máirtín Ó Cadhain's critical pamphlet *Páipéir Bhána agus Páipéir Bhreaca* (White papers and speckled papers) advanced an important discussion of the problems facing writers in Irish.

Periodicals

The *Lace Curtain: A Magazine of Poetry and Criticism* appeared until 1978 under the editorship of Michael Smith (1942–   ) and Trevor Joyce (1947–   ), championing neglected poets of an older generation such as Thomas MacGreevey (1893–1967), Denis Devlin, and Brian Coffey (Denman 1987, 140).

Poetry

No Continuing City was Belfast poet Michael Longley's first collection. Educated at Trinity College (as was his wife, Edna Longley [1940–   ], the literary critic) in classics, Longley taught school before going to work for the Arts Council of Northern Ireland (Murphy and MacKillop 1987, 388). The economical form of his poems recalls Emily Dickinson.

1970

The Social Democratic and Labour party (SDLP), Catholic and nationalist, was founded in Northern Ireland, bringing into the political arena many of the civil rights activists who demonstrated in the streets in 1968, most notably John Hume. At the other end of the political spectrum, Ian Paisley and William Beattie were the first Protestant Unionist members of Parliament elected to the Stormont Parliament outside Belfast. In the moderate middle, the Alliance party (a relatively small group dominated by moderate Protestants) was formed in April.

The IRA split into two separate factions, the Officials (more strongly socialist and led by Cathal Goulding) and the Provisionals (Republicans led by Seán MacStiofáin and committed in the traditional way to overthrow of British rule in Northern Ireland by violent means).

The Ulster Defence Regiment (UDR) was a military force in

Northern Ireland that was supposed to be an improvement over the abusive government enforcers, the "B Specials"—but a number of B Specials were recruited into the UDR (Hickey and Doherty 1987, 575).

The separation between public opinion in the Republic and IRA activity in Northern Ireland was underscored when Fianna Fáil taoiseach Jack Lynch dismissed two influential cabinet members (Charles Haughey, who later became taoiseach himself, and Neil Blaney [1922–   ] on the suspicion of involvement in IRA arms importation) and managed to survive politically not only their dismissal but also their subsequent acquittal (T. Brown 1985, 281).

Drama

Samuel Beckett's *Breath* was produced at the Oxford Playhouse in England. Focused on breathing and "expiration" (in more than one sense) and coming the year after his Nobel Prize, this short, spare play underscored Beckett's movement toward increasingly brief and final statements.

Education

President Eamon de Valera dedicated the arts block at the new suburban Belfield campus of University College, Dublin (O'Donnell 1986, 25).

Fiction

In her novel *A Pagan Place,* Edna O'Brien returned to the landscape and period of *The Country Girls* (1960), but as described by a narrator who tells her own story in the second person ("you").

Irish Language and Literature

In his final collection of stories, *An tSraith Dhá Tógáil* (The Swath raised up), Máirtín Ó Cadhain offered for the first time fully urban stories in Irish.

Periodicals

Innti (With it) was a journal of poetry in Irish founded at University College, Cork (Nic Pháidín 1987, 81).

Atlantis was a quarterly on literature and culture headed by Seamus Deane along with Derek Mahon, Hugh Maxton (W. J. McCormack, 1947–   ), Augustine Martin, and Michael Gill (Denman 1987, 142).

Poetry

John Montague's *Tides* appeared.

The first volumes of poetry from the Gallery Press appeared. With Gallery, Peter Fallon (1951–   ) demonstrated that an Irish publisher could actually survive while publishing mostly poetry.

1971

Brian Faulkner (1921–77) took over as Northern Ireland's prime minister in March, replacing James Chichester-Clark. In August hundreds of northern Catholic nationalists were interned— imprisoned without trial—and at least fifteen people died in violence shortly thereafter. The Long Kesh internee prison— subsequently infamous as the site of harsh treatment of IRA interners and hunger strikes by prisoners—was opened near Lisburn, county Antrim, in September (O'Donnell 1986, 30). No Protestants were interned even though the Protestant Ulster Volunteer Force (UVF) and Ulster Defense Association (UDA) had by this time become active as mirror images of the Provisional IRA.

Ian Paisley and Desmond Boal founded the Democratic Unionist party (DUP) in Belfast as a harder-line Protestant alternative to the Unionist party, which the DUP felt had made too many concessions to the Catholic minority in the North. Paisley—a minister educated at the fundamentalist Bob Jones University in South Carolina who founded his own version of a Presbyterian church—swiftly rose to prominence as leader of the hard-line Protestant opposition. No leader has been more popular among large numbers of the Protestant working class and conservative middle class.

In April a march from county Kerry to Dublin was organized in protest over the government's neglect of the Gaeltacht or Irish-speaking areas (O'Donnell 1986, 28).

By this year an estimated 416,676 people lived in Belfast, but because of unemployment and the "troubles" (the popular euphemism for the three-way guerrilla war among the IRA, the British army, and Protestant paramilitaries), Belfast's population would decline by 26.6 percent over the next ten years (Todd 1989, 46). In the Republic, it was announced in December that 69,462 people were unemployed—the highest number in two decades (O'Donnell 1986, 31). In the years since then, unemployment figures have further worsened, and concomitantly the numbers of people emigrating to England, America, and elsewhere have swelled to crisis proportions.

In contrast to the 1950s, when population declined, by this time the Republic's population was more than 160,000 higher than in 1961, at 2,978,248—in contrast to Belfast, and largely a reflection of the Republic's economic growth during the 1960s. Migration from the countryside to the cities (especially Dublin) and larger towns was underscored by the fact that 52 percent of that population now lived in towns of more than 1,500, as opposed to 32 percent in 1926, 41 percent in 1951, and 49 percent in 1966 (T. Brown 1985, 257–58).

A survey found that 95.5 percent of Catholics "claimed to have attended Mass the previous Sunday" (Beale 1987, 14).

Women formed the first women's liberation group in Dublin, and this subject was the main topic on RTE's popular Saturday evening program "The Late Late Show" in March. Thanks largely to the institutionalization of the "special position" of the Catholic church in the Republic's 1937 constitution, "contraception was illegal, divorce was banned in the Constitution, and abortion was a criminal act. Single mothers and separated women were ineligible for welfare payments, and women were openly discriminated against in education, employment, and the tax and welfare systems. A marriage bar was in operation in the Civil Service and other occupations, forcing women to give up their jobs on marriage. Women had few rights under family law, and were in a highly vulnerable position if their marriages broke down. The illegitimacy law stigmatised children born out of wedlock, and their mothers with them" (Beale 1987, 3–4).

In May women organized a "Contraceptive Train" to Belfast in defiance of the governmental ban in the Republic. Forty-seven women "took over two carriages on the Dublin-to-Belfast train. When they arrived in Belfast they headed for chemist [pharmacy] shops and bought large quantities of whatever contraceptives they could find. When the train arrived back in Dublin that evening the women brandished condoms and creams at the Customs officials, who decided against a confrontation and waved them through, to cheers from the crowd that had turned out in support" (Beale 1987, 107).

Aer Lingus, the Irish national airline, became one of the first major Irish employers to offer equal pay for equal work to women (O'Donnell 1986, 27).

Bord na gCapall (The horse board) was established as an advisory agency on horse breeding (Hickey and Doherty 1987, 40). Only a rural, farm-dominated country—one as obsessed with horses as Ireland, whose greatest poet, Yeats, used the horse as a leading image, even on his gravestone—would create such a governmental unit.

Architecture

The Institute for Advanced Studies building was erected in Dublin by the firm of Stephenson and Gibney (de Breffny 1983, 31).

Cultural Institutions

It was announced in July that Sir Tyrone Guthrie (b. 1900), the great theatrical producer who died earlier in this year, had left his family home in county Monaghan, Annaghmakerrig, to the nation to be used as a retreat for writers and artists (O'Donnell 1986, 29). This intent was subsequently carried out (see 1982 entry).

Drama

The rejuvenated Gate Theatre received a government subsidy and in general showed new signs of life.

Fiction

Francis Stuart's (1902–   ) major work, *Black List/Section H,*
was a nonfiction novel whose materials were very directly those of
Stuart's own life experiences since the 1920s. Virtually all of its
characters, such as Yeats, are given their real names—except for
the Kafkaesque protagonist "H" himself (Stuart's actual first
name is Henry), perhaps indicating that the author was least
confident of his own identity, which H constantly searches for in
the book.

Thomas Kilroy's novel *The Big Chapel* examined the role of
Father William Lannigan during the ecclesiastical controversies of
the 1870s in the town of Callen, county Kilkenny.

Christy Brown's (1932–81) *Down All the Days* was a vivid
autobiographical novel about the working-class Dublin youth of
this remarkable paraplegic writer, who was later immortalized in
the film *My Left Foot* (see 1990 entry).

Periodicals

The Provisional IRA began publication of *An Phoblacht* (The
republic)—a newspaper distinct from the IRA paper of the 1920s
and 1930s.

Prose Nonfiction

The Trinity College historian F. S. L. Lyons published *Ireland
since the Famine,* a fine example of the new kind of searching
economic and sociological analysis to which Irish historians were
now turning.

1972

On "Bloody Sunday," 30 January, thirteen Catholic civilians were
shot dead and at least sixteen others injured by British soldiers
after a banned civil rights march in Derry. Three days later the

British embassy in Dublin was burned to the ground on a day announced as a day of mourning in the Republic. Derry's Guildhall was wrecked by bombs in February. The death toll in Northern Ireland was 474 by the end of the year. On 24 March, British prime minister Edward Heath suspended the Northern Ireland parliament at Stormont in favor of direct rule by a secretary of state (William Whitelaw), thereby bringing to an end the complete Protestant home rule granted in 1920. Eleven days earlier, an Amnesty International report found that concerning treatment of interned Catholic prisoners, the "ill-treatment used amounted to brutality" (quoted in Darby 1976, xvi).

Ireland's application for membership in the European Economic Community was accepted in January, and ratified by a five-to-one popular vote in a May referendum. The twenty-six-county southern republic had prospered during the same years in which the six-county northern state had exploded. While nationalist lip service to the ideal of a united Ireland continued, privately many people in the Republic were indifferent about the North and understandably devoted instead to their own newfound well-being. The twenty-six counties were 95 percent Catholic (with the small number of Protestants fairly well assimilated rather than alienated), and the Republic had become a remarkably unified, stable state. Its population was over three million for the first time in fifty years, and the average marrying age was 23.5 for women (opposed to 29.1 in 1929 and 25.9 in 1957) and 25.6 for men (34.9 in 1929, 29.4 in 1957) (Foster 1988, 594). Population growth was to remain by far the largest in Dublin, with increasing numbers of rural people resettling there and (to a lesser extent) in Cork and Galway.

December referenda lowered the voting age to eighteen and removed the reference to the "special position" of the Catholic church in the Republic's constitution (O'Donnell 1986, 39).

At the end of the year, a government Commission on the Status of Women advanced forty-nine recommendations and seventeen suggestions "designed to eliminate all forms of discrimination against women in the fields of employment, social welfare, education, the taxation code, property rights, and in all areas of central and local administration" (quoted in Beale 1987, 4–5). Progress in realizing these goals, however, would be very slow.

The long-standing, popular, Quaker-run Bewley's Cafes of

Dublin converted itself into a workers' cooperative (the "Bewley Community"), with all employees with at least three years of service able to hold shares.

Fiction

Brian Moore's *Catholics,* a short novel whose subsequent CBS television adaptation did much to increase Moore's international fame, was set on an island off the county Kerry coastline in the near future, at Muck Abbey, where the Latin Mass and private confession are still practiced despite the contrary edicts of an increasingly secularized church.

Jennifer Johnston (1930–   ) made an impressive debut with her first published novel, *The Captains and the Kings,* in which a friendship between an Ascendancy widower and a working-class Catholic boy is destroyed by the boy's parents.

Edna O'Brien's novel *Night* presented the Molly Bloom–like monologue of Mary Hooligan, a middle-aged woman who recalls her life.

Aidan Higgins's *Balcony of Europe* was a novel focused on an Irish painter's life abroad.

Film

Ardmore Studios International was formed near Dublin out of the remains of the closed Ardmore Film Studios. John Huston was one of the directors of the new company (O'Donnell 1986, 32).

Irish Language and Literature

In April Radio na Gaeltachta, a new government-funded station, began broadcasting about twenty-five hours a week in Irish throughout the country. Appropriately enough, a ten-minute address by President Eamon de Valera was its first broadcast.

Poetry

Thomas Kinsella published his broadside poem *Butcher's Dozen* in protest over "Bloody Sunday" and the subsequent defensive government report on it.

Seamus Heaney's *Wintering Out*, Kinsella's *Notes from the Land of the Dead*, Derek Mahon's *Lives*, John Montague's *The Rough Field*, and Eiléan Ní Chuilleanáin's *Acts and Monuments*—five important collections by five prominent contemporary Irish poets—all appeared in the same year. Heaney's collection showed a newly heightened attention to human relationships and the power of words. Several of Kinsella's poems focus on encounters between a boy and his grandmother, exploring the polarities of youth and age, innocence and experience. Mahon's title poem was dedicated to Heaney and his poems showed a devotion to contemporary use of classical form. Like Kinsella's, Montague's volume has a familial focus, in this case superimposed on a historical landscape in county Tyrone in the north of Ireland. Ní Chuilleanáin's collection, her first, won the Patrick Kavanagh Award.

Prose Nonfiction

On the one hand, as noted above, much outrage over "Bloody Sunday" was expressed in the Republic; on the other hand, continuing evidence of the detachment of southern opinion from the North could be found in the government minister and writer Conor Cruise O'Brien's (1917–   ) book *States of Ireland*. In his typically maverick fashion O'Brien argued that the idea of a united Ireland was a hopelessly romantic notion that Ireland could no longer afford in the face of the harsh realities of Irish life and the conflicting interests represented by the different constituencies in the island.

Further "revisionism" could be found in the Reverend Professor Francis Shaw's essay in *Studies* entitled "The Canon of Irish History: A Challenge." Shaw argued that Pádraic Pearse (whose death had been commemorated at the half-century mark in 1966, when the original draft of Shaw's essay had been withheld by the editor) had evidenced a certain megalomania and a heretical Christ complex, and generally debunked much of the mythos of modern Irish nationalism (T. Brown 1985, 287–88). Shaw's critique was taken up by a number of subsequent Irish historians (the "revisionists").

1973

In the Republic a coalition government comprised of Fine Gael and its minority partner, Labour, came to power and held office for the next four years, with Liam Cosgrave as taoiseach and Erskine Childers (son of the rebel slain in 1922) as president. In the North a March referendum confirming Northern Ireland's continuance in the United Kingdom was boycotted by most Catholic voters. In November the British secretary of state, William Whitelaw, announced a new executive of six (Protestant) Unionists, four (Catholic) SDLP members, and one (moderate Protestant) Alliance party member; and in December a "Sunningdale agreement" by the pro-executive parties was adopted.

Ireland formerly joined the European Economic Community (EEC), as approved the year before. EEC membership served to continue the steady internationalization of the Irish economy as encouraged by Seán Lemass, taoiseach in the early 1960s.

A second Irish television channel was recommended, and it began broadcasting five years later.

The Irish Supreme Court ruled that a married couple's right to privacy included the right to import contraceptives for their own use (Beale 1987, 107).

Drama

Hugh Leonard's (1928–   ) play *Da,* a tribute to his adoptive father, was published and enjoyed its first production at the Olney Theater, near Washington, D. C. Five years later it won a Tony Award, and was extremely successful in long runs in Dublin, London, New York, and elsewhere. Leonard (born John Byrne in Dublin) noted, "I wrote the play to pay off a debt to my father. But the play made me successful as a writer and since I couldn't have written it without my father, the debt's now greater than ever" (quoted in Owens and Radner 1990, 630). Recalling Brian Friel's *Philadelphia, Here I Come!* (1964), which divided its protagonist into separate "Public" and "Private" characters, *Da* utilizes "Charlie Now" and "Charlie Then," with the younger and older son occasionally conversing together. Leonard is a very popular playwright and television scriptwriter.

Clearly echoing the outrage over the previous year's "Bloody Sunday" in Derry City, Brian Friel's play *The Freedom of the City* re-created a similar occurrence in Derry in 1970 from the point of view of three people who were killed by the British Army. In documentary fashion, the play ended with an inquest judge's defensive exoneration of the army.

Irish Language and Literature

Satisfactory performance in Irish on the leaving certification exam at the end of secondary schooling was now no longer required, but Irish remained a required subject.

Codladh an Ghaiscigh (Sleep of the warrior) was a collection of poems by Máire Mhac an tSaoi.

Fiction

John Banville's novel *Birchwood* focused on the narrator's attempt to sort out his Big House family history—which is continually thwarted by Banville's deliberate subversion of chronology—on his search for his supposed twin sister, and on his picaresque adventures with the circus, directed by a character named Prospero.

Eilís Dillon's novel *Across the Bitter Sea* and its sequel *Blood Relations* (1977) dealt with Ireland during the period between Fenianism and the Civil War, adding the valuable perspective of women to the male-dominated world of the Irish historical novel.

The Gates was Jennifer Johnston's first novel (though published second), focused on a girl and her uncle living in a decaying ancestral home.

A Ball of Malt and Madame Butterfly was Benedict Kiely's second collection of stories.

Music

By this date Ireland's own musical "fab foursome"—Christy Moore, Andy Irvine, Donal Lunny, and Liam O'Flynn—were well established as the traditional music group Planxty (a word referring to a tune on behalf of one's patron: "Planxty Irwin" translates as "to the health of Irwin"). They were playing to large audiences throughout the country, and had become as popular as the older group the Chieftains and more appealing to the younger generation. Throughout the 1970s Planxty was the most popular of several excellent traditional music groups that were to include Clannad (a Donegal group that fused jazz with the Gaelic tradition), De Danaan (a Galway-based group of string musicians), the Bothy Band (partly a spinoff of Planxty), and others.

Poetry

At the precocious age of twenty-one, northerner Paul Muldoon (1951–) published his first collection, *New Weather* (Murphy and MacKillop 1987, 406). He is one of a group of poets, including Seamus Heaney, educated at Queen's University, Belfast. Muldoon's stylish poems are rooted in Irish tradition.

New Poems 1973 by Thomas Kinsella and *An Exploded View* by Michael Longley were published.

1974

In the North, a coalition executive government headed by Unionist party leader Brian Faulkner took office but was swiftly opposed by hard-line, anti-power-sharing Protestants of the Official Unionist and Democratic Unionist splinter parties, who withdrew from the Northern Ireland Assembly in protest against Faulkner's executive. Subsequently a general strike against the executive was called by the Ulster Workers' Council. In March Merlyn Rees became the new British secretary of state in the North. In May the executive coalition collapsed because of Unionist resignations, and direct rule from London was restored (Darby 1976, xviii).

The People's Liberation Army began as a left-wing splinter of the Official IRA (see 1970), and in the following year became known as the Irish National Liberation Army (INLA) (Hickey and Doherty 1987, 250).

In the Republic Cearbhall Ó Dálaigh (1911–77) became the fifth president of Ireland.

Former minister for external affairs Seán MacBride—a leading human rights and international peace activist, cofounder of

Amnesty International, former United Nations representative in Namibia—shared the Nobel Peace Prize with former Japanese prime minister Eisaku Sato. MacBride was the first Irishman to win this award.

Glencree Peace Centre opened in old barracks and reformatory buildings in county Wicklow. It was begun by a group of Quakers, Catholics, and others as a place for people from the North to retreat, negotiate, and rejuvenate.

Taoiseach Liam Cosgrave encouraged the defeat of his own Fianna Fáil government's Bill for the Control of the Importation, Sale, and Manufacture of Contraceptives, by seventy-five votes to sixty-one (O'Donnell 1986, 51).

Fiction

John McGahern's novel *The Leavetaking* concerned a teacher's last day at a Dublin school before leaving for England after being dismissed because his civil-law marriage to an American divorcée is not recognized by the Irish state or school system. This novel was based in part on McGahern's departure into exile after the banning of *The Dark* (1965) and his own firing.

Jennifer Johnston's novel *How Many Miles to Babylon?* examined the friendship of an upper-class boy and a lower-class boy, which survives early family obstacles only to be brought to an end in World War I, when one is told that he must direct the firing squad of the other (condemned to death after going AWOL).

Film

Paistí ag Obair (Children at work), a Gael-Linn documentary film by Louis Marcus about Dublin Montessori schools, was nominated for an Academy Award (O'Donnell 1986, 48).

Irish Language and Literature

It was announced that fluency in Irish was no longer compulsory in the Irish civil service.

The periodical *Scríobh* (Writing), which published such critics in Irish as Seán Ó Tuama, originated and continued until 1984.

Poetry

The *Collected Poems* of Austin Clarke (who died in March) was a volume dominated by his highly productive last twenty years.

Also published in the year of his death, Padraic Fallon's (1905–74) volume *Poems* was marked by the influence of the Gaelic tradition and the shadow of Yeats.

The verses in Richard Murphy's volume *High Island* were anchored to the physical and symbolic setting of the islands around Cleggan, county Galway.

1975

In October the Protestant Ulster Volunteer Force (UVF) took eleven lives in a single day. British Northern Ireland Secretary Merlyn Rees outlawed the UVF shortly thereafter, for the second time. Protestant bombs killed a man and injured five others at Dublin Airport in November (O'Donnell 1986, 61, 62).

After retiring from public life two years earlier, Eamon de Valera (b. 1882) died and was buried in Glasnevin Cemetery in Dublin after a huge state funeral.

Unemployment in the Republic exceeded 100,000 for the first time since 1942 (O'Donnell 1986, 56).

Ireland's first mastectomy center was opened in Dublin in October (O'Donnell 1986, 61).

Architecture

Michael Scott was awarded the Royal Gold Medal in London, earlier won by such famous architects as Frank Lloyd Wright (de Breffny 1983, 31).

Cultural Institutions

The government's Arts Council provided awards or stipends, for the first time, to four writers.

President Cearbhall Ó Dalaigh dedicated the new Project Arts Centre in Essex Street in Dublin. It became a forum for innovative drama (and art) much like the Abbey had been at the turn of the century.

Drama

The Irish Theatre Company was founded to bring plays to small towns and to mount productions at the Abbey. The Druid Theatre was begun in Galway. This theater became perhaps best known in the 1970s for its strikingly authentic productions of plays by Synge, under the direction of Garry Hynes (artistic director today of the Abbey).

Film

The National Film Studio was established by the Republic—but subsequently sold in 1982 (de Breffny 1983, 64).

Poetry

Seamus Heaney's *North* appeared. Heaney continued to focus on earthy, often ancient settings and to write for the ear, exploring the sensuous possibilities of language.

As in his subsequent collection *The Great Cloak* (1978), Montague's poems in *A Slow Dance* were more direct and explicit than in his previous collections.

Michael Hartnett published *A Farewell to English,* announcing in the title poem that henceforth he would publish only in Irish.

He thus joined the growing body of writers publishing in Irish during this period. Hartnett felt that Irish was the language that "reminds us" that "we are human" and "not a herd," and was now convinced that the Irish language should not be "concealed or killed" or only preserved from the past, "microfilmed to waste no space." He believed that as such an act of independence and defiance, Irish could be "our final sign." Hartnett thereby linked language, politics, and aesthetics.

He insisted that "the act of poetry / is a rebel act." Although he has not completely kept to his oath not to publish any more poetry in English, Hartnett did subsequently produce a lively body of work in Irish.

Eavan Boland's collection of poems *The War Horse* appeared, as did Derek Mahon's *The Snow Party,* Eiléan Ní Chuilleanáin's *Site of Ambush,* and Paul Durcan's *O Westport in the Light of Asia Minor.*

1976

Christopher Ewart-Biggs, British ambassador to Ireland, and British civil servant Judith Cooke were assassinated by a bomb near Dublin in July (O'Donnell 1986, 66–67).

In August three Catholic children were killed in Andersonstown, Belfast, by a car whose IRA driver had been shot dead by British soldiers. Shortly thereafter the children's aunt, Máiréad Corrigan, joined a Protestant woman, Betty Williams, and began a "Peace People" movement. Their rallies and marches were soon joined by thousands of people. Corrigan and Williams won the 1976 Nobel Peace Prize as a result. The Peace People's movement continued into the 1980s, though it never again approached its early level of popularity and acclaim.

In October Anne Dickson was elected leader of the Unionist party of Northern Ireland, becoming the first woman to lead a political party in Ireland. In the same month Máire Drumm, a former Provisional Sinn Féin vice-president, was shot dead in a Belfast hospital (O'Donnell 1986, 68, 70).

In December Patrick Hillery (1923–   ) was sworn in as the sixth president of Ireland (O'Donnell 1986, 71).

Drama

Thomas Murphy's *The Sanctuary Lamp* was staged at the Abbey.

Fiction

The veteran Seán O'Faoláin's collection of stories *Foreign Affairs* appeared.

At the other end of the spectrum, young Neil Jordan's (1950–   ) first collection of short stories, *Night in Tunisia* (focusing on petty lives via striking imagery, as in the story "Last Rites"), was published.

Michael McLaverty's *The Road to the Shore and Other Stories,* like his *Collected Short Stories* two years later, was a collection that helped to make his short fiction, much of it published many years earlier, more available and better known. Maeve Kelly's (1930–   ) *A Life of Her Own* contained stories about strong-minded, self-sufficient women.

Doctor Copernicus was the first of John Banville's series of long novels of ideas focused on imaginative scientists—also to include *Kepler* (1980), *The Newton Letter* (1982), and *Mefisto* (1986).

The Ikon Maker was Desmond Hogan's (1951–   ) first novel, wherein a mother suspects that her son's school friend committed suicide because her son refused to have sex with him—and goes in futile search of her exiled son.

Irish Language and Literature

Breandán Ó hEithir's (1930–91) *Lig Sinn i gCathú (Lead Us into Temptation)* was a novel that received perhaps more attention than any other novel in Irish since Máirtín Ó Cadhain's *Cré na Cille* (1949). It concerns a University College, Galway, student named Martin Melody who makes love to a barmaid and escapes his mother and his brother (a priest) by leaving Galway for Dublin and America. The names of Ó hEithir's characters—Martin Melody, Stella Walsh, Billy O'Grady, Larry de Lacy—reflect his frank acceptance of bilingualism, involving the incursion of English into spoken and written Irish.

It was calculated that during the year ending in September, broadcasting in the Irish language on Irish television represented only 10 percent of the total, with half of that small portion taken up by brief, obligatory news broadcasts in Irish (commonly prefacing fuller accounts in English). During the year there was only one hour of feature material and only three hours of children's shows in Irish (T. Brown 1985, 271–72). Radio Telefís Éireann was charged to encourage use of the native language, but these statistics demonstrate the demise of idealistic intentions in the face of U.S. and British broadcasting—and the hegemony of the English language in general. This remained largely the case even though the *Report of the Committee on Irish Language Attitudes Research,* a government-funded sociological study published the year before, found that the majority of the people of the Republic valued the Irish language and felt that its survival was important to national identity.

Periodicals

In Dublin magazine was launched as a fortnightly guide to entertainment and culture in the capital (O'Donnell 1986, 65).

Books-Ireland, a book-review organ as well as forum for information about the Irish publishing industry, commenced monthly publication that continues today. The very appearance of such a magazine was evidence of the dramatic growth of Irish publishing.

Poetry

The New Estate was the first collection of Belfast poet Ciaran Carson (1948–   ); *Teresa's Bar,* a collection by Dubliner Paul Durcan; and *Man Lying on a Wall,* one by Michael Longley of Belfast.

Prose Nonfiction

The first volume of the ongoing *New History of Ireland* (edited by T. W. Moody [1907–84], F. X. Martin, and F. J. Byrne) was published by Oxford University Press.

1977

Fianna Fáil leader Jack Lynch once more became taoiseach, serving as prime minister for the next two years.

An opinion poll of lay Catholics in the Republic found that 74 percent believed that abortion is always wrong. "A further 21 percent agreed that it was generally wrong, leaving a mere 5 percent who thought otherwise" (Beale 1987, 13).

Drama

Thomas Kilroy's play *Talbot's Box* examined the Dublin working-class mystic and saint Matt Talbot.

Fiction

Francis Stuart's novel *A Hole in the Head* recounted some features of the northern troubles—with Belfast thinly disguised as "Belbury," the IRA as the "B.A.M.," and the Protestant UVF (Ulster Volunteer Force) as "L.D.F."—at the same time that the protagonist, Barnaby Shane, has a relationship with Emily Brontë, whom Stuart adopts as an emblem of Celtic melancholy.

Similarly, Benedict Kiely's *Proxopera* was a novella exposing and attacking an IRA bombing.

Jennifer Johnston's *Shadows on Our Skins* focused on a schoolteacher who is beaten after she becomes engaged to a British soldier.

James Plunkett's second novel, *Farewell Companions,* encompassed the world of its author's youth from the 1920s until the 1950s, in an alternately nostalgic, playful mode.

Irish Language and Literature

Eoghan Ó Tuairisc's last novel, *An Lomnochtán* (The naked person), was an autobiographical bildungsroman focused on his childhood in the 1920s.

Niall Ó Dónaill's (1908–) major new Irish-English dictionary, *Foclóir Gaeilge-Béarla* (Tomás de Bhaldraithe, advisory editor) was released by the government.

Periodicals

The *Crane Bag* began its twice-yearly appearances (continuing until 1985) under the editorship of Mark Patrick Hederman and

306 Modern Irish Literature and Culture

Richard Kearney (1954–   ). Following the earlier example of O'Faoláin's the *Bell,* the *Crane Bag* was the liveliest forum for literary and cultural debate during the period.

Poetry

Mules by northerner Paul Muldoon included poems such as "Lunch with Pancho Villa," in which he meditates on the act of writing poetry in the midst of violence: "Look, son. Just look around you. / People are getting themselves killed / Left, right and centre / While you do what? Write rondeaux?"

Cork, a collection by Eiléan Ní Chuilleanáin, was published, and Gallery Books brought out her selected poems *The Second Voyage* (subsequently reissued with revisions by Wake Forest University Press in 1981).

1978

Amnesty International published a report documenting mistreatment of IRA suspects at the Castlereagh Royal Ulster Constabulary (RUC) station in the North (O'Donnell 1986, 79).

The Irish Medical Association estimated that 48,000 women were using the pill. Women "were ignoring the Church's opposition to contraception because they found that the rhythm method was not sufficiently reliable, and they wanted to use the safer methods now available" (Beale 1987, 106).

Post Office and Aer Lingus workers returned to work after lengthy strikes.

Drama

Joe Dowling succeeded Tomás MacAnna as artistic director of the Abbey in April.

Fiction

Michael MacLaverty's *Collected Short Stories* appeared.

Val Mulkerns's (1925–   ) first volume of stories, *Antiquities,* was published.

Elizabeth Bowen's Irish Stories was a compilation of eight earlier works from the oeuvre of this major Anglo-Irish talent (most of whose works were set in England).

Irish Language and Literature

Bord na Gaeilge (the Irish language board) was established by the government. Aindrias Ó Muimhneacháin published *Seanchas an Táilliúra (Stories from the Tailor)*, a collection of tales in Irish collected at midcentury by Seán Ó Croinin from the great county Cork storyteller, "the Tailor," Timothy Buckley, who had been celebrated in Eric Cross's book *The Tailor and Ansty* (1942).

Dubliner Micheál Ó Siadhail's (1947–   ) first collection, *An Bhliain Bhisigh* (The year of recovery), was published. Ó Siadhail was lecturer in Irish at Trinity College for four years and subsequently worked on the language at the Dublin Institute for Advanced Studies.

1979

Charles Haughey took over control of the Fianna Fáil party from Jack Lynch (who had fired him from his cabinet nine years earlier) and became taoiseach, serving as prime minister for two years— at the beginning of a period of nearly constant elections with the prime ministership alternating between Haughey and Fine Gael leader Garret Fitzgerald (1926–   ).

In the North, John Hume became leader of the Social Democratic and Labour party (SDLP). The IRA assassinated the emblematic British Lord Louis Mountbatten and killed eighteen British soldiers in a single day, 27 August (O'Donnell 1986, 83).

In the Republic a two-week national bus strike occurred in January, and a six-day national postal strike (the first in over fifty years) in June (O'Donnell 1986, 81).

In the Republic, contraceptives were still legal only for married women, and available only at government-sponsored family planning clinics. Nonetheless, the birth rate for married women aged fifteen to thirty-four had dropped by 20–25 percent since 1971, and had decreased 33 percent for women aged thirty-five to thirty-nine and 40 percent for women aged forty to forty-four—indicating that "women are having fewer children, and having them earlier in their marriages" (Beale 1987, 54).

Aer Lingus's first female pilot, Grainne Cronin, flew from Frankfurt to Shannon in April, and Dublin's first women bus conductors took up their posts in October (O'Donnell 1986, 82, 85).

In his first and only appearance in Ireland, Pope John Paul visited Dublin in September, attracting hundreds of thousands to a huge gathering in Dublin's Phoenix Park.

Drama

Set like most of his other plays in the generic town of "Ballybeg" in county Donegal, Brian Friel's *Aristocrats* focused on the various responses of a family to the death of their father or paterfamilias.

Graham Reid's (1945–   ) *The Death of Humpty Dumpty* was staged at the Peacock Theatre.

Fiction

Seán O'Faoláin's final novel, *And Again?*, was a playful fantasy that demonstrated his considerable artistic versatility and endurance. After almost getting hit by a truck that kills a young boy instead, James J. Younger receives in the mail an offer from the gods to relive his life backward, an offer he cannot refuse, "to decide, once for all, whether what you humans call Experience teaches you a damned thing." This storyline leads to some hilarious complications—as Younger shrinks into infancy and finally evaporates in a matchbox—as well as thought-provoking meditations on life and art.

John McGahern's novel *The Pornographer* told the ribald, frequently comic tale of a Dublin writer of pornography who survives his beloved aunt's death and his guilt-ridden affair with a woman who moves to London and has his child there. The protagonist finally decides to move back home to the countryside and marry a nurse with whom he has fallen in love.

The Old Jest was a novel by Jennifer Johnston in which eighteen-year-old Nancy Gulliver befriends a kind, mysterious older man whom she finds in the hut that she has fixed up near her home—and then witnesses his shooting by British Black-and-Tan soldiers.

Irish Language and Literature

Breandán Ó Doibhlin (1931–   ) focused his novel *An Branar Gan Cur* (The untilled field) on a train journey from Dublin to Derry by a young university lecturer who thinks despairing thoughts about Ireland.

Michael Hartnett, who had announced in *A Farewell to English* (1975) that henceforth he would publish only in Irish, published his first Gaelic collection, *Adharca Broic* (The badger's horns), under his Irish name of Micheál Ó hAirtneide.

Poetry

As in his earlier volume *North,* Seamus Heaney in *Field Work* included several poems about the problems of his native Northern Ireland, but he did so here in a new, plainer style.

Michael Longley's *The Echo Gate* was also published, and *Poems 1962–1978* by yet another gifted Ulsterman, Derek Mahon, also appeared. Like Heaney, Mahon characteristically takes inspiration from elsewhere—the Danish bogs in Heaney, Samuel Beckett in Mahon—and turns it compellingly back on Northern Ireland.

Belfast poet Medbh McGuckian (1950–   ) won the Poetry Society competition for "The Fitting" and (in the following year) an Eric Gregory Award. She has written memorably of the natural landscape and sexuality in such volumes as *The Flower Master* (1982) and *Venus and the Rain* (1984) (Murphy and MacKillop 1987, 402).

Richard Murphy's *Selected Poems* appeared.

1980

A survey conducted for the European Values Study Group showed that the rate of regular mass-going by Catholics had fallen to the (still very high) rate of 82 percent overall, and 72 percent among young people, from the overall claimed rate of 95.5 percent nine years earlier (Beale 1987, 14).

Art

A major exhibition by county Kilkenny artist Tony O'Malley, one of Ireland's foremost contemporary painters, was sponsored by the Arts Council.

Drama

Brian Friel's *Translations* was the opening production of the Field Day Theatre Company in Derry (founded by Friel and the actor-director Stephen Rea), and a very impressive and popular play that also enjoyed successful runs in New York, Boston, and elsewhere. As D. E. S. Maxwell noted soon after Field Day's inception, "Field Day has no theatre of its own, and assembles its cast from play to play. Its practice has been to open in Derry, then to tour, first in the North, then the South" (1984, 186). *Translations* focuses on the cultural and linguistic conflicts that ensue when a team of early nineteenth-century British soldiers and cartographers arrive in Ballybeg (the recurrent setting of Friel's plays) in county Donegal, encountering a Gaelic-speaking community centered on a hedgeschool taught by a colorful old schoolmaster and his son. The British are assisted by the schoolmaster's other son, who returns home after many years away to help them find English "equivalents" for the placenames in the area. The British officer with whom he works falls in love with a local young woman and is killed; the play ends with inevitable disaster awaiting Ballybeg. Friel manages the impressive feat of writing a "bilingual" play entirely in English, with audiences and readers always clear about which speeches are meant to be in Irish.

According to Field Day itself, by the time *Translations* was produced, "the initial project for a new theatre and a new audience had been widened. Four others [in addition to Stephen Rea] were invited to join the company as directors—Seamus Heaney, Tom Paulin (1949–   ), David Hammond, and Seamus Deane. In brief, all the directors felt that the political crisis in the

North and its reverberations in the Republic had made the necessity of a reappraisal of Ireland's political and cultural situation explicit and urgent" (Field Day Theatre Company 1985, vii).

Fiction

Julia O'Faoláin's novel *No Country for Young Men* merged contemporary politics with 1920s backgrounds in recounting the doomed love affair between an Irish-American academic and IRA supporter and an impressive Irishwoman who is burdened with an alcoholic, impotent husband.

The novel *The Past* by Neil Jordan, who has since become a filmmaker (see 1981 entry), examined fairly traditional materials —the story of characters living through the days of the Abbey Theatre and the birth of the Irish Republic—but in a thoroughly nontraditional way. The narrator presents his fantasies about the lives of his ancestors, moving from confusion to hypothesis to doubt, finally implying that he can be sure neither of who his father is nor of who he himself is.

Irish Language and Literature

An Runga (The rung), Micheál O Siadhail's second collection, appeared.

Máire Mhac an tSaoi's *An Galán Dubhach* (The black smoke) was also published.

Poetry

Eavan Boland's collection *In Her Own Image,* Thomas Kinsella's *Peppercanister Poems 1972–1978,* Paul Muldoon's *Why Brownlee Left,* and Paul Durcan's *Jesus, Break His Fall* were published.

1981

Garret Fitzgerald became taoiseach, taking over at the head of a coalition government of the Fine Gael and Labour parties.

In January Bernadette Devlin McAliskey and her husband, Michael, were seriously wounded in a Protestant attack at their home in county Tyrone.

In May Bobby Sands (b. 1954) was the first of ten IRA hunger-strikers to die in Northern Ireland prisons in this year, setting off the largest public outcry since "Bloody Sunday" in 1972 and immortalizing Sands and his compatriots as Pearse-style martyrs.

At long last, the Maternity Protection of Employees Act gave women in the Republic the legal right to fourteen weeks maternity leave and the right to return to the same job after having a child (Beale 1987, 154).

Cultural Institutions

Aosdána (Bold folk)—an exclusive organization of writers, musicians, and artists—was established. Membership was limited to 150 and some provisions were made for grants.

Fiction

In Brian Moore's novel *The Temptation of Eileen Hughes,* a Belfast shopgirl escapes the clutches of her wealthy employer, who is insanely infatuated with her, and the machinations of his nymphomaniacal, grasping wife.

Beyond the Pale was a collection of some of William Trevor's subtle Irish stories.

Film

The Irish Film Board was established by the Republic. Along with Britain's Channel 4, it funded the writer Neil Jordan's film *Angel,* "which must be considered a landmark in the history of the Irish film industry" (de Breffny 1983, 64).

Irish Language and Literature

Eoghan Ó Tuairisc published *The Road to Brightcity,* a translation of nine stories by Máirtín Ó Cadhain.

An Duanaire [Anthology]: Poems of the Dispossessed, a collection of translations by Thomas Kinsella and Seán Ó Tuama (1926–   ) of poems in Irish from the seventeenth to the nineteenth century, achieved great popular as well as scholarly success.

Nuala Ní Dhomhnaill's (1952–   ) first volume, *An Dealg Droighin* (The blackthorn spine), was published. Born in London to Irish parents, she was raised in the Irish-speaking area near Ventry, county Kerry, and studied at University College, Cork, with Seán Ó Tuama and John Montague.

Poetry

Eiléan Ní Chuilleanáin's poetry collection *The Rose Geranium* appeared.

1982

Out of divided election results, Charles Haughey managed to form another government.

Cultural Institutions

A house in county Monaghan left by Sir Tyrone Guthrie to the nation as a retreat for artists and writers opened its doors as such, under the joint sponsorship of the Irish and Northern Irish Arts Councils (T. Brown 1985, 354).

Fiction

Jennifer Johnston's novel *The Christmas Tree* focused on the fading consciousness of Constance Keating, who is dying of cancer.

Irish Language and Literature

Gleann an Ghleann (Valley of the valley) was the first collection by young poet Michael Davitt (1950–   ).

Periodicals

Theatre Ireland was founded in Northern Ireland, drawing funds from both northern and southern Irish Arts Councils and becoming an important national forum for critics and other theater people.

Poetry

Eavan Boland's collection *Night Feed* was published, as were Derek Mahon's *The Hunt by Night,* John Montague's *Selected Poems,* and *The Selected Paul Durcan.*

1983

Garret Fitzgerald (elected at the end of 1982) took office as taoiseach, again replacing Charles Haughey, and continuing their musical-chairs act with the prime ministership.

The New Ireland Forum—formed by the Social Democratic and Labour party in Northern Ireland and all three leaders of the Republic's major political parties—began their meetings (extending over nearly a year) to see if they could solve the Northern Ireland crisis. Their major recommendations were rejected by British Prime Minister Margaret Thatcher in the following year.

The number of births fell to 66,802 from 74,388 in 1980; writing not long thereafter, Terence Brown noted that "in the present economic climate it seems that marriages are being postponed and families restricted" (1985, 329).

By a two-to-one majority, a referendum in the Republic passed a constitutional amendment insisting on "the absolute right to life of every unborn child from conception" (quoted in Beale 1987, 115).

Fiction

Bernard MacClaverty's (1942–   ) novel *Cal* was a popular success, as was its subsequent film version. Its protagonist is a young northern Catholic who seeks to atone for his role as driver of the car in the IRA shooting of the husband of a beautiful young woman—with whom he falls in love, before she learns of his guilt and he is finally arrested. William Trevor's experimental Big House novel, *Fools of Fortune,* deals with the Quinton family. After one of the Quintons' workers was found hanging from a tree with his tongue cut out for informing to the British during the Anglo-Irish War, Willie Quinton's Ascendancy but nationalist father was shot by the British, and Willie has spent most of his life in exile after revenging this shooting.

Aidan Higgins's *Boenholm Night-Ferry* was an epistolary novel about an Irish writer's affair with a Danish poet.

Clare Boylan's (1948–) *Holy Pictures* was a racy novel of Irish girlhood, recalling Edna O'Brien's early novels.

Irish Language and Literature

Diarmaid Ó Súilleabháin's novel *Ciontach* (Guilty) was written in the form of a jail journal and dedicated to its model, the author's Republican uncle, Diarmaid Ó Drisceoil. *Aistear* (Journey), published in the same year, examined the experiences of several ordinary people in the moments surrounding death.

Nuala Ní Dhomhnaill's collection *Fear Suaithinseach* (A remarkable man) was published by An Sagart.

Literary Criticism

Field Day published three pamphlets "in which the nature of the Irish problem," according to the group's own description, "could be explored and, as a result, more successfully confronted than it had been hitherto" (Field Day Theatre Company 1985, viii): Tom Paulin's *A New Look at the Language Question,* Seamus Heaney's *An Open Letter,* and Seamus Deane's *Civilians and Barbarians.* Heaney's was a broadside poem addressed "To Blake and Andrew, Editors, / Contemporary British Verse, / Penguin Books, Middlesex"; in it he expressed his reluctance to be celebrated as a major "British" poet in such anthologies as Penguin's and Norton's.

Poetry

Quoof was a collection by Paul Muldoon.

1984

While exposed to the winter weather and in hiding at the Grotto of Our Lady in Granard, county Longford, a fifteen-year-old girl named Ann Lovett gave birth to a baby boy, and both she and the baby died shortly afterward. No one in the town except for one friend admitted knowing that she had been pregnant. The nation-wide uproar over this case "focused attention yet again on the atmosphere of shame, guilt, secrecy, and punishment which surrounds women who are pregnant outside marriage" (Beale 1987, 57).

Fiction

The Railway Station Man was a novel by Jennifer Johnston in which middle-aged, widowed Helen Cuffe falls in love with Roger Hawthorne, a gentle Englishman devoted to restoring the town's railway station, but she loses both Roger and her son in an IRA bombing.

Val Mulkerns's *The Summerhouse* was a Big House novel with a difference: it blended five different narrators to expose the nasty interactions of a genteel Catholic (rather than Protestant) family, suggesting that the family itself, not history, is to blame for the failure of this Big House.

Light a Penny Candle was the first of Maeve Binchy's (1940–   ) best-selling novels, which have also included *Echoes* (1985), *Firefly Summer* (1987), *Silver Wedding* (1989), and *Circle of Friends* (1991). Binchy is also well known as a very popular columnist in the *Irish Times*.

Desmond Hogan's novel *A Curious Street* spun an interesting variation on the conceit of the indefinitely receding mirror-images—with the novelist presenting a narrator who whose subject is a novelist writing a strangely romantic, Cromwellian historical novel with a protagonist who tends to overlap with everybody else.

Liam O'Flaherty (b. 1896) died in Dublin on 7 September.

Irish Language and Literature

Anois (Now), a new Irish-language newspaper, took the place of *Inniu.*

Literary Criticism

Field Day published another set of three critical pamphlets: Seamus Deane's *Heroic Styles: The Tradition of an Idea,* Richard Kearney's *Myth and Motherland,* and Declan Kiberd's (1951–   ) *Anglo-Irish Attitudes.*

Poetry

Michael Hartnett's *Collected Poems: Volume One* was published, with the second volume appearing two years later.
The Dead Kingdom was a collection by John Montague.

1985

At the end of the year, Taoiseach Garret Fitzgerald and British Prime Minister Margaret Thatcher signed the Anglo-Irish Agreement at Hillsborough Castle, county Down. It outlined consultative roles of the London and Dublin governments in the administration of Northern Ireland, and was soon met by large-scale protests by northern Protestants. Unionist M.P. Harold McCusker vented his feelings in a speech later published under the title "Waiting Like a Dog: The Gates of Hillsborough" (Deane et al. 1991, 3: 372).

Drama

Frank McGuinness's (1956–   ) *Observe the Sons of Ulster Marching towards the Somme* was a powerful, impressionistic play about World War I and Ulstermen's role in it. It bears comparison with O'Casey's 1928 play *The Silver Tassie.*

Modern Irish Literature and Culture

Fiction

A summer school was held in county Donegal to examine and celebrate the career of the novelist and socialist leader Peadar O'Donnell. O'Donnell attended and remarked humorously that it was like being at his own wake; he died in the following year.

Francis Stuart's *Faillandia* was a fable in novel form attacking the narrow puritanism of Irish church and state, particularly the anti–divorce referendum campaign at the time (see 1986 entry).

In his novel *Nothing Happens in Carmincross*, Benedict Kiely sent to Ireland an Irish-American academic who traverses the countryside northward to witness both his mother's death and a brutal IRA bombing, flying back to New York at the end with a drink in his hand, a sadder if not wiser man.

Mary Leland's novel *The Killeen* focused on the lives of two women during the political turmoil of the 1930s, culminating in one of their children's horrible death and shameful burial in the *killeen,* a graveyard for unbaptized children.

Donegal fiction writer Patrick McGinley's (1937–   ) novel *The Trick of the Ga Bolga* was dedicated "To Myles" (na gCopaleen: Flann O'Brien). As in O'Brien's novels, characters frequently exchange identities in this novel and in McGinley's other ones (*Bogmail*, 1978; *Goosefoot*, 1982; *Foggage*, 1984; and *The Red Men*, 1987).

Irish Language and Literature

Mícheál Ó Brolacháin's *Pax Dei* was a futurist novel in Irish presenting an Orwellian vision of a bleak postindustrial future.

Annraoi de Paor's *Buan ar Buairt* (Forever vexed) was a quirky study of an Irish academic.

Music

The Irish rock group U2 gave a concert to a packed house in Croke Park in Dublin early in their meteoric rise to world fame. This band has often treated Irish politics and problems in their songs—as in, for example, "Sunday Bloody Sunday," concerning Bloody Sunday in Derry (see 1972 entry).

Dubliner Bob Geldof organized a worldwide popular music "telethon" that raised $100,000 for African famine relief.

Poetry

Michael Longley's collected *Poems 1963–1983* appeared.
Derek Mahon's *Antarctica* was published.
The Berlin Wall Café was a collection by Paul Durcan; *Songs of the Psyche* and *Her Vertical Smile,* volumes by Thomas Kinsella; *The Price of Stone,* one by Richard Murphy.

1986

Des O'Malley, a former Fianna Fáil minister, founded the Progressive Democrat party.
In June a much-debated referendum on divorce, after lengthy and large-scale campaigns on both sides of the issue, upheld the illegality of divorce in the Republic by a nearly two-to-one popular vote. Divorce remains illegal in Ireland today.

Film

The world premiere of the Irish-made film *Eat the Peach,* about an Irishman obsessed with Elvis Presley, took place in the Savoy Cinema in Dublin (O'Donnell 1986, 129).

Irish Language and Literature

Dónal MacAmhlaigh's novel *Deoraithe* (Exiles) examined the lives of three people waiting in a Galway pub for their train to Dublin.
Raven Arts published Nuala Ní Dhomhnaill's *Selected Poems* (translated from the Irish by Michael Hartnett), with a dual-language edition following two years later.

Poetry

The Journey was a collection by Eavan Boland.
Paul Muldoon's *Selected Poems* also appeared.

1987

Fianna Fáil leader Charles Haughey once again took over from Fine Gael leader Garret Fitzgerald as taoiseach, and remained as Irish head of government until February 1992.

Fiction

Jennifer Johnston's novel *Fool's Sanctuary* was yet another fictional indictment of the IRA, in which Miranda Martin loses her IRA lover to gunmen after he tips off Miranda's brother about an IRA plot to kill him.

Irish Language and Literature

The publisher Sairséal Ó Marcaigh brought out *An Cion Go Dtí Seo* (My share so far), poems by Máire Mhac an tSaoi.

Michael Davitt's bilingual collection *Selected Poems / Rogha Dánta 1968–1984* also appeared.

Poetry

Thomas Kinsella's *Out of Ireland* and *St. Catherine's Clock,* Paul Muldoon's *Meeting the British,* and Paul Durcan's *Going Home to Russia* all were published.

1988

Drama

Brian Friel's *Making History* took as its subject the "flight of the earls" at the beginning of the seventeenth century, with a focus on Hugh O'Neill. O'Neill was a crafty Donegal chieftain who successfully operated as a middleman between England and the Gaelic aristocracy, and then led the struggle to save the traditional Gaelic way of life. Friel focuses on O'Neill's increasing despair following his defeat at the Battle of Kinsale in 1601, and his later years of exile, as encapsulated in a final scene set in Rome. O'Neill's compatriot and friend Red Hugh O'Donnell serves as a racy secondary character in this play.

Irish Language and Literature

Micheál Ó Siadhail's instructional book *Learning Irish* was based on his work on the language at the Dublin Institute for Advanced Studies. Subsequently, however, this poet and former Trinity College lecturer in Irish—now convinced that the language is doomed to inevitable extinction—has become a full-time poet dedicating himself to "English literature" (in his own words), publishing the volume *The Chosen Garden* (1990). Ó Siadhail has thus followed a course opposite from that of Michael Hartnett, who earlier decided to stop writing in English and to begin writing in Irish.

Poetry

Medbh McGuckian's collection of poems *On Ballycastle Beach* was issued, as was Thomas Kinsella's *Blood and Family,* John Montague's *Mount Eagle,* and Michael Hartnett's *Poems to Younger Women.*

1989

Recent net emigration from the Republic peaked at about 46,000 people in this year (Tynan 1991), reflecting a crisis in Ireland and creating problems in the countries to which these people emigrated. Many illegal (as well as legal) Irish immigrants remain in the United States today.

Drama

Garry Hynes, formerly director of the Druid Theatre in Galway, was appointed the artistic director of the Abbey Theatre.

Samuel Beckett (b. 1906), who claimed to have been born on Good Friday, died just before Christmas.

Film

Cinema enjoyed rapid growth in Ireland. A survey of the nations of the European Economic Community showed that "whereas aggregate admissions to European cinemas rose to 637 million in 1989, an increase of 3.6 percent over 1988, in Ireland admissions were up by 16.7 percent to a total of 17.5 million" (Kennedy 1990, 115).

Poetry

Carcanet Press published Eavan Boland's *Selected Poems.* *The Mirror Wall* was a volume by Richard Murphy.

1990

Senator Mary Robinson became the first woman to be elected president of Ireland.

Art

Women artists received increased attention in a number of shows. Surveying "The Arts in Ireland, 1990," Brian P. Kennedy noted that "both critical and public attention were accorded to Elizabeth Magill's paintings of weird and wonderful objects, to the heavily textured pictures of Gwen O'Dowd, to the mature and meditative work of Anne Madden, and to the sculptures of Kathy Prendergast, Éilís O'Connell and Vivienne Roche. The most remarkable talent to emerge in the past year or so has been the Cork-born sculptor Marie Foley" (1990, 114).

Drama

At the Abbey, Brian Friel's play *Dancing at Lughnasa* filled the theater for weeks and also played very successfully at the Royal National Theatre in London, returned to the Abbey in September 1991, and opened on Broadway in New York to rave reviews in October 1991. Dedicated "in memory of those five brave Glenties women," the play was also performed in Friel's presence at its

original setting in Glenties, county Donegal (Friel's hometown
and fictional "Ballybeg" in many of his plays) at the Patrick
MacGill Summer School in August 1991, where Friel and his work
comprised the subject for the week. *Dancing at Lughnasa* focuses
on five sisters and their interactions, with the focal point of the
play provided by a scene where they all throw themselves into a
liberatory harvest dance at Lúnasa (or "Lughnasa," August).
Seamus Heaney's first play, *The Cure at Troy,* based on
Sophocles's *Philoctetes,* was also well received.

Fiction

John McGahern's novel *Amongst Women* received very positive
reviews and won the *Irish Times*-Aer Lingus Irish Literature Prize
for fiction.

James Plunkett's third novel, *The Circus Animals,* was a
sequel of sorts to his *Farewell Companions* (1977). It focused on
Frank McDonagh, a somewhat autobiographical liberal journalist
struggling to make his way in the conservative, church-dominated
Ireland of the 1950s, and his friend Lemuel Gulliver, an older man
who develops into a kind of father-figure and benefactor to Frank
and has inherited his own father's obsession with Jonathan Swift.

Film

My Left Foot—Noel Pearson and Jim Sheridan's (1949–   ) film
about the paraplegic, working-class Dublin novelist Christy
Brown—received five Oscar nominations; Daniel Day Lewis as
Brown won Best Actor and Brenda Fricker won Best Supporting
Actress as his mother. At the end of the year the same duo released
a powerful screen version of John B. Keane's 1965 play *The Field,*
starring Richard Harris as the tragic rural patriarch Bull McCabe,
and Fricker as his wife. Five other Irish-made films by Irish
directors were released in Irish cinemas in this year, reflecting the
growth of Irish film (Kennedy 1990, 116).

Music

The National Symphony Orchestra, "formerly the Radio Telefís

Éireann Orchestra, was inaugurated on January 5 . . . amid great enthusiasm" (Kennedy 1990, 117).

In popular music, Sinéad O'Connor took "the number one slot in Ireland, Britain, and the United States with her single 'Nothing Compares 2U' and her album *I Do Not Want What I Haven't Got*. Ireland's world-conquering rock group, U2, was working on a new album (*Achtung Baby*) and gave no live performance in 1990, but the Hothouse Flowers and Something Happens gave their fans plenty to cheer about with live concerts and new albums. Bob Geldof was in form with his album *Vegetarians of Love*, as was Belfast rocker Van Morrison with *Enlightenment*, and Gary Moore with *Still Got the Blues*" (Kennedy 1991, 118).

Poetry

Ciarán Carson's *Belfast Confetti* received the Irish Literature Prize for poetry.

Paul Durcan's *Daddy, Daddy* won the Whitbread Prize for poetry (Kennedy 1990, 116).

1991

According to British statistics, 1,053 women with addresses in the Irish Republic had abortions in the United Kingdom during the first three months of the year (Ferrie 1991).

At the end of July, 261,400 people in the Republic were unemployed. This was the highest recorded figure in the country's history, and it had never been as high as 250,000 before this year; indeed, "people look back with a touch of wry nostalgia at a time when the former Taoiseach Jack Lynch could say that the Taoiseach's place was out of office if unemployment reached more than 100,000" (Tynan 1991). In September the total number registered as unemployed was 258,700, or 20 percent of the work force (Ferrie 1991).

The Republic endured postal and bus strikes.

Multiparty talks including the (Protestant) Unionist and (Catholic) SDLP (Social Democratic and Labour) parties were held in Northern Ireland. In August the largest demonstration against IRA violence since the Peace People events in 1976 was held in county Louth near the northern border. Several thousand people attended this rally to protest the killing of Thomas Oliver, a local farmer, by the IRA for allegedly giving information about the IRA to police.

Cultural Institutions

The Irish Museum of Modern Art opened in premises at the Royal Hospital, Kilmainham, in Dublin.

The Dublin Writers Museum opened late in the year at a site on Parnell Square.

Dublin was designated as "European City of Culture" for this year.

Fiction

Seán O'Faoláin died in Dublin after an eminently distinguished life of ninety-one years; born in 1900, he grew up with the century and became the most influential Irish man of letters after Yeats.

Literary Criticism

The Field Day Anthology of Irish Writing, a massive three-volume collection edited by a team of twenty-two scholars led by general editor Seamus Deane, appeared to considerable acclaim but also sharp criticism in Ireland over the fact that all twenty-two editors were male and that the anthology's many thematic sections included none specifically on women writers or feminism as a theme or movement. This collection of Irish writing since the Middle Ages reflected Deane's conviction, in particular, that Irish literature—like Irish culture—contains a variety of divergent traditions, consistently marked by conflicts of class, nationality, and language.

Poetry

Eavan Boland's seventh volume, *Outside History,* appeared.

1992

Following repeated rumors about earlier phonetaps on journalists and other political difficulties, in February Charles Haughey resigned as taoiseach and head of the Fianna Fáil party. Albert Reynolds, a low-key, moderate Fianna Fáil member and former minister, was elected as Haughey's replacement.

Within days of coming to power, Taoiseach Reynolds found himself faced by the most heated controversy in several years. A fourteen-year-old Irish girl who had become pregnant from a rape was told by officials in the Republic that she could not proceed with an abortion in England because of the Republic's strong anti-abortion laws, after her parents had phoned to ask if the doctors should preserve any evidence since the rape case was still to go to trial. Angry demonstrations against this order ensued in Dublin and several cities in other countries, with many pointing out that the EEC guarantee of free movement of citizens throughout EEC countries outweighed the ban on abortion in the Republic. At the very end of February, the Irish Supreme Court granted an appeal, leaving the girl free to obtain (as she reportedly did) an abortion in England (the traditional site of recourse for thousands of Irish women). This episode provoked a new, ongoing debate on Irish law concerning these problems.

Drama

In the same month, Thomas Murphy's *Conversations on a Homecoming* opened at the Abbey.

SECONDARY WORKS CITED

....

Note: As specified above and explained in my introduction, the following is a list of the secondary works cited in my text. As such it does not list any of the hundreds of primary, literary works that I mention throughout my chronology. Please see my introduction for advice on where to find bibliographical information about Irish fiction, poetry, drama, and other literary texts.

Æ [George Russell]. 1923. "The Lessons of Revolution." *Studies* 12 (March): 1–6.

Akenson, Donald H. 1975. *A Mirror to Kathleen's Face: Education in Independent Ireland, 1922–1960.* Montreal: McGill-Queen's University Press.

Barry, F. V., ed. 1931. *Maria Edgeworth: Chosen Letters.* Boston: Houghton Mifflin.

Bartlett, Thomas, ed. 1988. *Irish Studies: A General Introduction.* Totowa, N.Y.: Barnes and Noble.

Beale, Jenny. 1987. *Women in Ireland: Voices of Change.* Bloomington: Indiana University Press.

Becker, R. S. 1986. "George Moore: An Exile from the Noivelle Athènes." *Éire-Ireland: A Journal of Irish Studies* 21.1 (Summer):146–51.

Beckett, J. C. 1966. *The Making of Modern Ireland, 1603–1923.* New York: Knopf.

Boylan, Henry, ed. 1988. *A Dictionary of Irish Biography.* 2d ed. New York: St. Martin's.

Brady, Anne M., and Brian Cleeve, eds. 1985. *A Biographical Dictionary of Irish Writers.* New York: St. Martin's.

Brewer, Betty Webb. 1983. "'She Was a Part of It': Emily Lawless (1845–1913)." *Éire-Ireland* 18.4 (Winter):119–31.

Brown, Malcolm. 1972. *The Politics of Irish Literature: From Thomas Davis to W. B. Yeats.* London: Allen and Unwin.

Brown, Stephen J. 1919. *Ireland in Fiction: A Guide to Irish Novels, Tales, Romances, and Folklore,* Vol. 1. Reprint. Shannon: Irish University Press, 1969.

Brown, Stephen J., and Desmond Clarke. 1985. *Ireland in Fiction: A Guide to Irish Novels, Tales, Romances, and Folklore,* Vol. 2. Cork: Royal Carbery Books.

Brown, Terence. 1985. *Ireland: A Social and Cultural History, 1922–1985.* Rev. ed. London: Fontana.

Butler, Marilyn. 1972. *Maria Edgeworth: A Literary Biography.* Oxford: Clarendon.

Cahalan, James M. 1976. "The 'Preacher of Ideas': Michael Davitt, 1881–1906." *Éire-Ireland* 11.1 (Spring):13–33.

―――. 1979. "Tailor Tim Buckley: Folklore, Literature, and *Seanchas an Táilliúra* [Stories from the Tailor]." *Éire-Ireland* 14.2 (Summer):100–18.

―――. 1983. *Great Hatred, Little Room: The Irish Historical Novel.* Syracuse: Syracuse University Press / Dublin: Gill and Macmillan.

―――. 1988. *The Irish Novel: A Critical History.* Boston: Twayne/ Dublin: Gill and Macmillan.

―――. 1991. *Liam O'Flaherty: A Study of the Short Fiction.* Boston: Twayne.

"Charles Lever." 1872. *Dublin University Magazine* 80 (July):104–9.

Clarke, Austin. 1935. "Irish Poetry Today." *Dublin Magazine* 10. 1 (January–March):26–32.

Cole, Alan. 1962. "Acting at the Abbey." *University Review* 2.13:37–52.

Connolly, James. 1910. *Labour in Irish History.* Reprint. New York: Donnely, 1919.

Cronin, Anthony. 1982. *Heritage Now: Irish Literature in the English Language.* Dingle, County Kerry: Brandon.

Darby, John. 1976. *Conflict in Northern Ireland: The Development of a Polarised Community.* Dublin: Gill and Macmillan / New York: Barnes and Noble.

Deane, Seamus, et al., eds. 1991. *The Field Day Anthology of Irish Writing.* 3 vols. Derry: Field Day Publications.

de Breffny, Brian, ed. 1983. *Ireland: A Cultural Encyclopedia.* London: Thames and Hudson.

Denman, Peter. 1987. "Ireland's Little Magazines." In *Three Hundred Years of Irish Periodicals,* eds. Barbara Hayley and Edna Mckay, 123–46. Mullinger, County Westmeath: Lilliput.

de Valera, Eamon. 1946. *Ireland's Stand, Being a Selection of the Speeches of Éamon de Valera during the War (1939–1945).* Dublin: M. H. Gill.

Dietrich, Richard F. 1989. *British Drama, 1890 to 1950: A Critical History.* Boston: Twayne.

Doherty, J. E., and D. J. Hickey. 1989. *A Chronology of Irish History since 1500.* Dublin: Gill and Macmillan.

Doyle, Paul A. 1968. *Seán O'Faoláin.* New York: Twayne.

"Dublinienis." 1871. *Dublin Builder* 13.283 (1 October):250–51.

Eamon de Valera States His Case: Interview Reprinted from the "Christian Science Monitor," Boston, U.S.A., May 15th, 1918. 1918. Dublin: Sinn Féin.

Ellis, P. Berresford. 1973. *A History of the Irish Working Class.* New York: Braziller.

Ellmann, Richard. 1982. *James Joyce.* Rev. ed. New York: Oxford University Press.

———. 1988. *Oscar Wilde.* New York: Knopf.

Fallis, Richard. 1977. *The Irish Renaissance.* Syracuse: Syracuse University Press.

Fallon, Gabriel. 1957. "Dublin's Theatre Festival." *Threshold* 1.3 (Autumn):75–81.

———. 1955. "The Future of the Irish Theatre." *Studies* 44 (Spring):92–100.

Fallon, Gabriel, and Derek Mahon, eds. 1990. *Contemporary Irish Poetry.* London: Penguin.

"The Famine in the Land." 1847. *Dublin University Magazine* 29:501–40.

Fanne an Lae (The break of day). 1898. 1.1 (8 January). First issue of this newspaper.

Ferrie, Liam, ed. 1991. *Irish Emigrant,* no. 244 (7 October). Electronic-mail newsletter sent from Galway, Ireland.

Field Day Theatre Company. 1985. *Ireland's Field Day.* London: Hutchinson.

Finneran, Richard J., ed. 1976. *Anglo-Irish Literature: A Review of Research.* New York: Modern Language Association.

———, ed. 1982. *Recent Research on Anglo-Irish Writers.* New York: Modern Language Association.

Finneran, Richard J., George Mills Harper, and William M. Murphy, eds. 1977. *Letters to W. B. Yeats.* 2 vols. New York: Columbia University Press.

Fitzpatrick, W. J., ed. 1888. *Correspondence of Daniel O'Connell, the Liberator: Edited with Notices of His Life and Times.* 2 vols. London: John Murray.

Flanagan, Thomas. 1966. "The Big House of Ross-Drishane." *Kenyon Review* 28:54–78.

Foster, John Wilson. 1991. "Natural Science and Irish Culture." *Éire-Ireland* 26.2 (Summer):92–103.

Foster, R. J. 1988. *Modern Ireland, 1600–1972.* London: Penguin.

Frazier, Adrian. 1990. *Behind the Scenes: Yeats Horniman, and the Struggle For the Abbey Theatre.* Berkeley: University of California Press.

Garratt, Robert F. 1986. *Modern Irish Poetry: Tradition and Continuity from Yeats to Heaney.* Berkeley: University of California Press.

Greacen, Robert. 1947. "Trends in Irish Poetry." *Irish Bookman* 1.7 (February):58–63.

Harmon, Maurice. 1968. *Modern Irish Literature, 1800–1967: A Reader's Guide.* Chester Springs, Penn.: Dufour, 1968.

———. 1977. *Select Bibliography for the Study of Anglo-Irish Literature and Its Backgrounds: An Irish Studies Handbook.* Dublin: Wolfhound.

———. 1985. "The Era of Inhibitions: Irish Literature 1920–1960." In *Irish Writers and Society at Large,* ed. Masaru Sekine, 31–41. New York: Barnes and Noble.

Hayley, Barbara. 1987. "'A Reading and Thinking Nation': Periodicals as the Voice of Nineteenth-Century Ireland." In *Three Hundred Years of Irish Periodicals,* eds. Barbara Hayley and Enda McKay, 29–48. Mullingar, County Westmeath: Lilliput, 1987.

Hayley, Barbara, and Enda McKay, eds. 1987. *Three Hundred Years of Irish Periodicals.* Mullingar, County Westmeath: Lilliput.

Herr, Cheryl, ed. 1991. *For the Land They Loved: Irish Political Melodramas, 1890–1925.* Syracuse, N.Y.: Syracuse University Press.

Hickey, D. J., and J. E. Doherty. 1987. *A Dictionary of Irish History, 1800–1980.* Rev. ed. Dublin: Gill and Macmillan.

Hogan, Robert, ed. 1980. *Dictionary of Irish Literature.* Westport, Conn.: Greenwood.

Hogan, Robert, and James Kilroy, eds. 1975. *Modern Irish Drama: A Documentary History: Vol. 1. The Irish Literary Theatre, 1899–1901.* Dublin: Dolmen / Atlantic Highlands, N.J.: Humanities.

———, eds. 1976. *Modern Irish Drama: A Documentary History: Vol. 2. Laying the Foundations, 1902–1904.* Dublin: Dolmen / Atlantic Highlands, N.J.: Humanities.

———, eds. 1978. *Modern Irish Drama: A Documentary History: Vol. 3. The Abbey Theatre: The Years of Synge, 1905–1909.* Dublin: Dolmen / Atlantic Highlands, N.J.: Humanities.

Hogan, Robert, and Michael J. O'Neill, eds. 1967. *Joseph Holloway's Abbey Theatre: A Selection from His Unpublished Journal "Impressions of a Dublin Playgoer."* Carbondale: Southern Illinois University Press / London: Feffer and Simons.

Hogan, Robert, Richard Burnham, and Daniel P. Poteet, eds. 1979. *Modern Irish Drama: A Documentary History: Vol. 4. The Rise of the Realists, 1910–1915.* Dublin: Dolmen / Atlantic Highlands, N.J.: Humanities.

"Ireland in 1880." 1880. *Dublin University Magazine* 95:77–82.

"An Irish Educationalist—Mr P. H. Pearse." 1913. *Irish Review* 2 (January):608–9.

Irish Times. 1 December 1823. First issue of this newspaper.

Jeffares, A. Norman. 1982. *Anglo-Irish Literature.* London: Macmillan.

Joyce, James. 1902. "James Clarence Mangan." *St. Stephen's* 1.6 (May):116–18.

Kain, Richard. 1962. *Dublin in the Age of William Butler Yeats and James Joyce.* Norman: University of Oklahoma Press.

Kelly, John, and Eric Domville, eds. 1986. *The Collected Letters of W. B. Yeats: Vol. 1. 1865–1895.* Oxford: Clarendon.

Kelly, Major. 1921. "Notes on the Tactical Employment of the

Thompson Submachine Gun in Guerilla Warfare." *Óglaigh na hÉireann* (Youth of Ireland [the Irish Volunteers]) 1.2:12–16.

Kennedy, Brian P. 1990. "The Arts in Ireland, 1990." *Éire-Ireland* 25.4 (Winter):111–19.

Kilroy, James F., ed. 1984. *The Irish Short Story: A Critical History.* Boston: Twayne.

Kilroy, Thomas, ed. 1975. *Seán O'Casey: A Collection of Critical Essays.* Englewood Cliffs, N.J.: Prentice-Hall.

Lapisardi, Frederick S., ed. 1991. *The Plays of Eva-Gore Booth.* San Francisco: Mellen Research University Press.

Lemass, Seán. 1959. *The Role of the State-Sponsored Bodies in the Economy.* Dublin: Institute of Public Administration.

Lubbers, Klaus. 1980. "Die Erzählprosa des modernen Irland" (The fiction of modern Ireland). In *Einführung in die Zeitgenössische Irishche Literatur* (Introduction to contemporary Irish literature), eds. J. Kornekius, E. Otto, and G. Stratmann, 63–78. Heidelberg, Germany: Carol Winter/ Universitätverlag.

————. 1985. *Geschichte der irishchen Erzählprosa von den anfängen bis zum ausgehenden 19. Jahrhundert* (A history of Irish fiction from the beginnings to the end of the 19th century). Munich: Wilhelm Fink.

MacCana, Proinsias. 1980. *Literature in Irish.* Dublin: Department of Foreign Affairs.

McCarthy, Patrick A. 1983. "The Moore-Joyce Nexus: An Irish Literary Comedy." In *George Moore in Perspective,* ed. Janet E. Dunleavy, 99–116. Totowa, N.J.: Barnes and Noble; Naas, County Kildare: Malton; Gerrards Cross, England: Colin Smythe.

McCrum, Robert, William Cran, and Robert MacNeil. 1986. "The Irish Question." In *The Story of English,* 163–93. New York: Elisabeth Sifton / Viking.

MacDonagh, Donagh. 1936. Review of *Ploughman and Other Poems* by Patrick Kavanagh. *Ireland Today* 1.6 (November):85–88.

MacEoin, Gearóid. 1969. "Twentieth-Century Irish Literature." In *A View of the Irish Language,* ed. Brian Ó Cuív, 57–69. Dublin: Stationery Office.

McHugh, Roger, and Maurice Harmon. 1982. *Short History of Anglo-Irish Literature from its Origins to the Present Day.* Totowa, N.Y.: Barnes and Noble.

MacLiammóir, Micheál. 1946. *All for Hecuba: An Irish Theatrical Autobiography.* London: Methuen.

Malone, Andrew. 1931. "The Irish Theatre in 1930." *Dublin Magazine* 6.2 (April–June):1–11.

———. 1933. "The Irish Theatre in 1933." *Dublin Magazine* 9.3 (July–September):45–54.

———. 1936. "The Irish Theatre in 1935." *Dublin Magazine* 11.1 (January–March):48–59.

Mangan, James Clarence. 1847. "Anthologia Hibernica." *Dublin University Magazine* 29:239–50, 624–34.

Marcus, Phillip. 1970. *Yeats and the Beginning of the Irish Renaissance.* Ithaca, N.Y.: Cornell University Press.

Martin, Augustine. 1980. *Anglo-Irish Literature.* Dublin: Government of Ireland.

Maxwell, D.E.S. 1984. *A Critical History of Modern Irish Drama, 1891–1980.* Cambridge: Cambridge University Press.

Mikhail, E. H. 1981. *An Annotated Bibliography of Modern Anglo-Irish Drama.* Troy, N.Y.: Whitson.

Miller, J. Hillis. 1982. "From Narrative Theory to Joyce, from Joyce to Narrative Theory." In *The Seventh of Joyce,* ed. Bernard Benstock, 3–4. Bloomington: Indiana University Press / Brighton, England: Harvester.

Miller, Liam. 1966. "Eden and After: The Irish Theatre, 1945–1966." *Studies* 55 (Autumn):231–35.

Moore, George. 1900. "The Irish Literary Renaissance and the Irish Language." *New Ireland Review* 13 (April):65–72.

———. 1901. "The Irish Literary Theatre." *Samhain* 1 (October):13–15.

Murphy, Maureen O'Rourke, and James MacKillop, eds. 1987. *Irish Literature: A Reader.* Syracuse, N.Y.: Syracuse University Press.

Nation. 1842. 1.1 (15 October). First issue of this newspaper.

Newman, Peter R. 1991. *Companion to Irish History, 1603–1921: from the Submission of Tyrone to Partition.* New York: Facts on File.

Nic Pháidín, Caoilfhíonn. 1987. "Na hIrisí Gaeilge" (The Gaelic journals). In *Three Hundred Years of Irish Periodicals*, ed. Barbara Hayley and Enda McKay, 69–85. Mullingar, County Westmeath: Lilliput.

O'Brien, Darcy. 1976. "In Ireland after *A Portrait*." In *Approaches to Joyce's "Portrait": Ten Essays*, ed. Thomas F. Staley and Bernard Benstock, 213–37. Pittsburgh: University of Pittsburgh Press.

Ó Broin, Tomás. 1979. "*Deoraíocht*: Saothar Eispresiunach" [*Deoraíocht*: an expressionistic work]. *Feasta* 32.6:13–19.

Ó Cadhain, Máirtín. 1971. "Irish Prose in the Twentieth Century." In *Literature in Celtic Countries*, ed. J. E. Caerwyn Williams, 139–51. Cardiff: University of Wales Press.

Ó Canainn, Tomás. 1978. *Traditional Music in Ireland*. London and Boston: Routledge.

O'Casey, Seán. 1919. *The Story of the Irish Citizen Army*. Dublin: Maunsel.

O'Connor, Frank. 1967. *A Short History of Irish Literature: A Backward Look*. New York: Putnam.

Ó Cuív, Brian, ed. 1969. *A View of the Irish Language*. Dublin: Stationery Office.

Ó Danachair, Caoimhín. 1969. "The Gaeltacht." In *A View of the Irish Language*, ed. Brian Ó Cuív, 112–21. Dublin: Stationery Office.

O'Donnell, Jim. 1986. *Ireland, the Past Twenty Years: An Illustrated Chronology*. Dublin: Institute of Public Administration.

O'Faoláin, Seán. 1940. Introduction. *Bell* 1.1 (October):6–8.

Ó Fiaich, Tomás. 1969. "The Language and Political History." In *A View of the Irish Language*, ed. Brian Ó Cuív, 101–11. Dublin: Stationery office.

Ó Háinle, Cathal. 1984. "'The Inalienable Right of Trifles': Tradition and the Modernity in Gaelic Writing since the Revival." *Éire-Ireland* 19.4 (Winter):59–77.

Ó Muirithe, Diarmaid. 1977. *The English Language in Ireland*. Dublin: Mercier.

Oram, Hugh. 1983. *The Newspaper Book: A History of Newspapers in Ireland, 1649–1983*. Dublin: MO Books.

Owens, Cóilín D., and Joan N. Radner, eds. 1990. *Irish Drama 1900–1980*. Washington, D.C.: Catholic University Press.

Pearse, Pádraic H. 1922. *Political Writings and Speeches. Collected Works of Pádraic H. Pearse*. Dublin: Maunsel and Roberts.

Powell, David. 1971. "An Annotated Bibliography of Myles Na Gopalien's (Flann O'Brien's) 'Cruiskeen Lawn' Commentaries on James Joyce." *James Joyce Quarterly* 9.1 (Fall):50–62.

"The Present Crisis." 1833. *Dublin University Magazine* 1.1 (January):1–10.

Review of *The Cock and Anchor,* by Joseph Sheridan LeFanu. 1835. *Dublin University Magazine* 26 (November):607–25.

Review of "Congal," by Samuel Ferguson. 1872. *Dublin University Magazine* 80 (October):385–400.

Review of *Guests of the Nation,* by Frank O'Connor. 1932. *Dublin Magazine* 7.1 (January–March):71.

Review of *Juno and the Paycock* and *The Shadow of a Gunman,* by Seán O'Casey. 1925. *Studies* 14:493–95.

Sheeran, Patrick F. 1976. *The Novels of Liam O'Flaherty: A Study in Romantic Realism.* Atlantic Highlands, N.J.: Humanities Press.

Shenfield, Margaret. 1962. *Bernard Shaw: A Pictorial Biography.* New York: Viking.

Sloan, Barry. 1982. "Samuel Lover's Irish Novels." *Études Irlandaises* 7:31–42.

Smyth, Ailbhe, ed. 1989. *Wildish Things: An Anthology of New Irish Women's Writings.* Dublin: Attic.

Synge, John Millington. 1898. "A Story from Inishmaan." *New Ireland Review* 10 (November):153–56.

Thompson, William Irwin. 1967. *The Imagination of an Insurrection: Dublin, Easter 1916: A Study of an Ideological Movement.* New York: Oxford University Press.

Todd, Loreto. 1989. *The Language of Irish Literature.* New York: St. Martin's.

Tynan, Maol Muire. 1991. "No Brakes to Halt the Upward Trend." *Irish Times,* 12 August, p. 10.

"Ulster and the Unity of Ireland." 1921. *Irish Review* 1.2 (11 November):15–16.

Wall, Maureen. 1969. "The Decline of the Irish Language." In *A View of the Irish Language,* ed. Brian O Cuív, 81–90. Dublin: Stationary Office.

Whyte, J. H. 1971. *Church and State in Modern Ireland, 1923–1970.* Dublin: Gill and Macmillan.

Wolff, Robert Lee. 1979a. "The Fiction of the 'O'Hara Family'." Introduction to *The Denounced,* by John Banim, v–lii. New York: Garland.

336

Secondary Works Cited

———. 1979b. *"Knocknagow,* by Charles Joseph Kickham."* Introduction to *Knocknagow,* v–xi. New York: Garland.

———. 1980. *William Carleton, Irish Peasant Novelist: a Preface to His Fiction.* New York: Garland.

Yeats, W. B. 1886. "The Poetry of Sir Samuel Ferguson." *Dublin University Review* 2.11 (November):923–41.

———. 1899. "Plans and Methods." *Beltaine* 1 (May):6–9.

———. 1901. Introduction. *Samhain* 1 (October):10.

———. 1902. "Notes." *Samhain* 2 (October):3–10.

———. 1903. "Notes." *Samhain* 3 (September):7.

INDEX

••

362

Index

"Sisters, The" (J. Joyce), 155, 179
Site of Ambush (Ní Chuilleanáin), 302
Sive (J. B. Keane), 267
Skerrett (O'Flaherty), 22, 221
Sketches of Irish Character (Hall), 74
Slater, William, 97
Sleep of the King, The (Cousins), 148
Slow Dance, A (Montague), 301
Smith, Michael, 287
Smith, Terence, 249
Smock Alley Theatre, 34–35, 46, 47, 48, 50, 52
Snow Party, The (Mahon), 302
Social Democratic and Labour party (SDLP), 287, 307, 314, 324
Socialist party of Ireland, 134
Society for the Preservation of the Irish Language, 108, 112
"Soldier's Song, The" (Kearney and Heeney), 163
Some Experiences of an Irish R.M. (Somerville and Ross), 140–41
Somerville, Edith, *24–25*, 65, 119, 130, 137, 140–41, 171, 181, 193, 204–205
Son of Learning, The (A. Clarke), 244
"Song of Wandering Aengus, The" (W. B. Yeats), 122, 142
Songs, Poems and Verses (Dufferin), 132
Songs of the Psyche (Kinsella), 319
Soul for Sale, A (Kavanagh), 17
South, Seán, 262
Spacious Adventures of the Man in the Street, The (O'Duffy), 207
"Speech from the Dock" (Emmet), 61
Spirit of the Nation, The, 85
Sport, 186

Spreading the News (Gregory), 16, 154
Spring Sowing, collection of stories (O'Flaherty), 22, 202
"Spring Sowing," individual story (O'Flaherty), 230
Squireen, The (Bullock), 151, 202
Stage Irishman, 49, 52
Stand and Give Challenge (MacManus), 225
Standard, 233, 244
Star, 122
Star Turns Red, The (O'Casey), 19, 176, 234
"Stare's Nest by My Window, The" (W. B. Yeats), 211–12
States of Ireland (Conor Cruise O'Brien), 295
Statesman and Patriot, 64
Staunton, Michael, 67
Steelboys movement, 48
Stephen Hero (J. Joyce), 184
Stephens, James (1825–1901), 96, 99, 101
Stephens, James (1882–1950), *25*, 115, 168, 169, 172, 174, 174, 177, 189, 200, 208, 211, 249
Sterne, Laurence, 50
Still Got the Blues (G. Moore), 324
Stories (F. O'Connor), 20
Stories of Liam O'Flaherty, The, 22, 262
Stories of S. O'Faoláin, The, 21, 266
Storm (O'Donnell), 21, 205
Stormy Hills, The (Corkery), 214
"Story from Inishmaan, A" (Synge), 137–38
Story of the Injured Lady, The (Swift), 40, 46
Story of the Irish Citizen Army, The (O'Casey), 19, 191
"Story by Maupassant, A" (F. O'Connor), 286
Story Teller's Holiday, A (G. Moore), 188–89